Batsford Chess Library

Secrets of Spectacular Chess

Jonathan Levitt and David Friedgood

With a Foreword by John Nunn

An Owl Book
Henry Holt and Company
New York

Henry Holt and Company, Inc.
Publishers since 1866
115 West 18th Street
New York, New York 10011

Henry Holt® is a registered
trademark of Henry Holt and Company, Inc.

First published in the United States in 1995 by
Henry Holt and Company, Inc.
Originally published in Great Britain in 1995 by
B. T. Batsford Ltd.

Library of Congress Catalog Card Number: 94-73165

ISBN 0-8050-3901-5 (An Owl Book: pbk.)

First American Edition—1995

Printed in the United Kingdom
All first editions are printed on acid-free paper.∞

10 9 8 7 6 5 4 3 2 1

Editorial Panel: Mark Dvoretsky, John Nunn, Jon Speelman
General Adviser: Raymond Keene OBE
Managing Editor: Graham Burgess

Contents

Part One: Background and Context

1 Introduction

Part Two: The Elements of Chess Beauty

2 Paradox

3 Depth

4 Geometry

Preface

An enormous amount of work has gone into this book and we hope there will not be many errors. Those that have crept through deserve some credit for having got by the efforts of both authors, Fritz 3, Graham Burgess and John Nunn. If you do spot any, please let us know, care of the publishers.

Apart from the introduction, for which responsibility lies entirely with Jon Levitt, every section of the book has been worked on by both authors. The work on the first draft was divided up as follows: David Friedgood – Chapters 2, 3, 4 and 8; Jon Levitt – Chapters 5, 6 and 7. The final chapter was something of a joint effort from the start.

A number of people have made suggestions, contributed ideas or helped in some way. We would especially like to thank:

Beverley Friedgood
Brian Stephenson
Kelly Collett
John Beasley
Gerald Hertneck
Julian Hodgson
David Norwood
Kevin of the Teachers
Peter Millican

It is the authors' privilege to have such a high-powered team working for the publishers: Graham Burgess and John Nunn. The job of a conscientious editor should never be underestimated and Graham has helped out in many ways besides. Having an eagle-eyed typesetter with a rating well over 2600 can also come in handy...

Jonathan Levitt and David Friedgood, *London 1995*

Symbols

+	Check
++	Double check
x	Capture
#	Checkmate
!	Good move
?	Bad move
!!	Excellent move
??	Blunder
!?	Interesting move
?!	Dubious move
Wcht	World Team Championship
Ct	Candidates
OL	Olympiad
Win	White to play and win
Draw	White to play and draw
P	Paradox
D	Depth
G	Geometry
F	Flow
#n	Mate in n moves
H#n	Helpmate in n moves
S#n	Selfmate in n moves
SH#n	Series helpmate in n moves
SH=n	Series helpstalemate in n moves
HM	Honourable Mention

Foreword

The question as to whether chess is a sport, an art or a science has been asked many times. As one might anticipate, such a general question doesn't admit a straightforward answer. Chess combines elements of all three, and different chess activities emphasize one or other of the three aspects. While over-the-board play undoubtedly emphasizes the sporting side, it is remarkable how often even hardened point-conscious grandmasters will proudly show off a 'beautiful' combination they have just played. It is clear that even the professional player, for whom a point may represent next month's rent, has a profound interest in the aesthetic side of chess.

But what exactly constitutes a 'beautiful' piece of chess? Very often players will agree that a particular game or combination is attractive, but equally often they are unable to describe the appealing ingredients precisely.

In this book, Jon Levitt and David Friedgood tackle the problem of isolating those elements of the game which contribute to chess beauty. I do not want to give away their secrets too soon, but I will say that their theory is very wide-ranging and

applies not only to the over-the-board game, but also to composed endgames and problems. Like the authors, I believe that their philosophy is an original contribution to the appreciation of chess aesthetics.

When I heard about this book, I was concerned that the result would be a kind of formula which one could use to assess the aesthetic impact of a game or composition. However, I am happy to say that while they have pinned down many fundamental aesthetic components, there is plenty of scope left for personal interpretation.

I will not talk further about the Levitt and Friedgood theory, because that is the subject of the rest of the book. Instead I would like to present some positions which had a particular aesthetic impact on me when I was a young player, and which helped to excite my interest in chess.

Taking practical play first, young players are quickly exposed to the classic combinations that are reprinted time and time again in books. These classics have percolated so deeply into the collective chess consciousness that it is normally only necessary to give the critical move or moves, and the game is instantly identified. For example, if I write 23...♕c3-g3!!, I would imagine that a majority of knowledgeable readers will have no difficulty identifying the game. One could continue with such puzzles almost indefinitely; I imagine that most club players will have no trouble with the first two sequences below, although the third is tricky:

1) **29...♕b6-b2! 0-1**

2) **30 ♗b2-a3! ♕e7xa3 31 ♘g3-h5+!**

3) **30...♕d7xh3+!**

Answers at the end of the foreword!

Only the most cold-hearted player could fail to be warmed by these famous combinations. When I was young I was especially impressed by the following 'classic':

W

E. Adams-C.Torre
New Orleans, 1920

This position looks fairly quiet, and one might expect that in the next few moves all the rooks will be swapped off along the open e-file, with a quick draw to follow. However, Adams found a combination which guaranteed his chess immortality:

17 ♗xf6   ♗xf6
18 ♕g4!

The first in a series of stunning sacrificial blows. White's queen is invulnerable due to Black's weak back rank, but for the moment Black is able to maintain the defence of e8.

18 ...   ♕b5

Over the next few moves White seeks to drive Black's queen off the a4-e8 diagonal and away from the defence of the rook on e8. Note that White's combination only works thanks to the circumstance that the rook on e1 is defended by a knight, thereby preventing ...♖xe2 at any stage.

19 ♕c4!!

Not content with putting his queen *en prise* to one black piece, Adams goes one better and offers it to two black pieces. Once again Black is forced to duck with his own queen.

19 ...   ♕d7
20 ♕c7!

There are problem-like elements to the protracted duel between the two queens. It is especially attractive that White's queen slides cheekily along the black rook's line of attack.

20 ...   ♕b5

21 a4!

Up to this point, White's moves haven't been that hard to find, but now White cannot make progress without introducing an extra element into the position. The obvious 21 ♕xb7? fails to 21...♕xe2 22 ♖xe2 (or 22 ♕xc8 ♕xe1+ 23 ♘xe1 ♖xc8) ♖c1+, when Black suddenly exploits White's own back rank. This element of counterplay adds to the combination's appeal – White isn't just raining punches onto a helpless opponent; he has to be precise or it could all go horribly wrong.

The pawn move deflects Black's queen onto a square which allows White to introduce the key new element. It would be hard to guess from the diagram that White's a-pawn would play such a vital role just five moves in the future.

21 ...   ♕xa4

22 ♖e4!

When I first saw this combination, I found the last two moves hardest to understand; it took me a few minutes to grasp what is going on. At first sight, 22 ♖e4 doesn't threaten anything, because 23 ♖xa4 can be met by 23...♖e1+ 24 ♘xe1 ♖xc7. But a closer look reveals that the threat isn't so much 23 ♖xa4, as 23 ♕xc8 (note that 23...♕xe4 loses to 24 ♕xe8+). This threat holds even

if Black relieves his back rank by 22...h6 or 22...g6. Nor can Black defend by 22...♖a8, because this removes the attack on White's queen and allows 23 ♖xa4. It follows that Black can only return to b5.

22 ...   ♕b5

What has White achieved with his last two moves? Remember that earlier on, White couldn't play ♕xb7 because of the reply ...♕xe2. The motivation for the last two moves is that White has transferred his rook away from the vulnerable e2-square with gain of tempo.

23 ♕xb7!   1-0

White has covered all the squares on the a4-e8 diagonal and Black faces a fatal loss of material. As you will learn later in this book, White's 21st and 22nd moves constitute what problemists call a foreplan, leading up to the mainplan 23 ♕xb7. Whilst it is understandable that problemists should wish to develop a precise language to describe such tactical manoeuvres, it is unfortunate that this jargon has the side-effect of making even relatively straightforward ideas seem very technical and difficult. An over-the-board player would probably describe a4 and ♖xe4 as 'a necessary preliminary manoeuvre to prepare the killing blow on b7' – much the same thing but in less technical language.

This combination had a profound effect on me. It suddenly seemed that chess was worth all the blunders and lost games, if only one could produce such a beautiful and profound combination. Unfortunately, I am still waiting.

My second example also had a big effect on me, although the contrast with the preceding position could hardly be greater.

W

A. Karpov-W. Unzicker
Nice OL 1974

Karpov faced a tricky problem in this typical Spanish position. White has a space advantage, but this is only useful if there are plenty of pieces on the board. If Black can exchange all the rooks along the a-file, then there will be less congestion in his position and he should have few problems holding the draw. At the moment it seems that Black is in an excellent position to challenge the a-file. His c8-rook and queen are well-posted, while the rook on e1 cannot

cross to the a-file because the b1-bishop gets in the way. In the hands of most players, this position would probably have petered out to a quick draw, but Karpov found an unusual and imaginative solution to the problem.

24 &a7!!

Once you have seen this idea, it appears very logical. White physically obstructs the open a-file in order to prevent the exchange of rooks. This gives White time to support the bishop on a7 using his other pieces, for example with &c2 and &ea1. White's queen might go to e3, or White might even triple his major pieces on the a-file. Black cannot emulate White's plan because of his lack of space. The blockading bishop is on a7, and so Black has no room to double rooks on his side of the bishop.

The reason such a plan is not seen more often is, of course, that normally Black would be able to attack the a7-bishop, forcing White to abandon his a-file ambitions. Karpov's unique perception was that, thanks to the position of Black's other pieces, this isn't feasible. After 24...&c7, for example, White plays 25 &e3 and it will take Black far too long to bring another piece to bear on a7. In the meantime White will have doubled rooks himself.

Once White has his major pieces lined up on the a-file, the bishop can move away and White will gain undisputed control of the open file.

24...♘e8 25 ♗c2 ♘c7 26 ♖ea1 ♛e7 27 ♗b1

This move opens the line d2-a2, so as to allow ♛xa2 after a possible exchange on a2.

27...♗e8 28 ♘e2!

Karpov knows that defending on two fronts is much harder than meeting threats in a limited area. Having secured a permanent advantage on the queenside, he now looks around for another way of inconveniencing Black. Unzicker's knight manoeuvres have been designed to counter the queenside menace, and as a result his knights have lost contact with the square e5. Karpov exploits this by preparing f4.

28...♘d8 29 ♘h2 ♗g7 30 f4

The second front is opened. Black should probably have exchanged on f4, so that at least one minor piece would gain some activity. However, even in this case White would have had a clear advantage.

30...f6?! 31 f5 g5

Now Black has permanent weaknesses on the kingside too, and it will only be a matter of time before Karpov breaks through on one side or the other.

32 ♗c2 ♗f7 33 ♘g3 ♘b7 34 ♗d1 h6 35 ♗h5 ♛e8 36 ♛d1 ♘d8 37 ♖a3 ♔f8 38 ♖1a2 ♔g8 39 ♘g4 ♔f8 40 ♘e3 ♔g8 41 ♗xf7+ ♘xf7 42 ♛h5 ♘d8 43 ♛g6 ♔f8 44 ♘h5 1-0

Before I saw this game, I had regarded positional manoeuvring as something that one undertakes reluctantly if no other option is available. Karpov's play convinced me that strategic ideas could have a beauty all their own, and were worth devoting more attention to. Up till 1974, my play had been heavily influenced by Tal and Alekhine, but it gradually became less one-sided, although I have retained a certain preference for tactics up to the present day.

My local library had a couple of books dealing with endgame studies, so at the same time that I was developing as a player, I was also introducing myself to the magic of studies. The following study particularly captured my imagination.

Draw
L. Kubbel, 1921
Listok Shakhmatnovo Kruzhka
Petrogubkommuny

Here one's instant reaction is to play 1 ♖e6 ♛xe6 2 ♘c5+, an impulse which dies as soon as one notices that 1...♛xe6 pins the knight. If the knight were not blocking the third rank, then one could play ♖a3+ and ♖b3, but the only really forcing knight move is 1 ♘c5+, and this fails to 1...♛xc5 2 ♖a3+ ♚b6 3 ♖b3+ ♚c6 and c3 is guarded by Black's bishop.

So the two most active moves fail, and no other move seems likely to do the trick. When solving the best endgame studies, there always comes a moment when it seems completely impossible to achieve the study's objective. In this study, the critical moment arises straight away.

I can well remember my delight when I hit upon the paradoxical key move.

1   ♘d4!!

Not only does this put the knight *en prise* to both Black's pieces, it is hard to imagine that Black's queen has no way to escape from the threats of 2 ♖e6 and 2 ♖a3+. I recall trying out all the queen's moves one by one, unable to believe the truth of the matter – apart from the immediate capture of the knight, Black's queen is trapped. The only non-trivial variation arises after 1...♛d8, but then 2 ♖a3+ ♚b7 (c5 and c7 are off limits, so the king can only hope to slip away from the checks via c8) 3 ♖b3+ ♚c8 leads to a position in

which White sacrifices his rook after all: 4 ♖b8+! ♚xb8 5 ♘c6+ drawing.

But now we should return to analyse Black's most obvious move.

1   ...   ♛xd4
2   ♖a3+   ♚b5

Black can only evade the rook checks by playing his king to the d-file.

3   ♖b3+   ♚c4
4   ♖c3+   ♚d5

No more checks, but now White can switch plans.

5   ♖d3!   ♛xd3
      Stalemate

This study possesses great charm and I often use it to introduce endgame studies to players who haven't met composed endgames before.

I hope that readers will gain as much pleasure as I have from the plentiful examples of spectacular chess provided by Levitt and Friedgood. Their theory successfully tackles a very difficult task.

Finally, those mystery games. If you didn't recognize 23...♛g3 as coming from Levitsky-Marshall, Breslau 1912, then you should spend more time studying the classics! The other three were: 1) Bernstein- Capablanca, Moscow 1914; 2) Botvinnik-Capablanca, AVRO (Rotterdam) 1938; and 3) Averbakh-Kotov, Zurich Ct 1953.

John Nunn, *London 1995*

Part One: Background and Context

Our Purpose

It is the authors' unashamed intention to overwhelm readers of this book with a wealth of dazzling and magnificent examples in such a way that they will come to share with us the joy and appreciation of beauty in chess for the rest of their lives!

This may sound over the top – it was written that way – but we actually mean it. After joining us on our guided tour round some of the beauty spots of the chess universe (games, studies and problems) we think there is a very good chance you will agree. We believe in the games and positions to be found in this book and hope that, with perhaps a little help from us, they will speak for themselves and convince you.

In fact we are even more ambitious. We also wish to attempt a theoretical analysis of chess beauty. In the first part we will isolate what we believe to be the important basic elements of that beauty and look at them one by one. In the second part we will bring those elements together in an orgy of spectacular chess. We will also look at some difficult and abstract questions of chess aesthetics. Hopefully that will also

interest the reader; if not it should be more than possible just to enjoy the examples.

As with much else that is worthwhile, taste develops with experience. We are aiming this book at the practical player, of whatever strength. Intelligent beginners should be able to follow a reasonable amount; however, some experience of chess is necessary before you can really begin to appreciate the game.

At the start of the journey there is a small hill to climb: learning the rules and developing some familiar patterns from play. After that it is downhill most of the way! It is probably the case that less playing experience is necessary before you can begin to enjoy problems (they are relatively independent of playing strength) and more is needed before studies can really be appreciated. The complexity of chess is such that one can appreciate the game on many different levels.

It is a great pity that the majority of competitive players have not become acquainted with the worlds of problems and studies. They are missing out. They have all the equipment necessary to derive great pleasure and yet they fail to do so. Why?

Many of them believe it will not help their game. Not a good reason anyway; in fact they could not be more wrong, as we will demonstrate.

The more this book reaches such people, the better. There is much of value in chess. Some of the positions in this book represent great triumphs of human ingenuity, persistence and sheer intellectual skill. Many beautiful surprises await you. Of course, chess is of great value to society as a competitive sport and as an educational tool, but our objective is to spread awareness of a completely different side to the game. If we succeed to some extent in that objective, it will do no harm.

The Importance of Chess Aesthetics

Just in case you were not completely convinced by the blurb on the back of this book – and it would be most worrying if you were – it is worth considering some of the points in more detail.

The case for chess aesthetics – the value of developing an eye for the beauty of the game – can be argued on several different levels. We will consider four of them:
  1) hedonism (pleasure-seeking);
  2) cultural/artistic value;
  3) educational and, crucially for the competitive player,
  4) practical value.

1) Hedonism

Bertrand Russell once wrote that strawberries, in themselves, were neither good nor bad. He went on to argue that, all other things being equal, the man who likes strawberries is at an advantage over the man who does not. He concluded "But the man who likes them has a pleasure which the other does not have; to that extent his life is more enjoyable and he is better adapted to the world in which both must live." As it is with strawberries, so it is with chess problems and studies. They are simply a great source of pleasure and delight to those who develop a taste for them. Quite a refined form of hedonism maybe, but one which, unlike strawberries, is readily available any time, any place. A book like Kasparian's *Domination in 2545 Endgame Studies* could give you hundreds of hours of entertainment and pleasure – at a price much cheaper, per hour, than strawberries. Seriously, there are a very great many studies, games and problems to enjoy and if you are not satisfied you can always create your own...

2) Cultural and Artistic Value

Paintings are generally accepted as a valid art form, and rightly so. There is every reason why chess composition should be treated in the same way. Just as paintings exhibit the skill and genius of their artists, so can chess positions show the brilliance, imagination and depth of thought of their composers. Some chess compositions require greater technical skill than others. There are different schools of chess composition as well as a great heritage and history to the development of the art.

It could be argued that paintings are simply pretty, and that alone is sufficient reason for looking at them. Such a limited view of art can also be applied to chess composition, but, even within these confines, there is more than enough 'justification' for its existence. Problems and studies help brighten up the intellectual world. That is something of great value.

The term 'art of chess' can mean two things: either true art (which is the meaning we will be using) or craft. The craft of chess, the skill by which you achieve victory, is something quite different.

3) Educational Value

As an experienced teacher of chess in schools, I (J.L.) am a great believer in the general educational benefit of our game. Apart from logical thinking and planning ahead, children also learn from the feedback they get in playing chess. They can see their own thinking process in action and can start to feel responsible for their own decisions. Good problems and pretty studies are a wonderful tool for anybody trying to teach chess to children. The puzzle element commands their attention and the surprising solutions can capture their imagination.

Of course, great games and endgame studies can also have a clear didactic value in teaching chess technique. However, there is more to it than that, and the next section is dedicated to sceptical competitive players who don't see the point in looking at chess composition.

4) Practical Value

'Will looking at problems and studies actually help me play better chess?' This is a question I have been asked many times. The answer is yes.

If you want to become a stronger player, following the example of Garry Kasparov might have its advantages. Let us hear a few things he has written about this subject (see, for example, the chapter entitled 'The Beauty of Chess' in the Batsford book *Learn Chess with Garry Kasparov*):

'I am fond of solving chess problems and, particularly, chess studies. Chess problems are full of paradoxes and original ideas.'

'There are some studies which I like to play through again and again.'

'Chess composition, the most beautiful and mysterious aspect of the art of chess.'

'It was the beauty and brilliance of tactical blows that captivated me in early childhood.'

'Chess for me is art.'

It is fairly clear from that barrage just how important the aesthetic side of chess has been in the development of Kasparov the player. He is by no means the only one. Smyslov, Botvinnik and Lasker have all composed endgame studies. Practically all world class players have an interest in this side of the game – it is part of what a true love for the game consists of.

Looking closer to home, the top English players (as of 1995) provide further examples. John Nunn is one of the world's best problem solvers and has written books on studies and problems. Jon Speelman is also a good solver (though not competitive) and has composed endgame studies. Michael Adams has entered British Chess Problem Solving competitions. Nigel Short sees chess as primarily a competitive sport with the artistry of the game as an important by-product. Julian Hodgson has a splendid eye for beauty in chess and has shown me several of the positions to be found later in this book. Jon Mestel is also a world class solver. To use an overworked pun, it

has been very hard to determine, in recent years, whether he is second to none or second to Nunn – their solving skills are that close. Internationally speaking, Grandmasters Benko and Timman are both brilliant study composers.

The correlation is very clear: a sophisticated aesthetic sense and appreciation of chess beauty go hand-in-hand with top-class play. For those not convinced by the empirical evidence, there are several plausible reasons why looking at chess problems and studies will improve your chess.

Firstly it should enhance powers of chess fantasy by building up the 'vocabulary' of tactical ideas and patterns. As Kasparov put it 'Chess problems are full of paradoxes and original ideas' – so even he came across ideas and 'vocab' he had not previously encountered.

Secondly, solving problems and studies requires very clear, logical, precise, goal-orientated thinking. Such thinking is very valuable, but not exclusively so, when playing chess at any level.

Thirdly, and perhaps most importantly, there is the question of motivation. Again, this is complex and there are several aspects worth considering (even if they are slightly tangential to the central theme of this book). I intend to show why motivation is crucial to competitive success, then to analyse motivation itself and, finally, to discuss why developing your aesthetic sense and fantasy will enhance your motivation.

The next section of this introduction, entitled 'Fantasy and Motivation', is divided into three. Only the final part fits the context of explaining why looking at studies and problems – or reading a book such as this – will help improve your chess; but the rest is necessary to put that final part itself into a slightly different context!

Fantasy and Motivation

The Importance of Motivation

It is helpful to consider an equation sometimes used by sports psychologists:

$$\text{Performance} = \text{Knowledge} + \text{Motivation}$$

In chess terms, the meaning of this is that a player's performance from one tournament to the next will vary entirely with his motivation. Knowledge builds up slowly over the years and does not vary much in a short time, whereas motivation has massive swings up and down, accounting for good and bad form. Of course, other factors, like luck, can play a part and the above equation

only holds as a rough approximation. Looking at my own results in recent years I have averaged about 2475 with several results over 2600 and several below 2350. In a match between myself in good form and myself in bad form, the statistical implication of the above figures is that good form would win something like 8½ to 1½. The moral is clear: competitive players should treat their motivation very seriously indeed and look for ways to improve it. It is not only intelligence, talent for the game, knowledge, understanding and physical fitness that count; will to win, pure unadulterated motivation can also count for enormous variation in the levels that different players reach.

Various Forms of Motivation

Not surprisingly, motivation varies both with time and from person to person. What makes one person tick may be of no consequence to another. But the question remains: why is it that so many people spend so much time on chess? I want to break the different types of motivation into two broad categories:

A) Power, success, glory, money, boosting ego, 'proving yourself', winning, point-scoring, increasing your rating, etc.

B) Reasons intrinsic to the nature of chess: love of the game, pleasure from the flow of ideas, satisfaction from playing a good game...

These two categories are not exclusive, mutually or otherwise. People could play for mental exercise or social reasons, for example. However, most motivation could be described either as type A (competitive) or type B (aesthetic). I am not trying to argue that type B is 'better' than type A. I do not go along with 'It's not winning that matters, its taking part' – in fact I regard that as unprofessional and dilettante – but nor do I endorse 'Winning isn't the main thing, it's the only thing!' That is simply unrealistic. The point is that type B motivation exists and is very important for many reasons, not least that it can help you gain type A success!

I gain pleasure from winning, even if the game was terrible, but I gain many times more pleasure from winning a good game. If the game is good technically (accurately played, say) perhaps that pleasure is partly type A since one could argue that it has a stronger ego-boosting effect. But if the game has a spectacular finish, an elegant and stylish episode or even a single surprising, powerful move I can get an enormously enhanced aesthetic kick. Incidentally, it is better, for practical reasons, to enjoy such things *after* the game, looking back at it. Enjoying them at the board, while you are playing, can

endanger the result! From what we can tell, most players, good and bad, have a similar experience. Winning in style generates enormous pleasure – a lovely, if occasional, reward for some of the pain and suffering involved in playing competitive chess.

Kasparov, perhaps currently the world's most strongly motivated player, is well aware of both types of motivation:

'I want to win, I want to beat everyone, but I want to do it in style!'

Type B motivation is crucial even for less ambitious mortals. If it were just a question of winning or losing, if it were not possible to play a brilliant game, to make an incredible queen sacrifice, to play the occasional shocking or outrageous move, then I suspect many people would not play chess. It simply would not be worth it: such a difficult game and with so few rewards.

It is clear that aesthetic, type B motivation is important for all chess players. If you can increase that motivation by increasing your knowledge and understanding of aesthetic ideas, your game should improve as well.

The Role of Fantasy

Many, many years ago I remember being particularly struck by the following position. I came across it as a young junior while reading the book *Practical Chess Endings* by Irving Chernev.

1.1   Win

A. Gurvich
Bakinski Rabochi 1927

It seems White cannot prevent the g-pawn queening, however...

    1 ♘e4!

Intending to meet 1...g1♕+? with 2 ♘f2+ forcing 2...♕xf2+ 3 ♕xf2 with a win. Black finds a better defence.

    1 ...   ♘d3!

So that 2 ♕xd3 g1♕+ leaves White with insufficient material advantage to win. White's only way to win is quite breathtaking:

    2 ♕f2!!   ♘xf2

If 2...♘f1, then 3 ♕h4+ wins. 2...g1♕ 3 ♘g3+ is also hopeless, so Black has to take the queen.

    3 ♘g3+!!   ♔g1
    4 ♘g5

A fabulous zugzwang. It is mate next move. Although my taste has

changed over the years, and different ideas 'turn me on' nowadays, the final position still makes a strong impression. (Later on in the book, once we have introduced our explanatory concepts, we will be able to discuss the aesthetic qualities of such examples in more detail. For the time being readers can judge the positions for themselves.)

I have to admit that I used to dream of winning important games with the above finish. I suspect the next position also found its way into my subconscious life of the time:

1.2   Win

F. Richter
Suomen Shakki 1953

A very difficult study to solve, since White starts paradoxically, by moving away from the action. Far more natural would be 1 ♔d7+, but it does not win. The position after 4 ♕f7! is an example of 'domination' and for that the king is needed on b7.

1	♔b7+!!	♚h7
2	♕h2+	♚g8
3	♕a2+	♚h7

Not 3...♚f8 4 ♕a8+ and 5 ♕xh8.

4   ♕f7!

Zugzwang. White wins since the black king and pawn cannot move (legally) and the black queen is captured if it moves anywhere along the eighth rank except g8. After 4...♕g8, 5 ♕h5 would be mate.

It was Freud who wrote that 'Fantasy is action in rehearsal.' Endgame studies are, essentially, well worked-out versions of other people's chess fantasies. You can imagine a composer thinking 'Would it not be fabulous if a chess game finished like this ... ?' As the Freud quote suggests, these fantasies have a practical function. Studies show the full potential of what is possible in chess, the heights to which it can aspire.

There can be very few chessplayers whose sense of wonder would not be awakened by positions such as the above. The positions in this book, and others, have motivated me generally, making me realize what a magical game chess is. They say chess is in the Russian soul; here is what Alexander Kotov thought of such positions (from his book *Play Like a Grandmaster*):

'... Chess combinations are a sort of dramatic work of art, full of tension and aesthetic content. It is for this facet of the game more than any other that millions of people throughout the world love chess.'

Chess may well be in the Dutch soul too. GM and journalist Hans Ree expressed the same sentiment much more succinctly:

'Chess is beautiful enough to waste your life for.'

The former French champion, endgame theorist and composer, André Chéron, warns the 'practical plodder' of his possible error:

'The player who would shun the artistic endgame would thereby deprive himself of a spiritual training which is as useful as it is pleasing. If to this disregard he adds that of the problem, he can compliment himself in the knowledge that out of the noble game of chess he has drawn only one third of its potential intellectual enjoyment.'

A Brief History of Beautiful Chess Ideas

In this book we will be looking at the positions themselves rather than the historical context in which they developed. To make up for that, this little section is offered as compensation. It should be stressed that this is a very brief, generalized and necessarily simplistic 'history', written only to provide the newcomer to composition with some perspective.

The art of chess composition has been around a very long time:

1.3   Win

Al-Adli, ninth century

Faced with various threats, White pulls off a tremendous 'swindle'.

1 ♘h5+!   ♖xh5
2 ♖xg6+!   ♔xg6
3 ♖e6#

A combination of which any modern club player would be proud. It could be presented as a study (White to play and win) or a problem (mate in three).

But hang on a second, didn't chess only reach its modern form in the fifteenth century? How can this position be genuine? In fact, the old form of chess, Shatranj, did not have queens or bishops as we know them today, but the above position contains only rooks, knights, kings and pawns – all of which moved much the same way over a thousand years ago as they will tomorrow.

H. J. R. Murray in his *History of Chess* (1913) looked at over 500 positions that cropped up in Arabic and Persian manuscripts dating back as far as the twelfth century. Few positions showed any economy of force; many involved king-hunts. Often, for dramatic and game-like significance, Black threatened mate in one, as in the above problem. There were many fine sacrifices and elegant mates.

Study composition did not reach such heights again until the nineteenth century. Kling and Horwitz established the term 'study' in their 1851 book which contained about 200 endgames. Prior to that, most endgame positions found in chess books were only for didactic purposes. By 1890 Alexei Troitsky (1866-1942) and Henri Rinck (1870-1952) – considered the fathers of the modern endgame study – were already active.

The famous Saavedra position dates from 1895. Saavedra did not in fact create the position; he simply discovered the paradoxical under-promotion 6 c8♖, contradicting published analysis 'proving' that the position was drawn. For that one beautiful move, his name will probably be more famous than any other grandmaster of the present era who fails to reach over 2700 standard! The study is, of course, a great one. Rich play out of a simple-looking position, a paradoxical twist at the end and an elegant flow to the logic of the solution. All from just four pieces – marvellous economy.

1.4   Win

F. Saavedra (Barbier)
Glasgow Weekly Citizen 1895

1   c7   ♜d6+

There is no other way to stop the pawn promoting. If, now, 2 ♞c5? then 2...♜d1! 3 c8♛? ♜c1+ wins the queen. 2 ♞b7? ♜d7 is only a draw.

2   ♞b5   ♜d5+
3   ♞b4   ♜d4+
4   ♞b3   ♜d3+

There is a minor dual here in that White could have played 4 ♞c3 ♜d1 5 ♞c2 ♜d4!, transposing.

5   ♞c2!   ♜d4!

No longer able to go 'behind' the king on the c-file, Black finds a surprise defence: 6 c8♛? ♜c4+ 7 ♛xc4 is drawn by stalemate! Saavedra found that White could still win:

6   c8♜!!

Threatens mate by 7 ♜a8+ ♜a4 8 ♜xa4.

6   ...   ♜a4
7   ♞b3

Threatens both the rook and the king (8 ♜c1 mate). There is no defence.

This century has seen prolific activity, especially amongst Soviet composers. Many themes have been exploited almost exhaustively. There now exist vast collections of high-class studies, a testimony to the enormous amount of work that has been put in by some of the great composers. You will see some of them later in the book, but here I want to present you with a personal favourite illustrating the theme of *Domination*, a term coined by its composer, Henri Rinck.

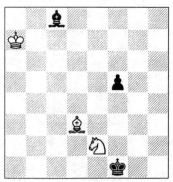

1.5   Win

H. Rinck
Las Noticias 1926

1   ♞b8!   ♝d7

The only square. After 1...♗e6, 2 ♘f4+ wins.

2 ♔c7　　♗e8

If 2...♗a4, 3 ♘c3+. The bishop and knight 'battery' against the black king controls all the black bishop's escape squares.

3 ♔d8　　♗f7

If 3...♗a4, then 4 ♘c3+, whilst 3...♗g6(h5) is met by 4 ♘f4+.

4 ♔e7　　♗g8

The hunt continues. Incredibly, all the bishop's squares are controlled, e.g. 4...♗a2 5 ♘c3+ or 4...♗b3 5 ♘c1+.

5 ♔f8　　♗h7
6 ♔g7

If you tried to compose a position where the white king chases a bishop to its doom (as in the above position) you would expect a board full of pieces. Rinck controls the play with just four more pieces (including the black king). Rich content with astounding economy – the bishop is dominated over more than half the light squares on the board. To my mind this position is a simply fabulous achievement.

Unusually, the above endgame has no introductory sequence (sometimes known as 'foreplay'!). It just starts in the middle of the essential action (a floating domination across the board). More often composers try to hide the main idea in order to make it harder to see, and to increase the element of surprise, but this study is exceptional, and is almost perfect presented as it stands. A natural gem!

The history of the game (and its famous players) is well known. It is interesting that the development of positional theory – the theory of Steinitz and Lasker; the hypermoderns; the dynamic Russian school – has gone hand-in-hand with the mushrooming of study art. Figures such as Richard Réti (1889-1929) have been significant in both.

Finally, moving on to the problem, the major advances on what had been seen a thousand years earlier by the Muslim world again came in the nineteenth century. One man in particular stands out: Sam Loyd (1841-1911). His problems were not only entertaining, original and elegant but also way ahead of their time in terms of thematic content. The following problem (known as the 'organ pipes') is a favourite of leading German Grandmaster Gerald Hertneck. Several beginners to whom I have shown the position also expressed their admiration for it, showing just how accessible Loyd's problems can be.

(see diagram on following page)

The solution **1 ♕a5!** sets up a striking zugzwang. The black pieces cannot help but get in each other's way: 1...♗d7 2 ♕d5#; 1...♗e6 2 ♕e5#; 1...♖e7 2 ♕xb4#; 1...♖d7 2 ♘f5#; and 1...♗c5 2 ♕a1# being

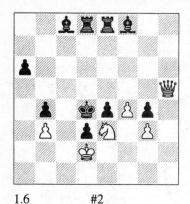

1.6   #2

Sam Loyd
Boston Gazette 1859

sample variations. The reader should go through every legal black move just to prove it really is mate in two. The 'organ pipes' – the formation from c8 to f8 – have since become an established idea seen in many more problems.

Going back to the practical value of solving problems, seeing surprising zugzwangs as in the above position can greatly help a player broaden his perspective. Weaker players tend to see the board only from their side, whereas stronger players are able to step inside the opponent's shoes from time to time and take both sides' plans into consideration. Karpov, for example, often reaches positions where all his opponent's moves have drawbacks. It is not (humanly) possible to solve the Loyd problem without looking at both sides' possibilities.

This century has seen a great deal of activity in problem composition. Many ideas and themes have been investigated almost to exhaustion. Some people claim it is now impossible to create a genuinely original mate in two. Others have resorted to 'fairy chess' to find new pastures. Towards the end of the book we will look at some unorthodox types of problem, but we will restrict ourselves to positions with regular chess pieces.

In the orthodox mate in three, Lev Loshinsky (1913-1976) is considered one of the greatest exponents. Some of his problems are extremely complex and sophisticated, yet still crisp and clear. In his book *Solving in Style* John Nunn described the following problem as 'perfect in every way'. To really understand such a problem takes time (at least half an hour probably), but it is well worth the investment. Except for its unusual quality, it is a typical modern mate in three.

(see diagram on following page)

Sooner or later practical players will have to face up to complicated problems with a board full of pieces. Forget your prejudices for just a few minutes and enjoy unravelling the mechanism of this problem – you will begin to see why it is necessary to have all those pieces to achieve the desired effect. The only way to force mate in three is as follows:

1.7   #3

L. Loshinsky
First Prize '64' 1974

1   ♖g6!

A surprising key, exposing the white king to various checks by moves of the f7 pawn (...fxg6; ...f6; ...f5). In fact, in view of the threat 2 ♘h3+ gxh3 3 ♗g3#, Black must move the f-pawn (1...♗f1 fails to 2 ♘e6+ fxe6 3 ♕f8#). There are now three variations all exploiting the intersection in the lines of action of the black pieces on the square d5. Bear in mind that the bishop on c4 prevents ♘e6# and the rook prevents e6#.

    a) 1...f5+ 2 ♗d5! with 2...♗xd5+ 3 e6# or 2...♖xd5 3 ♘e6# to follow.

    b) 1...f6+ 2 d5! ♖xd5 (2...♗xd5+ 3 e6#) 3 ♘e6#.

    c) 1...fxg6+ 2 ♘d5+! ♗xd5+ (or 2...♖xd5 3 ♕f8#) 3 e6#. Note that 2 d5? would fail to 2...g3!.

In other words, for each of the three different moves by the black

f-pawn, a different white unit plays into d5. Apart from the paradoxical element, the beauty of this problem lies in the depth and structure of the thinking needed to solve it. The solution displays great unity as well as a sort of 'conceptual geometry'.

Finally, to conclude this brief survey, I want to show another of my personal favourites. It is a mate in six from early in this century. Surprisingly, it is not as well known as its merits deserve.

1.8   #6

T. Nissl
Akademische Monatshefte
für Schach, 1910

The black king has no escape, but how does the white bishop get at it?

1   ♗h4!

Threatens 2 ♗e1+; the black rook stops this while keeping an eye on the d8 square.

    1 ...   ♖d1

    2   ♗g3!   ♖c1

Necessary to stop both ♗c7 and ♗e1.

3 ♗f4! ♖c2

And now the bishop returns to its starting square. Such a trip is known by the German term 'Rundlauf'.

4 ♗g5

The rook cannot cope any longer. It is not possible to prevent both 5 ♗d2 and 5 ♗d8 simultaneously, so White mates in two more moves e.g. 4...♖c8 5 ♗d2+ ♖c3 6 ♗xc3#.

Why is this problem special? If you imagine, starting from an empty board, trying to compose a position where the white bishop has to do a 'Rundlauf' (♗g5-h4-g3-f4-g5), you would expect the problem to need many more then seven pieces. Here it is achieved in a miniature with game-like material (it is a rook and opposite-coloured bishop ending with White a single pawn up). The interplay between the white bishop and the black rook is entertaining, the solution is very elegant and the setting is perfect. An underrated masterpiece.

Previous Work in the Field

Given the enormous number of books on chess and the importance of aesthetic taste (even if only for practical reasons), there is surprisingly little published and available material on this topic. [At least that is the case in English; a number of Russian composers have published their works in conjunction with their philosophy and methods.]

Probably the most significant work was done by Emanuel Lasker. In his *Manual of Chess* the former world champion devotes one part out of six (the others being 'Elements', 'Openings', 'Combinations', 'Positional Play' and 'Examples') to 'The Aesthetic Effect in Chess'. It is well worth reading for yourself, but basically his theory of chess aesthetics is quite clear. According to Lasker the aesthetic effect in chess depends upon the *achievement* of the pieces. The ideal is when the pieces achieve a difficult task of vital importance (in chess terms) and can do so in one way only. The greater the achievement, the closer to the ideal – the stronger the aesthetic effect. Economy is clearly important since, if fewer pieces can accomplish the same task, the greater the achievement. It is difficult to disagree with anything Lasker writes on chess aesthetics. In our book we will be trying to take the theory further. Lasker gives several examples (problems, studies and games) of which the following seems to be his favourite:

(see diagram on following page)

The position is a win for White if he can stay two pieces up, but he cannot prevent Black picking off one of the knights.

1 ♗e2!

1.9   Win

E. Ratner

Em. Lasker's Lehrbuch
des Schachspiels, 1926

The reason that this is the only square to win is already well hidden. 1 ♗f1 ♔b7+ 2 ♔h1 ♗d4 draws (compare this with the main line), while 1 ♗d3 ♔b7+ 2 ♔g2 ♗d4 3 ♘b3 ♗xe5 4 ♘a5+ ♔b6! 5 ♘c4+ ♔c5 6 ♘xe5 ♔d4! regains the piece.

1	...	♔b7+
2	♔g2	♗d4
3	♘b3	♗xe5
4	♘a5+	♔a8

The only square since 4...♔c8 allows 5 ♗g4+ and 6 ♘c6+.

5	♘c6	♗d6

It is not important where the bishop goes.

6	♗a6	g5

Now that his opposite number is trapped, the white king races to c8 to pick off his prey. Black's best chance lies in advancing his g-pawn. If White had played 1 ♗f1? this plan

would have drawn for Black, since 1...♔b7+ 2 ♔g2 blocks the bishop (see the note to move four). So White would have been forced to play 2 ♔h1, losing critical time for the final phase. Clever stuff, huh?

7	♔f3	♗f4
8	♔g4	♗d2
9	♔f5	♗f4

If the g-pawn moves White can just take it or, more dramatically, go straight for the mate anyway.

10	♔e6	g4
11	♔d7	g3
12	♔c8	g2
13	♗b7#	

'The white army is composed only of heroes ... The above composition comes near to the ideal' – Lasker. It is certainly a wonderful piece of chess action – not easy to solve since you have to take Black's play into consideration, too. It is particularly nice (and deep) the way White's first move is the only one to win. The black king is lured into the corner, trapped and executed in both a surprising and elegant fashion. The play has a pleasant flow to it, with each piece just succeeding in doing what it has to do. The general himself (the white king) closes in to finish off his counterpart.

Lasker's book was first published in England in 1932. Since then there have been several books consisting purely of artistic compositions with practically no commentary or theory except, perhaps, for a brief introduction. Roycroft's *Test Tube Chess* is an exception. The book focuses on studies and has a rich, rambling commentary which is well worth reading. Also excellent is John Nunn's *Solving in Style* which has many nice examples clearly and logically presented from the solver's point of view. We will be trying not to duplicate too many of the examples from these works, although some of them are such masterpieces that we feel compelled to use them. Neither Roycroft nor Nunn focus exclusively on aesthetic considerations and no 'theory of chess aesthetics' emerges in either book. We believe the theory in this book to be original.

Other books of interest include *Creative Chess* by Avni, the *Oxford Companion to Chess* (Hooper and Whyld) and one chapter of *Learn Chess with Garry Kasparov* where the World Champion gives his views on chess art. Avni's book contains an interesting selection of positions where unusual measures are called for, but again the positions are not looked at from an aesthetic or artistic viewpoint, but more from a psychological or 'creative thinking' slant. *The Oxford Companion* has interesting background material on composers and composition. As could be gathered from the quotes given earlier, Kasparov enthuses unreservedly about the beauty of the game. He gives some good examples too, but the five pages are not enough for him to reveal any deeper thoughts on the subject. For those interested specifically in problems, *Chess Problems; an Introduction to an Art* (Matthews, Lipton and Rice) can be recommended. It systematically surveys the problem field with some interesting general commentary too, but again there is no distinct aesthetic theory.

Philosophical Perspective: Art, Analogies and Taste

Beauty and taste have long been topics for heated philosophical debate. Plato, Hume, Kant and Wittgenstein have been among those tackling questions such as: What is art, what is its value? How do you define beauty? How is it perceived? Can taste be objective? Not surprisingly, these questions lead to further and still broader questions. There are many conflicting theories and partial answers involving terms such as 'imitation', 'expression', 'representation', 'form', 'symbolism', 'yūgen' and 'sōō'.

Our book will assume no previous knowledge of any of this, but, in case you were wondering, the Japanese Zeami Motokiyo (1363-1443) argued that the value of art lies in yūgen ('mystery and depth') and that the artist should follow the rule of sōō ('appropriateness to context') – a fine theory when applied to chess, and he probably never saw the game.

While reading up on aesthetics in general I was surprised just how well many of the theories applied to chess. It confirmed me in my view that chess composition is an art form to be reckoned with. Perhaps there are limits to what can be expressed (it is hard to show 'compassion' in a mate in two for example), but composition can evoke a wider range of responses than is commonly imagined. I've experienced surprise, astonishment, depth, pleasing geometrical patterns, humour and, of course, pleasure just looking at the solutions to positions. Naturally the competitive game can involve a range of other emotions (fear, relief, etc.), but that is not currently our concern.

Analogies

It is quite easy, and sometimes even useful, to draw analogies between chess and other forms of art. Take writing for example. If the game is likened to reality then the study is similar to the novel. There should be nothing irrelevant, no waste – both should, ideally, be crisp and clear and flow from start to finish carrying the solver/reader along. Extending the analogy further, problems (with their precise stipulation, 'unnatural' to the real game) would be like some form of more structured writing – limericks or sonnets perhaps.

To some extent it is possible to create criteria of aesthetic beauty applicable across the range of forms that beauty can take. Aquinas (around 1270) tried to define beauty as that which pleases solely in the contemplation of it, and which exhibits clarity, appropriate proportion and perfection. Around 1450, Leon Alberti (writing on architecture) proposed that beauty is an order or arrangement such that any change is for the worse. Such thoughts apply quite well to chess, too. Some of the criteria for chess beauty we develop in this book may apply to other fields (such as literature, music, paintings, cinema, architecture, the human form, fashion, nature...) but, if so, that would be purely accidental. They are designed to incorporate only the individual nature of chess composition (it is even necessary to have additional criteria for competitive chess). Ultimately, chess is its own language.

Chess, however, may prove to be a useful testing ground for more general aesthetic theories, in the same way as computer chess has been a measure for artificial intelligence. Chess, being a closed system, can be clear and testable, which gives it an advantage over many other fields.

Relaxation of Tension

Earlier we discussed the possible educational, cultural and practical value of chess art, but what causes the intrinsic pleasure when somebody appreciates a fine chess game? One interesting description (or theory) is that pleasure results from the relaxation of tension. The pleasure of winning is because of the great relaxation of tension when the game ends. A chess problem (or a murder mystery) can create a certain tension which is resolved as the solution becomes clear, as the elements fall into place. Music can create a tension which results in pleasure as the brain processes and understands it. If the music is too simple, by the time you have heard it a couple of times it fails to create any further tension and consequently no further pleasure. If it is too complex, you may never resolve it and hence never enjoy it.

The ability to understand the content of something, be it a sequence of chess moves, a film, or a piece of music, is crucial to deriving pleasure from it. Of course, this ability to perceive the order and reasonableness of a chess sequence (or the harmony in music, or the consistency of a film) will depend on how sophisticated the viewer/listener is. You cannot expect to enjoy any form of chess without, to some degree, understanding it. Weaker players need not despair though, since all this means is that they may need to spend a little longer in discovering the 'truth'. In chess composition the truth is not necessarily beautiful (the 'truth' has ruined many would-be beautiful ideas) but when the two coincide we have before us real chess art.

Recognizing Patterns

Broadly speaking, we regard pleasure as very much a part of the aesthetic experience. The greater the relaxation of tension, the greater that pleasure. Tackling the question of what causes pleasure on a neurological level is way outside the scope of our book.

Another theory (the first part of which is due to the Austrian Ernst Mach, around 1890) which helps to explain chess aesthetic pleasure runs as follows: in order to survive by intelligence, the human brain has become very quick at recognizing patterns, repetitions and symmetries. The ability to discover order has been crucial to the success of human beings and their brains have evolved in such a way as to be very good at it. A number of these geometrical ideas occur on the chessboard, and the brain enjoys discovering such order. Using familiar patterns to help resolve and sort out a chess position causes pleasure since the tension created by the (initially chaotic) position is reduced. As will be seen shortly, chess 'geometry' is one of the key elements of our theory.

Taste

What creates tension in one brain, may or may not create tension in another. As pointed out above, people's ability to understand a piece of work may also vary. We have moved onto the difficult question of taste which Hume described as a peculiar kind of 'emotionally inspired discrimination'. It may vary because of intelligence, it may vary with experience, but one thing is for sure: it certainly varies! Is there such a thing as objectively good taste? Yes, we believe so. It is simply a lazy option to dismiss the subject with something like 'beauty is in the eye of the beholder'. Some chess games are better than others, some literature is 'good' and some 'bad'. Of that much we are reasonably convinced, but proving it is another matter. Perhaps, dear reader, you feel you have good taste in music (and that there is some objectivity about that taste) but could you prove it?

Rules of Assessment

Believe it or not, people have actually attempted to create a formula for the assessment of mate in two chess problems. Feed in a couple of positions and the formula decides which is the better one! We believe this is going too far. Formulating guiding principles is not easy, but if you can do it successfully (usefully), fine. Having rigid rules for assessment, an absolute formula, is another matter. Rules for assessment would imply associated rules for creation. There would be no creativity or freedom left and the art-form would be stifled. Even if the price you have to pay for freedom is that 99% of what is produced is garbage, it seems better to have that freedom than a rigid set of rules. Paradoxically, the attempt to have such rules for art generally may have helped the development of chess. Communist states greatly restricted the freedom of their artists ('socialist realism') and many frustrated and talented minds turned their attention to our politically neutral game. It was not just the Soviet *players* who were way ahead of the rest of the world, but also their problem and study composers.

So, although the choice of positions in this book was dictated by our taste, and we will often try to say why we like certain aspects of those positions, do not expect to find any clear rules for assessment. For the reasons given above we think it better not to undertake such a task. In other words, we will only partially be attempting to validate our judgements. We neither are, nor wish to be considered, arbiters of taste.

Balance and Tension

In most art forms, introducing tension while maintaining balance is a delicate matter. How does the notion of 'balance' apply to chess and chess composition?

At the start of a game of chess, two equal armies stand facing each other across the board. There is a balance between the forces (and resources) available to Black and White. With good play, that balance is maintained. After a serious blunder, the balance is upset and the other side obtains a winning position. There have been many grandmaster games where a symmetrical type of position is reached, the pieces are swapped off and the game heads inexorably towards a draw. Such games fail to capture the interest since, although balance is maintained throughout, there is no tension. It is far more exciting when there is a balance between conflicting elements after, for example, a sacrifice. Perhaps then there could be a balance between initiative and material. Broadly speaking, the greater the tension and the longer the balance is maintained, the more 'interesting' the game.

But where is the balance in a White to play and win study? Here the notion is quite subtle, and in fact the 'rules' of creating a sound study ensure a certain balance. For a sound study, there must be only one solution (if there are two ways to do it, the study is 'cooked'). If White does not have sufficient resources there will be no win. Too many resources and there will be several wins. The 'balance' must be just right so that there is precisely one win. Similar considerations apply to problems with stipulations such as 'mate in two'. There must be a balance of force such that there is a unique solution (assuming the problem is sound). This could also be regarded as 'economy of solution'.

Here is a tricky one for you: place the white king on a6, the black king on a8 and a white rook on h1. White to play and mate in one! Here, in the sense discussed above, there is a balance – the problem is sound with a unique solution (1 ♖h8, heartfelt congratulations). However it is trivial and does not deserve a diagram, since there is practically zero tension. Because there is no tension, there is no pleasure in finding the solution (resolving the tension) and no aesthetic effect (perhaps a complete beginner might think otherwise; these notions are relative to the observer). It is the composer's job to play around with the balance and thereby create as much tension as possible.

Our four Elements and why we have introduced them

In this book we are going to consider four basic elements:

1. Paradox
2. Depth
3. Geometry, and
4. Flow.

These terms will be defined more fully (with many examples) when we come to the individual chapters dedicated to each of them, but for the present, the following should help you to understand what we mean by them.

1. Paradox

Surprise, outrageousness. An immediate confrontational tension is created. The response to a paradoxical move might be 'How can this be possible?' or 'That simply cannot work!'. An example would be the move 2 ♕f2!! in the solution to the Gurvich study (see the first example in the book) or the underpromotion 6 c8♖!! in the Saavedra position. To win by such means is a heroic form of achievement, and, other things being equal, the more paradox in the play, the better.

2. Depth

Subtlety, complexity. A deep move is one which is not obvious (though not necessarily paradoxical) and for which the point is well hidden. Initially one does not understand it, and later the response is 'Ah, so that was the point!'. In the study by Ratner given earlier, the move 1 ♗e2! would qualify as being deep. In the Richter position 1 ♔b7!! is both paradoxical (moving away from the action) and deep. Depth relates to the complexity of what is being achieved. Again, other things being equal, the deeper the moves, the stronger the aesthetic effect. A game with no deep moves at all might be enjoyable the first time you see it, and maybe even a second time if it is good for other reasons; but some degree of depth is required to generate sufficient tension to count as a true masterpiece that can be played over many times with pleasure.

3. Geometry

Patterns, repetitions, echoes, mutual interferences between a rook and a bishop ... The response might be 'Oh, what a pretty pattern!'. An example of mainly geometrical play would be the Nissl position (see the end of the brief history section). Here the bishop jockeys with the rook (in what could be described as a geometrical duel) while completing a diamond-shaped 'Rundlauf' (♗g5-h4-g3-f4-g5). In the Sam

Loyd 'Organ Pipes' mate in two, the mutual interference on lines and diagonals would also be called geometrical. As explained earlier, the brain is good at spotting such patterns and the prettier the pattern that is involved in achieving something, the better (the tension is resolved in a pleasing, aesthetic fashion).

In our extended meaning of 'geometry', any striking pattern or special feature could be included. For example, if during the solution to a problem one side promotes pawns to each of the four possible pieces (♕, ♘, ♖, ♗ – this is known as 'Allumwandlung') this would be a 'pattern' or feature that the brain might easily recognize. Many tasks and special effects achieved by composers fall into this broader 'geometry' which is not restricted entirely to its spatial sense.

4. Flow

Smoothness of movement. It relates to the length of the sequence of moves for which the tension is dynamically maintained. For example in the Rinck position (see history section), the play flows across the board as the king chases the bishop for a whole series of moves. The degree of tension (or 'area' of tension) could be seen in terms of length × depth. The response to flow might be something like: 'Whoosh! I'm being carried along!', and again, the more flow the stronger the aesthetic effect. Often, in top class studies, an elegant flow is abruptly halted by a paradoxical finish.

These four factors are relatively independent of one another and have come about after a sort of 'instinctive factor analysis' of our experience of beautiful chess ideas.

What is the point of this categorisation? Basically to help us communicate about tension and the aesthetic effect in chess and chess composition. Games, studies and problems exist regardless of how we try to describe them. There is nothing 'real' about our categories; they are just words and one should not expect too much from them. As with any descriptive theory, if the categories prove helpful in communication, they will be useful and will survive. If not, they will die and we would have failed in our task. Certainly your co-authors find the categories useful. With surprising consistency and clarity we agree as to which of the four elements (one, two, three or all four of them) are present in a piece of chess action. The categories help us identify and pinpoint the tension-creating features of the play and thus to talk more usefully about aesthetic issues (and it is never that easy to talk about such abstract matters).

Limitations of our Method

We should point out that our method is completely useless for classifying games or positions since any number of our elements (zero to all four) might be involved in a single piece of chess action. To classify positions, another approach to aesthetics would be needed, i.e. one where the objective content of the 'work of art' is considered. In the case of chess this might involve such classifications as 'mate', 'zugzwang', 'positional draw', 'perpetual check' and the like. John Nunn takes such an approach in his book *Tactical Chess Endings*. There have been books looking at a single theme, e.g. Kasparian's *Domination in 2545 Endgame Studies*.

Our approach is different. We are looking at the aesthetic response to the position and our categories are designed to help us do that. Aspects such as 'originality', 'economy', 'difficulty', 'spectacularity' and so on are part of the 'language of criticism' applied to works as a whole. We will be using such terms, but they are not fundamental elements of our approach. However a few basic thoughts should be articulated:

Originality

Naturally, when judging chess composition, originality is very important. After all, the easiest way to compose a great endgame study is to pick an earlier masterpiece and adapt it slightly! The new but unoriginal study might be just as good, if judged by purely aesthetic criteria, but would (rightly) be disparaged by the critics if the 'anticipation' was noticed. Knowing whether something is original depends on the ability to research what has gone before and on a judgement as to how similar one idea is to another. We shall not be tackling such questions.

Economy

Economy of material is a necessary condition of good composition. Anything wasted or 'heavy' immediately jars the aesthetic eye. We will be assuming the reader understands this concept without further explanation and the reader may assume that none of the composed positions in this book have unnecessary material. We will only point out when compositions are particularly striking in their use of force.

Economy of time is another, more subtle, notion. Repeating moves or winning by a long-winded method detracts from the artistic quality of a game. In problems it would be considered bad if a mate in three showed something that could be exhibited in a mate in two. Generally speaking, economy is more about 'form' rather than aesthetic content itself.

Achievement

Earlier we pointed out that Lasker based his theory of chess aesthetics on the notion of 'achievement'. Actually, achievement is a very tricky concept to deal with, since it comes in several forms. One could talk of achievement of the pieces as part of the objective content of the chess. Then there is achievement of certain 'tasks' within the world of composition. Players and solvers can achieve things too. Within the language of criticism one can also talk of the achievement of the position as a whole and whether the composer succeeds in realising his intention. It is quite easy to confuse these different types of animal and, to avoid communication difficulties, it is probably best not to rely on this notion too heavily.

Completeness

It is possible that there are forms of achievement not conveniently dealt with by our four elements. We believe our elements can be easily applied to almost all aesthetic chess positions, but it is difficult to be 'complete'. Chess art is a rich field and it is natural that there will be positions which defy attempts to categorize or explain their appeal. We considered adding a fifth element dealing with the appreciation of special forms of achievement ('special effects') but decided that it was not sufficiently useful. Of course, one could artificially achieve completeness by adding a fifth element that deals with everything not dealt with by the other four, but that would be even more pointless!

One further drawback to the approach of looking at aesthetic response is that such response is relative. To some extent we are relying on the notion of the typical man in the street, one who just happens to have a fair degree of chess sophistication and experience. Presumably an orang-utan would experience no aesthetic response when presented with a piece of chess art (although there might be some rudimentary awareness of geometrical patterns). Despite this relativity, a certain consensus between experienced chess minds is hoped for, since we could not get anywhere without it.

We hope you'll forgive the theoretical and heavy nature of this last section. In that sense it should be the worst part of a book which is, essentially, example driven. It is, of course, possible just to enjoy the positions without having any artistic or philosophical context in which to place them, just as it is possible (and fairly normal) to play good chess without worrying about the place of the game in society.

Jonathan Levitt, *London 1995*

Part Two: The Elements of Chess Beauty

Before attempting to describe the elements of chess beauty in detail, it is necessary to clarify a fundamental issue: what precisely is the entity to which we apply the description 'beautiful'?

This question is surprisingly tricky to answer, because we customarily use the term so broadly and loosely. We might apply it to a game or composition as a whole, to a particular sequence of moves, a line of play, or an individual move. In compositions particularly, we often describe a group of variations or a thematic idea as beautiful.

The issue is encapsulated by Tarrasch's famous epigram, 'The beauty of a move lies in the thought behind it'. As all chessplayers will know, the 'thought behind' most moves includes other move-sequences, which, the player hopes, justify his choice. In this book we are not only concerned with the individual moves which constitute the actual game or solution, but also with their underlying ideas. These ideas, themselves fleshed out as move-sequences, not only provide each actual choice with its rationale but often form an important part of its aesthetic context.

To help us define more precisely what we are talking about when we discuss aspects of a game or composition, it is helpful to introduce the concept of the move-set. We define a *move-set* as either:

(a) a sequence of moves, of length of at least one, or

(b) a collection of sequences taken together, such as in a problem which has a number of variations triggered by a key move. In short, a move-set is a group of moves which we arbitrarily create because the moves in it share common features which we wish to single out. It is important to note that this grouping may well contain moves which are 'virtual', i.e. in a sense do not actually occur in the game or composition, but which are part of the rationale of the moves that do.

The diagram will help make the concept of a move-set clear.

(see diagram on following page)

The solution runs:

1   ♔e3+   ♚b3

If the king goes to the fifth rank, then 2 ♖xh5 wins the black queen.

Win

H. M. Lommer
Die Schwalbe, 1965

2 ♖xh5!

Anyway!

2 ...   ♛xf7
3 ♖b5+

Black has four alternative king moves:

A: 3 ...   ♚a4
      4 ♘xc3#

B: 3 ...   ♚c4
      4 ♘xa3#

C: 3 ...   ♚a2
      4 ♘xc3+   ♚a1
      5 ♖b1#

D: 3 ...   ♚c2
      4 ♘xa3+   ♚c1
      5 ♖b1#

The idea of this little work is to show a theme which is much more often seen in problems than in studies: starflights. By this is meant the four possible moves of the black king in answer to 3 ♖b5+ – they form the geometrical shape of a star. After each of these king moves, referred to in composer's jargon as *flights*, there should be a distinct and unique White continuation for the theme to be fully shown. Thus the move-set comprising the four variations beginning with Black's third move represents the thematic content. The play prior to that (and any alternatives worthy of note) constitutes another move-set, usually referred to as the *introduction* to the study.

2 Paradox

'One should always be a little improbable.' *Oscar Wilde*
'Surprise is the greatest gift which life can grant us.' *Boris Pasternak*

The first of our elements, Paradox, carries, we believe, the most powerful impact on the chessplayer's emotions. A succinct dictionary definition of the meaning of the word is sufficient for our purposes: 'A phenomenon that exhibits some conflict with preconceived notions of what is reasonable or possible...'

Sometimes chess moves can go so strongly against instinct that the player is left visibly shaken by the 'impossible' move. He realises with a jolt that the move is not only possible, but also good.

Such paradox is, of course, relative and depends on the player being sufficiently experienced to have acquired preconceived notions. The stronger those preconceptions, the stronger the sensation of paradox. An obvious queen sacrifice is no longer paradoxical to a grandmaster, but a move that allows a weakening of the pawn structure might be. More developed players have more sophisticated 'rules'. The nature of paradoxical moves remains the same, though: such moves break the rules.

The most prevalent type of paradox is the **paradox of material**, which we shall examine first. After that we review an interesting variety of paradoxical effects classified under the broad category of **rule-breaking**. At the end of the chapter we shall look at an example of a special type of paradox – **set play** – which plays an important role in many modern chess problems.

The Paradox of Material

The type of paradox most frequently seen in the game as played is also, quite naturally, the kind which is dearest to the chessplayer's heart: the paradox of material. The following 'page of paradox' should give you a clear idea of what we mean.

In 2.1, White has to put all his pieces *en prise*, while in 2.2 the surprising queen offer sets up three pretty mates. In 2.3 the shocking key gives Black the choice of capturing the rook or giving a check. The two positional draws are more complex. In 2.4 White can oscillate his bishop between the two safe squares d6 and e5, with a knight fork on f7 as

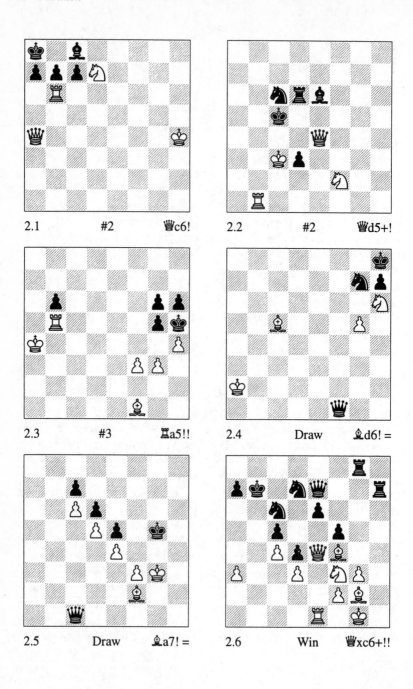

| 2.1 | #2 | ♕c6! | 2.2 | #2 | ♕d5+! |

| 2.3 | #3 | ♖a5!! | 2.4 | Draw | ♗d6! = |

| 2.5 | Draw | ♗a7! = | 2.6 | Win | ♕xc6+!! |

protection. 2.5 shows a position where Black can make no progress since his king cannot infiltrate on either side of the board. Careful defence suffices to hold the draw. An alarming aspect of this position for King's Indian lovers is that the pawn structure is typical of that opening. In 2.6, Norwood finishes off his opponent with a dashing queen sacrifice. The black king is chased all the way up the board and mated in the corner.

Here are the sources, together with detailed solutions to the longer positions:

2.1: V. Aleksandrov, special commendation, Kubbel Memorial Ty 1991.

2.2: F. Giegold, *Kristall* 1962.

2.3: H. W. Grant, *Evening News* 1942.

The variations of this problem run 1...b5+ 2 ♗xb5 gxh4 (or 2...g4) 3 ♗e8#, or 1...bxa5 2 ♗e2 g4/gxh4 3 fxg4/f4#.

2.4: End of a study by G. Zakhodiakin, 1st Prize, *Shakhmatny Listok* 1930.

2.5: From a study by V. A. Chekhover, 14 Commend, USSR Champ. 1948.

2.6: From a game D. Norwood – S. Marsh, Walsall Kipping 1992: 1 ♕xc6+!! ♔xc6 2 ♘xd4+! ♔b6 3 ♖b1+ ♔a6 4 ♗b7+ ♔a5 5 ♗d2+ ♔a4 6 ♗c6+ ♔xa3 7 ♗c1+ ♔a2 8 ♖b2+ ♔a1 9 ♘c2#.

Now try solving one for yourself – and do not be afraid to sacrifice in your search for the solution. You can remain a control freak even with limited means!

2.7   #5

A. Dreyers
6th-7th Place, Champ.
Latvian SSR, 1957

Diagram 2.7 is a typical composer's interpretation of material paradox:

    1 ♘h3!   **♔xh1**

    2 ♔f3!

Note how White has to get the timing of his moves right.

    2 ...   **g4+**

    3 ♔g3   **gxh3**

    4 ♔f2   **h2**

    5 ♘g3#

White has only three pieces apart from his king, yet to force mate in five he has to sacrifice two of them – a fine achievement. Did you manage to solve it? Such problems, in which

Black is restricted to a single move at each turn, are by their nature relatively easy for the experienced solver.

The next example shows a typical two-mover paradox.

2.8   #2

G. H. Goethart, 4th Prize
The Problemist 1952

The key is **1 ♕a6!!** which not only offers the queen to two black pieces, but also gives the king a flight square on c5 – with check! The purpose of this incredible move is simply to shut off the black rook from the a7 bishop, threatening mate by **2 ♖b5#**.

If **1...♖xa6** then **2 ♖xa6#**, while **1...♗xa6** creates a second flight on c4 but allows the double check **2 ♖b4#**.

The problem also demonstrates a rule-breaking type of paradox with **1...♔c5+** ('don't allow the black king to move' and 'don't allow Black

to give check' are the 'rules' which are implicit in this sort of position), which is met by **2 ♖b2#**, shutting off the a1-bishop.

A very clever geometrical variation occurs after **1...♗b5**. This move again vacates c4, but it also shuts off the white rook, preventing **2 ♖b4#**. On the other hand, it interferes with the black rook's ability to interpose on c5, so White can play **2 ♖c6#**.

As far as the game as played is concerned, the paradox of material is clearly top of the pops, covering all categories of sacrifice from the Queen's Gambit to the goriest conceivable combination. Its essence lies in the fact that, to be successful, a sacrifice involves the investment of something tangible in exchange for something abstract – an advantage in time or position – which turns out ultimately to be the more important. Much has been written about sacrifice in chess. Here we will merely state that, other things being equal, to have a preponderance in material is to have an advantage; therefore, to sacrifice material and thereby to obtain an advantage appears paradoxical.

At its best, the paradox of material is the stuff of which immortal games are made. At its worst, it is redundant, a gesture towards art where a more prosaic course is the more effective.

As an example of sacrifice in the game, we give here a combination of a sort which is comparatively infrequent: the motivation of the sacrifice is entirely to gain time. (Most combinations naturally involve a strong time element, but there is generally at least one major positional element resulting from the sacrifice, such as a line opening or a square blocking).

Study Diagram 2.9 from White's point of view.

2.9   W

A. Alekhine – C. H. O' D. Alexander Nottingham 1936

If you imagine the white queen on d2 instead of g5, White would have the combination 1 ♗xf5!. Then, if Black did not capture, he would soon lose owing not only to the pawn deficit, but even more because of the raking white bishops. On the other hand, playing 1...gxf5 2 ♘xf5 would leave Black with the awful choice of losing the queen (2...♛g6 3 ♘e7+, or 2...♛f7 3 ♘h6+), or the king after 2...♛h8 3 ♘h6+ ♚g7 (note that 2...♛h8 was a selfblock) 4 ♛g5#. With the queen on g5, however, White cannot play 1 ♗xf5? since 1...gxf5 gains time for Black because his queen threatens White's. If he prepares the combination with 1 ♛d2, White will give Black time to defend, e.g. with 1...♖be8, or even 1...♚h8, which remove one or both of the knight forks given in the hypothetical variations above. What White needs is a means of removing his queen with tempo, i.e. with gain of time, so that Black is unable to defend because he has his hands momentarily full. This Alekhine achieves with admirable elegance as follows:

1 e4!   **♘xe4**

A counter-combination which seems to win the pawn. Black has no alternative, since otherwise the bastion on f5 collapses without compensation. Note that 1...fxe4 2 ♗xd7 loses Black a piece.

2 ♛c1!

Of course, Alekhine had foreseen Black's last, with which he attempts to limit the damage by giving up a small amount of material: 2 ♗xg7? ♘xg5 3 ♗xf8 ♘xh3+ 4 ♚g2 ♚xf8 5 ♚xh3 ♘f6 and, although he has lost the exchange, Black is winning a second pawn, whilst the 'oomph' has gone from White's position. The text is even more convincing than 2 fxe4 ♕xb2 3 exf5 (3 ♗xf5 ♕g7) 3...♕f6 4 ♕xf6 ♘xf6 5 fxg6, which also gives an advantage.

2 ...   **♘ef6**

Forced – both queen and knight were attacked.

3 ♗xf5!   **♔h8**

Black dare not capture the bishop because of the variations given above, and now, even though he is not a pawn ahead, Alekhine shows that his powerful bishop pair gives him an overwhelming advantage.

4 ♗e6   **♗a6**
5 ♖fe1   **♘e5**
6 f4   **♘d3**
7 ♖xd3!

Finishing the game with a flourish although, given the position, this particular paradox has little surprise value.

7 ...   **♗xd3**
8 g4

Black resigned. There is nothing to be done about the forthcoming catastrophe on the long diagonal.

For our last example of traditional sacrifice we have chosen a celebrated game in order to subject it to a fresh scrutiny. Diagram 2.10 arose in the famous game Averbakh-Kotov, World Championship Candidates Tournament, Zurich 1953.

Both players have been massing their pieces on the kingside, but Black appears to have some way to go: the ♖b8 and the ♗e7 particularly

2.10   B

Y. Averbakh – A. Kotov
Zurich Ct 1953

seem to require further deployment. So much greater, then, the thrill of Black's next:

30 ...   **♕xh3+!!**

White must capture, since after 31 ♔g1 ♖h6 it is all over.

31 ♔xh3   **♖h6+**
32 ♔g4   **♘f6+**
33 ♔f5   **♘d7**

When Kotov sacrificed his queen, he must have foreseen this position and that the threat of 34...♖f8+ 35 ♔g4 ♖g8+ 36 ♔f5 ♖f6# is very hard to parry. In the heat of the moment, and perhaps because he was not a problemist, Kotov failed to play a prettier winning blow whose logic is shared by many a problem's key move: **33...♘g4!?**. The idea is that, because the knight's move is merely required to clear a line and its destination does not matter much, it might as well shut off the ♖g2 and prevent it from moving to g5, which is indeed the defence found by Averbakh in the game.

We shall return to analyse what might have happened had Kotov played this second paradoxical move after we have studied the rest of the game. As we shall see, 33...♘g4 is not at all easy to calculate against a ticking clock. Kotov's choice is indeed good enough for a win and bears out his fine judgement and perception in playing the queen sacrifice. And it is precisely this judgement that makes this game such a worthy beauty prize winner: because the sacrifice could not be calculated to a conclusion, it is elevated above the status of a 'mere' combination – pretty though that would have been.

34	♖g5!	♖f8+
35	♔g4	♘f6+
36	♔f5	♘g8+
37	♔g4	♘f6+

Kotov repeats the position to gain time on the clock. Taking care to avoid a threefold repetition, he performs a similar operation after capturing the d5-pawn. Such procedures might be regarded as aesthetic blemishes, but this would be very harsh, given the fact that Kotov and Averbakh are playing the game, not composing it.

38	♔f5	♘xd5+
39	♔g4	♘f6+
40	♔f5	♘g8+
41	♔g4	♘f6+

42	♔f5	♘g8+
43	♔g4	♗xg5

Black has regained some of the sacrificed material and threatens the 'quiet' 44...♗e7 followed by 45...♘f6+ 46 ♔f5 ♘d7+ 47 ♔g4 ♖g8+ 48 ♔f5 ♖f6#. White's pieces are so cut off by the pawn-chains that, as in many problems, there is very little they can do in the available time to stave off the inevitable. For example, White can attempt to disrupt proceedings with **44 ♗g3 ♗e7 45 ♗xf4**, but the continuation would be 45...exf4 46 ♘xf4 ♖h4+ 47 ♔g3 ♖hxf4 and the material balance has swung decisively in Black's favour.

44	♔xg5	♖f7!

Yet another delightfully 'quiet' continuation, threatening mate in two by 44...♖g7+ and 45...♖f6#. The desperate attempt 45 ♘xf4 fails to 45...♖g7+ 46 ♘g6+ ♖gxg6+! (not 46...♖hxg6+? 47 ♔h5 and the queen sneakily guards h6!) 47 ♔f5 ♘e7#.

45	♗h4

To guard the f6 square. The position highlights the feature which is the foundation of the queen sacrifice: only the bishop defends the white king and Black is actually material ahead – where it counts.

45	...	♖g6+
46	♔h5	♖fg7
47	♗g5	♖xg5+
48	♔h4	♘f6

Black has arranged to win the bishop under circumstances where the white king remains in a mating net. Next to go is the knight.

49 ♘g3   ♖xg3
50 ♕xd6

Because of Kotov's repetition-avoidance procedure on move 38, Averbakh survives a couple more moves than he should have done.

50 ...   ♖3g6
51 ♕b8+   ♖g8
White resigns

Let us now consider the position after the beautiful alternative move 33...♘g4!? *(2.11)*.

2.11   W

White's only defence is:

34 ♘xf4

Now Black must avoid playing **34...♖f8+?** 35 ♔xg4 ♖g8+ 36 ♘g6+ ♖gxg6+ 37 ♔f5 ♖h5+ 38 ♖g5 ♗xg5! 39 ♔g4! ♗xd2+ 40 ♔xh5, which may be insufficient to win. This variation shows the down-side of 33...♘g4 – if the knight were still

in existence, Black would be winning easily. Instead, the correct continuation is quite 'problem-like':

34 ...   ♖g8!

Threatening 35...♖f6#.

35 ♘h5   ♖hg6!
36 ♕g5

The only way to stop mate.

36 ...   ♗xg5!
37 ♔xg4

and now a discovered check by the ♗g5 leads to the win of the ♖g2 and a comfortably winning advantage of the exchange for Black.

It is evident that this line is not clearly better or worse than the best play which could have occurred after 33...♘d7. Comparing them aesthetically, we note that the two variations share the attribute of 'quiet play'. 'Quiet' play is paradoxical, because you expect the side who is down in material to keep checking and/or capturing so as to give his opponent's superior force no time to enter the fray. But the 33...♘g4 variation is the prettier, because it possesses more paradoxes: the further sacrifice of the knight and the refusal to capture the white knight after 34 ♘xf4. In addition, there is the point of 33...♘g4 – the shut-off of the ♖g2.

There is, however, an aesthetic flaw in this game. The existence of two equally strong alternatives undermines our satisfaction with the sacrifice. It implies that the sacrifice was, in a sense, too strong, and the defender really stood very little chance. Just how serious this flaw is for the aesthetic value of the game is largely a subjective matter. In a composition, on the other hand, the alternative would be labelled a 'dual' and might well have a grave effect on the evaluation of the work. The key difference is the sporting element, which provides this brilliancy prize-winning game with the poetic licence to make light of this defect.

Underpromotion

Underpromotion – promoting to a piece other than the queen – is a form of the paradox of material, and a particularly delightful one. It is a great favourite among composers in all genres. The aesthetic possibilities are very numerous in spite of the fact that there are so few motivations for underpromotion. In fact, there are just three logical reasons for underpromoting (we are not counting whimsical or 'sadistic' purposes):

(1) Stalemate avoidance;

(2) Positions where a knight is more effective than a queen;

(3) Self-stalemate.

Diagram 2.12 is a particularly fine illustration of stalemate avoidance:

1	c8♗!!	b3
2	♗g4	b2
3	♗d1!	♔xb1
4	♗b3#	

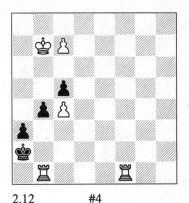

2.12   #4

O. von Krobshofer
Source unknown

The underpromotion is necessary to give Black the move 3...♔xb1, and only a bishop fits the bill. The paradox is particularly impressive in this example because it *appears* so easy to mate in four starting with 1 c8♕.

Diagram 2.13 shows the idea in study form.

(see diagram on following page)

1 ♗a4   ♘g4!!

One of the finest black moves in this book! It has an incredible look about it that stamps it as a sure-fire candidate for the chapter on Depth, which follows. Let us first dispose of the much saner-looking 1...♘c4. White continues as you would expect: 2 a6 (2 ♗b3 ♔e7 transposes) 2...♘b6 (2...♘e5 3 ♔c7 and the pawn promotes) 3 ♗b3+ ♔e7 4 a7 ♔d6 5 ♔b7 ♔c5 6 e5 winning.

2 ♗d1!!

2.13   Win

*G. A. Nadareishvili, 1st Prize
Drosha Tourney 1965*

This is starting to look like a game between a salesman and his prospect. The salesman, playing White, is trying very hard not to win, without making it too obvious, but his opponent appears to be too weak! In fact, the two are top-flight grandmasters, because look what would have happened had White proceeded as normal: 2 a6? ♔g6! 3 a7 ♔h5! 4 a8♕ g6! and White cannot prevent 5...d1♕ 6 ♗xd1 stalemate. The text move interrupts this fiendish plan by attacking the knight, but since Black does not lose a tempo, it is not yet clear what it achieves.

2   ...   ♘f2

It makes no difference whether the knight chooses this square or e3.

3   ♗b3+   ♔g6

Black insists on building his stalemate trap, and indeed this is his only chance.

4   a6   ♘g4
5   a7   ♔h5
6   a8♖!!

Now White has a sufficient material superiority to win, and at the same time it is possible to foil the stalemate trap:

6   ...   g6
7   ♖a1   d1♕
8   ♖xd1

and wins.

But why could White not underpromote in the line beginning 2 a6 (see note to White's second move)? Because in that line, the bishop was left on a4, obstructing the rook's path to a1; underpromotion would therefore not have helped White avoid stalemate. The manoeuvre beginning 2 ♗d1 was designed to transfer the bishop to b3 without loss of time. The mechanism whereby this was effected is not easy to discern; it resembles sleight of hand!

Underpromotion occurs quite often in actual play, and not always in the endgame either. Diagram 2.14 occurred after the following moves: **1 d4 d5 2 c4 e6 3 ♘f3 dxc4 4 ♕a4+ ♘d7 5 e4 ♘f6 6 ♘c3 a6 7 ♗xc4 ♖b8 8 ♕c2 b5 9 ♗e2 ♗b7 10 0-0?** *(2.14)*, provoking an original combination:

10   ...   b4
11   e5

White is committed to this, else the ♗e4 is lost.

11   ...   bxc3

2.14　　　　　B

Xu Jun – V. Ivanchuk
Lucerne Wcht 1993

12　exf6　　　cxb2!
13　fxg7

Both sides have desperado pawns. White has little choice, as 13 ♗xb2 ♘xf6 leaves him a pawn down with a poor position.

13 ...　　　　bxa1♘!!

This clever resource wins material, for after 14 ♕c3 ♗xg7 Black comes out with an extra rook. If instead 13...bxa1♕?, 14 gxh8♕ and White can view the future with confidence.

14　gxh8♕　　　♘xc2

White has not lost a piece; Black has gained one! Ivanchuk went on to win.

Our next example shows the least common reason for underpromotion.

White is not merely busted materially, his king is also trapped.

1　a8♗+!!

2.15　　　　Draw

A. Hurtig
2nd Prize, Schackvärlden 1943

A megaton paradox. Not only is the underpromotion in itself surprising, but we have the extra shock: White refrains from queening with check, giving him an apparently promising counterattack! In fact, after 1 a8♕+? ♔c8, White eventually runs out of steam: 2 b7+ ♔d7 3 ♕d5+ ♔e7 4 ♕xd8+ ♔xd8 5 ♕xb8+ ♔e7 6 ♕f8+ ♔xf8 7 b8♕+ ♔e7 8 ♕f8+ ♔xf8 9 hxg8♕+ ♘xg8 and Black avoids stalemate by releasing the g4 square. Other lines also boil down to the same problem: White is unable to rid himself of all his pieces whilst keeping the stalemate net intact.

On the other hand, what does the promotion to bishop achieve?

1　...　　　　♔c8
2　b7+

Now we see that White's first two moves have immobilized two men –

an achievement when you are playing for stalemate!

2	...	♚d7
3	♕d5+	♚e7
4	♕e5+	♚f8
5	♕xg7+!	♚xg7
6	h8♗+!!	

Beautifully echoing the strategy of the first move. Is chess too easy? If 6 h8♕+?, then 6...♚f8! 7 ♕g7+ ♚e8! 8 ♕e5+ ♘e7 9 ♕h8+ ♘hg8 and again White runs out of checks.

6	...	♚f8

If 6...♚xh8, then 7 g7+ ♚h7(xg7) stalemate.

7	g7+	♚ moves
	Stalemate	

The two promoted bishops are imprisoned by knights' pawns, themselves blocked by black pieces.

Winning with Limited Material

One of the more charming forms of the paradox of material is when success is achieved in spite of an apparent insuffiency of force. Diagram 2.16 is a classic of this kind.

Even though White has a material advantage, this is well short of a winning one. However, the bishop 'dominates' the knight (see Chapter 7 for a closer look at the domination theme) and the battle revolves around White's attempts to win it and Black's to rescue it.

1	♘e5!

White resists the temptation to

2.16   Win

A. & K. Sarychev, 3rd Prize
Vecherny Moskva 1930

rush up the board with his king. This move sets about erecting an invisible barrier to cut the black king off from his knight.

1	...	♚g7
2	♗d8!	

Preventing ...♚f6.

2	...	♚f8
3	♚f2	♚e8
4	♗a5	♚e7
5	♚e3	♚d6
6	♚d4	

The white king arrives in the nick of time. Black may now retreat by 6...♚e7 after which the knight is lost: 7 ♚c5 ♚f6 8 ♘d7+ followed by 9 ♚c6. Or he may save his knight:

6	...	♘c7
7	♗b4#	

A glorious and surprising checkmate effected in mid-board by a force with which it is difficult to bring about mate even against a lone king! The study also benefits from the quiet and clear introductory play.

The few versus the many: Positional Draw

Another aspect of the paradox of material is the idea of an outnumbered force successfully resisting a superior one. Our next example demonstrates the concept of **positional draw**, where the final position is a draw despite the presence of a normally winning material advantage. In Diagram 2.17, White's difficulty is the ♙c2 on the brink of promotion.

2.17   Draw

G. N. Zakhodiakin, 3rd Prize Chigorin Memorial 1950

1 ♖c7!

A pleasingly paradoxical refusal to remove the ♙e7 with check: 1 ♖xe7+? ♔f6 2 ♖c7 (2 ♖e1 ♖b1 wins) 2...♖b8+ 3 ♔d7 ♖b7! wins;

compare this position with that reached in the solution.

1 ...   ♖b8+
2 ♔xe7   ♖b7!

A well known tactic in ♖+♙ endings: the black rook decoys the white one by pinning it.

3 ♖xb7   c1♕
4 ♔e6+   ♔g6

Black gets nowhere by going to the back rank: 4...♔f8 5 ♖b8+ ♔g7 6 ♖b7+ repeats the position.

5 h5+!

A paradox-enhancing sacrifice.

5 ...   ♔xh5

Worse is 5...♔g5, which allows White's next to be a check, thus gaining time.

6 ♖g7!!

Surprisingly, the position is now drawn. The black king is pinned down and White has only to maintain this condition to achieve the draw, as the lone queen cannot break through the mutual protection of the king and rook. This type of positional draw, in which Black cannot make headway despite a material superiority, is called a **fortress**. The 'page of paradox' showed two more fortresses. Other types of positional draw include perpetual check and repetition of moves or position.

Breaking the Rules

This grouping of paradoxes focuses on the types of preconception which make paradoxes what they are. It looks at moves and ideas which are counter-intuitive, in that they either:

(1) break a rule (or rules) which we assume apply to the position, or

(2) appear to be irrelevant in the light of such rules. This category may be considered as something of a catch-all since, for example, a sacrifice breaks the rule 'don't lose material' while 'irrelevant' moves break the implicit rule that one should be doing something useful.

Let us review some relatively straightforward examples. In Diagram 2.18, White's has only one move to force a draw:

2.18   Draw

A. & K. Sarychev, 1928-II
Commended, Shakhmatny Listok

1 ♔c8!!

This move might have its equals, but for sheer paradoxicality it takes some beating. Even after eliminating the natural alternatives (1 c8♕? ♗f5+ 2 ♔c7 ♗xc8; 1 ♔d6? ♗f5; 1 ♔e6? ♔e4! 2 c8♕ ♗f5+) one's mind rebels against this apparently irrational move. And when the reasoning behind the move is revealed, one continues to marvel at its sheer magic: in a position of stark simplicity, the best move turns out to be one which apparently works against White's only counterplay by blocking his pawn's promotion square, whilst deliberately moving the king out of the 'square' of Black's pawn.

The point of the move is that if White merely maintains the status quo, Black will be able to bring his king over to usher his pawn to promotion, meanwhile protecting the latter with the bishop from c8 if necessary. For example: 1 ♔d6 ♗f5 2 ♔e5 ♗c8 3 ♔d5 ♔f4 4 ♔c5 ♔e5 5 ♔b6 ♔d6 and wins. After 1 ♔c8, on the other hand, the pawn is winkled out from b7 and the bishop can no longer protect it from the blockading square c8:

1 ...   **b5**

If 1...♗e4?, 2 ♔b8 wins the pawn by diverting the bishop to deal with the promotion threat.

2 ♔d7!   **b4**

If 2...♔e4, then 3 ♔d6 ♗f5 4 ♔c5 ♗d7 5 c8♕, while 2...♗f5+ is a transposition of moves.

3 ♔d6   **♗f5**
4 ♔e5!

Thus White gains a vital move to re-enter the 'square' of Black's pawn by attacking the bishop that stops White's pawn from queening.

4 ...   **♗d7**

The precise position of the bishop no longer matters.

5 ♔d4

And Black is helpless to prevent the loss of his last pawn, e.g. 5...♗e6 6 c8♕ ♗xc8 7 ♔c4, or 5...b3 6 ♔c3 ♗e6 7 c8♕.

So far, our examples have focused on a move-set comprised of a single move, and indeed this is by far the most common experience of paradox in chess. The next example, however, demonstrates that a more subtle form of paradox can apply to an entire sequence as well.

2.19   Win

G. Kasparian (end of study)
=2nd Prize, Urdski Rabochi 1946

White plays to win the knight as follows:

1 ♖b6   **♘d8**

If Black plays 1...♘a5 or 1...♘c5, then 2 ♖b5(+).

2 ♖d6   **♘f7**

After 2...♘b7 3 ♖d7 ♘a5 (or 3...♘c5), 4 ♖d5+ again wins the knight.

3 ♖d7   **♘g5**

3...♘e5 4 ♖d5 wins while if 3...♘h8, 4 ♖h7 dominates the knight in the corner.

4 ♖e7!

and wins by zugzwang – Black's legal moves all lose the knight.

Part of the paradoxical nature of this little work lies in the fact that the technique used for trapping the knight represents the very antithesis of the one which is usually effective in standard ♖ vs ♘ endings. In general, the strong side attempts to separate the knight from the defending king, and the weak side strives to bring them together, making mutual defence possible. Here, Black's jubilation at the knight's arrival in a safe haven is very short-lived because of a special feature of the position whereby the black king is hemmed in.

The Kasparian study also serves to emphasize the point originally made about the dependence on the 'preconceived notion' for the existence of the paradox. If one did not know about the standard approach to the conduct of ♖ v ♘ endings, one would certainly miss some of the point of this composition. And so it often is in art (and in life?): the greater your knowledge, the greater your pleasure.

Although technically there must be a relationship between paradox and difficulty, after some practice you become adept at reading the signs. In the case of No. 2.8 for example, an experienced solver would probably spot the idea of sacrificing the queen as well as providing a flight with check quite quickly, simply because he knows that it is the sort of effect that composers generally try to achieve. Yet the ease of solution would not spoil the impact of the paradox; it is merely that the enjoyment takes a different form – the joy of recognition instead of the delight of discovery, perhaps?

With this point at the back of your mind, see how long it takes you to solve the next example – or at least spot the likely key move. Don't be put off by the fact that it is a 3-mover by the great Sam Loyd!

Did you first consider and then discard any totally idiotic (and therefore 'problem-like') moves? (Example: 1 ♕d4?). Did you bother to consider any totally un-problem-like moves? (Examples: 1 ♕a6+?, 1 ♕c4+?). Did you then plump for the merely semi-idiotic key move?

1 ♕h7!

This move again carries no threat, but, whatever Black plays, White continues with **2 ♘d6** and selects his

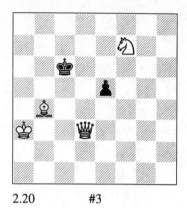

2.20   #3

S. Loyd
Baltimore Dispatch 1859

mating move according to where the prey arrives.

Examine this little masterpiece for a while. Get the hang of its mechanism, appreciate the way it operates. Yet even when you have mastered it completely, an element of mystery still remains: why is it that this move, with its obscure character, is the only one that works? What is it about the inner logic of chess that makes such paradox possible?

An impressive example of rule-breaking occurred in the game **Kamsky-Karpov**, *Dortmund 1993*.

This position arose after the following moves in a fashionable variation of the Caro-Kann Defence:

1 e4 c6 2 d4 d5 3 ♘d2 dxe4 4 ♘xe4 ♘d7 5 ♘g5 ♘gf6 6 ♗d3 e6 7 ♘1f3 ♗d6 8 ♕e2 h6 9 ♘e4 ♘xe4 10 ♕xe4 ♘f6 11 ♕h4 *(2.21)*

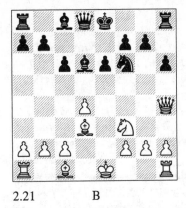

2.21   B

White has succeeded in provoking the weakening of Black's kingside by ...h6. His last move depends on the tactical circumstance that this pawn is pinned, so that Black cannot play the very troublesome 11...g5 because of 12 ♗xg5.

Karpov now played:

11 ...   ♔e7!

This move is paradoxical for the following reasons: the position appears entirely normal and we expect Black to proceed with the completion of his development and the freeing of his position with ...c5. The move played, so far from promoting these aims, violates the elementary principle that the king is unsafe in the centre and is liable to interfere with the communications of the other pieces; moreover, the ♘f6 now stands pinned.

Of course Karpov realized that all these considerations were subordinate to the fact that the ♖h8 is now defended by Black's queen, so that 12...g5 is playable and a threat of enormous power; not only will the white queen be driven back into a dangerous position, but in some lines the pawn can follow through to g4 harrying the knight on f3. Kamsky was unable to find a complete solution, and indeed your authors have analysed the position and have failed to find an improvement on his play.

12 ♘e5

Giving up a pawn to a simple combination, in the hope that the two bishops and superior development will offer White prospects of exploiting the position of Black's king.

12	...	♗xe5
13	dxe5	♛a5+
14	c3	♛xe5+
15	♗e3	b6
16	0-0-0	g5
17	♛a4	c5

and after some ups and downs Karpov triumphed on move 49.

Zugzwang

For many chess enthusiasts, the prettiest – certainly the most poignant – paradox of all is that of zugzwang. Normally, having the right of making the next move is an advantage: you can make progress, improve your position, generate threats, and defend against your opponent's. Yet, just once in a while, you might blunder into that embarrassing situation where you can only wish it were not your turn to play. Suddenly the right to move has become an onerous duty.

Because the unit of time in chess is the move (or, pedantically, the half-move), this situation, which breaks the rule that it is desirable to have the move, can be termed the **paradox of time**.

We have had a preview of zugzwang with Kasparian's No. 2.19. See if foreknowledge helps you to solve the next example, by the great 'Hypermodern' grandmaster, who was a very keen and successful study composer.

2.22   Win

Richard Réti
Hastings & St.Leonards Post 1922

White's plan is to capture Black's pawn whilst retaining both of his own. He must deal with the threat of 1...♔b5 picking up the a-pawn. Thus White begins with:

1 ♘d4+

Guarding b5. If instead 1 ♘b4+ ♔b5 2 a6 ♔b6, White's a-pawn is doomed as the bishop can dislodge the knight from its protection by playing to f8.

1 ...   ♔c5

This keeps the pawn under surveillance whilst also threatening the knight in certain circumstances (not immediately, since if Black were to capture the knight in this position, the white a-pawn would streak to promotion).

This is the critical position. The big question is: how does White make progress? If 2 ♔xh2, Black replies 2...♔xd4! 3 a6 ♗f4+ 4 ♔h3 ♗b8 and has time to capture the ♙a6. An improvement is 2 ♘b3+ ♔b5 3 ♔xh2, but it is still insufficient: 3...♗f4+ 4 ♔h3 ♔b4 5 a6 ♗b8 6 f4 ♔b5 and Black will again be able to capture the a-pawn, leaving the bishop enough time to prevent the f-pawn from promoting.

The strict answer to our question is, paradoxically, White cannot make progress! Fortunately, however, neither can Black, so White can maintain the status quo with the unexpectedly mild retreating move:

2 ♔h1!!

A very irrelevant-looking move! Let us review Black's possibilities: the only king move which does not allow the a-pawn to promote is 2...♔d6 and this is answered by 3

♘f5+ forking the bishop. All moves by the bishop, except to e3 where it will be captured by the lurking △f2, result in its loss to another knight fork on b3 or e6. There can surely be no chessplayer who would not exult in the chance to play a pure waiting move, a 'backward' one to boot, ♔g2-h1 – and in so doing force his opponent's resignation!

Now look at Diagram 2.23.

2.23   Win

A. S. Gurvich, 1st Prize
Alma-Atinskaya Pravda, 1959

This seems to be a perfectly innocent, rather drawish position with the reduced material and opposite-coloured bishops not offering much prospect of excitement.

1 ♗h5!

Threatening both the bishop as well as f7.

1 ...   ♗xc7

If the bishop shuns the pawn, things will be even worse for Black,

e.g. 1...♗h2 2 ♖xf7+ ♔d6 3 ♖f6+ picking up the rook.

2 ♖xf7+   ♔d8

Black again avoids 2...♔d6? 3 ♖f6+.

3 ♖xc7!

White now seems to have come out on top with a neat little combination, for if 3...♖xc7 then 4 ♗xe8, while if 3...♖f8+, 4 ♖f7, in both cases with a winning extra piece. But Black has one more arrow ...

3 ...   ♖g8!

Now both White's pieces are threatened, the rook directly and the bishop by 4...♖g5+. Surely both can't be saved?

4 ♖c4!!   ♖g5+
5 ♔e6!   ♖xh5
6 h4!

And White wins! It is Black's turn to move, he faces no threat, but 6...♔e8 allows 7 ♖c8#, while any rook move results in its immediate capture. Yet if it were White's move, he would be equally unable to escape the tentacles of zugzwang and would be obliged to let Black off with a draw.

Such a position, when whichever side has the move wishes it didn't, is a case of what is called **reciprocal** (or **mutual**) **zugzwang**. Large numbers of compositions are driven by this singularly attractive idea, but it seldom occurs in a game. Indeed, part of its allure, no doubt, derives from its rarity.

The Paradox of Set Play

From the earliest times, chess artists have explored paradoxical effects which rarely arise in play and never with the quality and intensity for which composition affords the opportunity. Consider Diagram 2.24:

2.24   #2

A. Volkmann, 1st Prize
Lippische Landeszeitung 1951

One of the first things the solver looks at when tackling a problem is the situation of the black king. Here there are two flights and, moreover, by moving to these squares the king discovers check from the ♗h7. Further examination shows that these two moves are each set with a specific mating retort: 1...♔e5+ 2 ♘cd3# and 1...♔g5+ 2 ♘e4#. Since the rook on f2 is not required for either of these mates, the solver might well essay the try 1 ♖d2, which is pleasingly paradoxical in

itself, giving up as it does the ♖+♘ battery. Black has against this the resource 1...♖h2! to which there is no answer. This will probably set the solver back somewhat, and it might be some time before he hits on the parallel idea of giving up the ♕+♘ battery – and the set mates with it – with the key move **1 ♕d2!** threatening 2 ♕d5#. Now 1...♔e5+ is met by 2 ♘g6# and 1...♔g5+ by 2 ♘fd3#.

We have seen this theme, the crosscheck theme, before in No. 1.7. Apart from the fact that the above position is 'only' a 2-mover, there is an important difference: in Loshinsky's problem, the key move was paradoxical because it allowed the black checks; here the checks exist already in the initial position. The paradox in the Volkmann is a horse of a different colour entirely: the key move unexpectedly 'sacrifices' the existing means of dealing with two very powerful black moves, changing them for quite different ones. In other words, the key appears to lose control of the position and this is surprising because it is something which any reasonable player would automatically struggle to retain; in reality, it substitutes a different control. This paradox of set play occupies a seminal role in the modern chess problem, yet it is hardly ever seen in anything approaching such clarity of expression in the endgame study, let alone in actual play.

Let us have a look at the rather special effect which a problem can produce using the paradox of set play combined with zugzwang.

2.25   #2

R. T. Lewis
The Problemist 1985

With Black to play, all the traps are set: 1...♗ random (e.g. 1...♗a7) 2 ♖e8#. If Black corrects his error of opening the rook's line to e8 by preparing to interpose on e7 with 1...♗d6, we have a selfblock instead, allowing the knight to relinquish its protection of d6 and deliver 2 ♘d8#. But it is White's move, and we seek in vain for a waiting move preserving the status quo, noticing that 1 ♖xb8? is stalemate. So what to do?

1 ♖a6!

This releases the apparent reciprocal zugzwang by invoking the paradox of set play: now 1...♗a7/c7 leads to 2 bxa7/c7# whilst 1...♗d6 leads to 2 ♘d8# as before. Such problems, in which the key move unexpectedly changes the set play and passes the zugzwang 'hot potato' to Black, are humorously called *mutates*. This one has the additional quirk that the position after the key is also a mate in two, solution 1 ♖a8!, of course!

3 Depth

'Some people take more care to hide their wisdom than their folly.'
Jonathan Swift

We have probably all at various times used the word 'deep' to describe a move or manoeuvre. What we mean by this is, simply, that the point is not obvious. In general, the reason why the point is not obvious is that it becomes clear only after an interval of some moves. Seeing the figure emerge from the marble, sometimes with a sudden shock of delighted revelation, sometimes with a gradually dawning glow of comprehension, can be one of the great thrills of the game.

In this chapter we examine various aspects of depth, in which the consequences of a move-set (usually but not always comprising a single move) are only revealed some considerable time later. Firstly, we look at the relationship between depth, length and breadth. Next we examine the ways in which a small difference in the position can make a big difference to the outcome. We also discuss the curious notion of 'negative depth', which could appeal to club players. Finally, we deal with some additional aspects of depth, in

particular its affinity to paradox and difficulty.

Depth, Length and Breadth

One indication of the depth of a move is the number of moves (length) before its point becomes clear. Other things being equal, the longer the sequence, the deeper the original move. As we shall see, however, other things are not always equal – depth is not as easy as that!

Our first example is a very basic illustration:

3.1   Win

S. Isenegger
Das 1x1 des Endspiels 1964

If White simply pushes his pawn, Black promotes his straight after, and the game is drawn. Instead, White can win with the cute 1 ♔e2!. This forces Black to play 1...♚h2, else White will be able to stop Black's pawn with 2 ♔f3, whilst his own is well beyond the reach of Black's king. Only now does White push his pawn, and we realize that this wins as it promotes on b8 with check! Note that 1 ♔f2? is a case of being hoist by one's own petard, as, after 1...♚h2, Black's pawn arrives on g3 with check, thus gaining time and promoting before White's. Note also that White could not postpone ♔e2: after 1 b4? g5 2 ♔e2? g4 Black's pawn prevents 3 ♔f3.

In spite of its simplicity, this example illustrates an important feature of depth. The length of the sequence following the 'deep' move is not the sole criterion of its depth. If, as here, the sequence is extremely simple (lacking in breadth), then the fact that it is of moderate length (5 moves) counts for relatively little.

Contrast this with the next example, which is an elaboration of a famous study by N. D. Grigoriev, *Shakhmatny Listok* 1934.

White has his back to the wall because his knight is trapped. However, if he attacks the b-pawn immediately, he can just hang on: 1 ♔a3 (or 1 ♔b3) 1...♔f7 2 ♔b4 ♔g7 3 ♔xb5 ♔xh7 4 ♔c4 and the king arrives in the nick of time to stop the remaining pawn from queening. So

3.2   Draw
David Gurgenidze
64 - Shakhmatny Obozrenie 1970

which of 1 ♔a3 and 1 ♔b3 is it to be? As in the best compositions, the answer, in the spirit of paradox, is the less natural move:

1 ♔a3!

This is less natural than 1 ♔b3 because, whilst the immediate objective is the b-pawn, it is common sense to choose a route which maintains more options, such as diverting to the kingside. Let us now see how play develops:

1 ...   ♚e6!

Black improves on 1...♔f7 and aims to occupy f5, whereupon the h-pawn can advance without fear of being overhauled by the knight. Thus if White continues with 2 ♔b4? Black wins straightforwardly but instructively as follows: 2...♚f5 3 ♘f8 – otherwise the pawn promotes unhindered – 3...h5 4 ♘d7 h4 5 ♘c5 h3 6 ♘d3 h2 7 ♘f2 ♚f4 8 ♔xb5 ♚f3 9

♘h1 ♔g2 and the white king looks on helplessly at the demise of his last officer. Thus White must react more energetically:

2 ♘f8+!   ♔f5

This is still the best square from which to keep the knight at bay.

3 ♘d7   h5
4 ♘c5   h4
5 ♘b3!!

Now we see why White's king avoided b3 on move one! Instead, 5 ♘d3 still doesn't work: 5...h3 6 ♘f2 h2 7 ♔b4 ♔f4 and we are back in the losing variation above.

5 ...   h3
6 ♘d2   h2

No better is 6...♔f4 7 ♘f1 ♔f3 8 ♔b4 ♔f2 9 ♘h2 ♔g2 10 ♘g4 ♔g3 11 ♘e3! h2 12 ♘f1+ and draws.

7 ♘f1!   h1♕
8 ♘g3+

forking the new queen.

Comparing Gurgenidze's study with Isenegger's, we observe that the sequence following the 'deep' move 1 ♔a3! and ending with the 'point' 5 ♘b3! is a move less than 1 ♔e2! followed by the march of the b-pawn. Nevertheless, the move 1 ♔a3 is patently 'deeper', in the aesthetic sense, than 1 ♔e2. This is no doubt because the point of 5 ♘b3 itself is harder to spot than that of 6 b8♕+. Also, such a knight manoeuvre is much harder to calculate than the straightforward advance of a pawn. The main reason for this is that there are more alternatives to eliminate when working out the main line. In other words, the variation is more complex.

There is an aspect of depth that we call *breadth*, and which is intended to capture the idea of complexity. In a 'broad' position the point can become clear even after just one move, but only when you have seen a number of variations. Certainly most two-movers would qualify as broad in this sense; the Loyd organ-pipes problem (No. 1.6) would be a typical example. To see the point of the key move, it is necessary to explore all Black's replies, particularly the mutual interferences among the rooks and bishops, before the position is completely unravelled.

Breadth, unlike depth, is not of itself aesthetic. When there is great unity between the variations (as in the Loyd), breadth is impressive – the content can be greatly magnified. Sometimes, though, breadth can just be messy and complex. For this reason breadth is not regarded as an aesthetic element; it can, however, enhance depth. Experiencing real depth can be like finding a needle in a haystack; it occurs at the moment when you see the point of the original move. The size of the haystack depends both on length and breadth.

Let us take a look at a more tactical example.

White begins with the slightly paradoxical...

3.3   Win

Mario Matous, 1st Prize
Shakhmaty/Šahs, 1979-80

1   ♔f2!

Ignoring the inferior, but tempting, 1 ♕xf1+ because there is nothing special after 1...♔h2. Similarly,
1 ♕h4+ ♘h2 leaves White without a
clear continuation. Also 1 ♔xf1??
♗a6 is worse than useless. Now
Black must cope with the threat of 2
♕xf1+ followed by a quick mate,
and natural defences like 1...♘h2
or 1...♕a6 lose to 2 ♗f3+!. Thus
Black's next is forced.

1   ...   ♗g2
2   ♗f3

This move really looks like it
overloads the black defenders, but he
hangs on with:

2   ...   ♕g7

Here the obvious move is 3
♕xf1+, but again it is not enough to
win: 3...♔h2 4 ♕g1+ ♔h3 5 ♗xg2+
♔h4 6 ♕h2+ ♔g5 and there is no
win. White therefore embarks on a

deep and pretty manoeuvre, making
clever use of the fact that the black
queen is tied to the defence of the
knight:

3   ♕h4+!

First forcing Black to block h2 ...

3   ...   ♘h2

... so that now ...

4   ♕h8!!

Not only threatening the queen,
but also preventing ...♕b2+, and of
course the white queen is immune
because of instant mate.

4   ...   ♕g6
5   ♕h7!   ♕g5
6   ♕h6!   ♕g8

We may now ask what this cute
pussyfooting is all about. The answer is that the black queen has been
driven back to g8, so that now the
continuation which did not work on
move 3, when the black queen was
on g7, does work:

7   ♕c1+   ♘f1
8   ♕xf1+   ♔h2
9   ♕g1+   ♔h3
10   ♗xg2+   ♔h4
11   ♕h2+   ♔g5
12   ♕g3+

and wins the queen!

This study again showed real
depth, in that White was able to improve on the 'normal' 3 ♕xf1+ by
first executing a lengthy sequence
that brought about a small change in
the position. Only once this change
was achieved did White return to 8
♕xf1+, having converted a drawing

line into a winning one. Later, in Chapter 8, we will see that this kind of depth is the essence of the Logical School of problem composition.

Small Change

As you can see from the examples above, it can be especially attractive when a small, subtle change in the position makes all the difference later. In the Isenegger, the change was the location of the black king on h2 instead of h1; in the Gurgenidze, the change was the availability of the b3 square, brought about by the white king's choice of a3 instead of b3 on move one; the Matous featured the persuasion of the black queen to occupy g8 instead of g7.

Sometimes, this small change is brought about by White's first move (as in the Gurgenidze). Of the two apparently equivalent possibilities, White must discover why only the one works. On other occasions (such as in the Isenegger and the Matous) the change is effected by a forcing sequence.

In the following example, the forcing sequence (or 'foreplan') is a mere one move, but the 'main plan' is staggeringly long. The position is of a type which is well understood by practical players.

With just heavy pieces left to slug it out on an open board, the general rule is: whoever has the move wins.

3.4   Win

Y. Hoch, 1st Prize
J. Mandil Memorial Tourney 1980

The obvious move is:

1	♖xf6+	♔a7
2	♕g7+	♕c7

This is forced; if 2...♔a8, 3 ♕b7 mate is not at all deep.

3	♖f7	♖c1+

Black has a series of spite checks, but there is a bolt-hole on h7 for the white king.

4	♔xg2	♖c2+
5	♔f3	

Avoiding the embarrassing error 5 ♔h3? ♖h2+ followed by ...♖g2+.

5	...	♖c3+
6	♔e4	

Again, White must play carefully, as 6 ♔g4? is met by 6...♖g3+.

6	...	♖c4+
7	♔d5	

Not 7 ♔f5? ♖f4+.

7	...	♖c5+
8	♔e6	♖c6+
9	♔f5	♖c5+

10 ♔g6

The fact that White can dither harmlessly here with 10 ♔f6 is of very little consequence aesthetically.

10	...	♖c6+
11	♔h7	

The king has arrived and White signs the scoresheet.

| 11 | ... | ♔xa6!! |

A rude shock – White had only bargained on the stalemate trap of 11...♔a8 12 ♕g8+! ♕c8 (12...♕b8 is also met by ♖f8) 13 ♖f8 winning.

12	♖xc7	♖xc7
13	♕xc7	

Stalemate!

Where did we go wrong? Checking backwards through the sequence, looking for an improvement, we will eventually arrive at ... move one! Surely one of the longest 'tries' on record!

| 1 | a5+!! | ♔xa6 |

1...♖c6 loses simply to 2 ♖xf6+ and Black can no longer interpose his queen on the next move.

2	♖xf6+	♔a7
3	♕g7+	♕c7
4	♖f7	

It really looks like we've cracked it now. White's deep first move has removed the stalemate trap we fell into before. Everything proceeds smoothly on the same lines as in the false trail, for a while...

4	...	♖c1+
5	♔xg2	♖c2+
6	♔f3	♖c3+
7	♔e4	♖c4+
8	♔d5	♖c5+
9	♔e6	♖c6+
10	♔f5	♖c5+
11	♔g6	♖c6+
12	♔h7	

Now if 12...♕b7!? there is the simple 13 ♔g8! (13 ♕b2+ also leads to a win).

| 12 | ... | ♔a8! |

This trap has a bit more life in it than on its first outing above.

| 13 | ♕g8+! | |

Of course, White must avoid the stalemate after 13 ♖xc7? ♖xc7 14 ♕xc7.

13	...	♕c8
14	♖f8	♖c7+
15	♔h8!	

The exclamation mark is for our delight at the way the position now 'echoes' that after 12 ♔h7.

| 15 | ... | ♔a7! |

An ingenious repetition of the stalemate resource in the try play line above, but one rank further up the board. It is this factor that makes all the difference:

| 16 | ♕g1+! | |

This is the resource which White lacked in the original 1 ♖xf6+ line. Black has no answer and must lose his queen and the game.

Hoch's work has several features to admire. We have already pointed out the 'echo' between the try and the actual play; this concept is further discussed in the Geometry chapter. There is also the paradoxical effect of the first move, sacrificing a white pawn rather than the much more obvious capture of a black one. And, as we shall understand more fully after Chapter 5, there is excellent flow in the long march of the white king.

What makes this study of special interest to us is the wonderfully long sequence separating the first move from its subtle point. One of the greatest studies of its kind – a real depth-charge!

Negative Depth

Up to now our examples have shown White – that is, the protagonist who succeeds – as the perpetrator of the deep moves. But Black can also make deep mistakes; when this happens we call it negative depth. One often sees the question raised – and not always answered – by the annotator of a game: where did he go wrong? The reason for a loss, or for drawing an apparently won position, can sometimes be very hard to pinpoint.

Chess is very much about just this phenomenon. First a weakness arises in your opponent's position, then, perhaps many moves later, you exploit it. For example, you are White and at some stage your opponent plays a useful-looking defensive move, ...h6. Play continues and for

some time this move plays no part in your calculations. Suddenly, events develop in such a way that ...h6 turns out to be a crucial weakening of Black's castled position. Utilizing this factor, you obtain a winning advantage.

Let us see how a problemist exploits negative depth for aesthetic effect in Diagram 3.5.

3.5 #4

*Nikolai Zharkov, 2nd Prize
Shakhmaty v SSSR, 1991*

First we note that Black's single flight, 1...♔d5, is set with the reply 2 ♕d1+ ♔e4 3 ♗f5#. This is not relinquished by the key **1 ♕h1!** which contains the neat threat **2 ♗c6+!** decoying the black queen away from the defence of c4: **2...♕xc6 3 ♘d2+ ♔xe5 4 ♘xc4#.**

To deal with this threatened combination, the black rook can be deployed to:

  a) protect c4 by 1...♖b4;

b) protect c6 – thus avoiding the decoy of the queen – by 1...♖b6 or

c) by 1...♖c7;

d) remove the threatening bishop from the scene altogether by playing 1...♖xd7.

Let us look at these four possibilities in turn. What weakness does 1...♖b4 create in Black's position? Would you believe a selfblock of the king? 2 ♕h4+ ♔d5 3 ♗xc5! (an unexpected 'quiet' move threatening 4 ♕d4#) 3...♔xc5 4 ♕d4#. But for 1...♖b4, this continuation would have made no sense. Now that you have seen the idea, can you spot the continuation after 1...♖b6? It is 2 ♗f5+ ♔d5 3 ♕d1+ ♔c6 4 ♕d7#, exploiting the prospective (i.e. not immediate) selfblock of the king by the rook on b6.

After 1...♖c7 we have 2 ♘h2+ ♔xe5 3 ♘g4+ ♔d6 4 ♕d1#. A pleasing long-distance mate, taking advantage this time of the selfblock on c7. Last, but not least, 1...♖xd7 2 ♘d2+ ♔xe5 3 ♕e4+ ♔d6 4 ♘e8#.

The theme of this problem is prospective selfblocks. It possesses a marvellous unity because all of the variations are introduced by the same black rook, a splendid feat of construction. But the point at issue is that all four variations showed a 'deep' weakening of the black position, not at all obvious at first sight. It is precisely this hiddenness which gives depth its special allure.

Further Aspects of Depth

At this stage, it is appropriate to introduce a distinction between our use of 'depth' and 'deep' on the one hand, and a looser usage which is common, on the other. This usage is characterized by such phrases as 'a deep combination'. The word 'deep' here is merely used as a synonym for 'long' and lacks connotations such as 'subtle' and 'profound' which we wish to convey with our more restrictive usage.

This fine distinction reveals a more substantive aesthetic issue. The kind of moves or manoeuvres to which we are referring in the context of depth are essentially finesses; they are clever and delicate. They do not so much trigger combinations as modify their result. The appeal of long combinations generally is not one of depth in our special sense, but one of flow – for which see later.

Returning to our discussion of depth as such, the hallmark of the truly deep move is the obscurity of its point. Other things being equal, the longer the sequence, the more obscure the point. But as we have seen, when other things are not equal, the point of a shorter sequence can be just as obscure, if not more so. It is perhaps debatable whether a two-mover can ever be truly deep, but it seems to us that a three-mover certainly can.

Consider for example Sam Loyd's (No. 2.20) which we discussed under Paradox. Although paradox was indeed its main impact, the point – that 2 ♘d6 could suffice to mate on the following move regardless of Black's first move – hardly leaps to the eye. Compare our next example:

3.6   #3

Fritz Giegold, 4th Prize
Oberfrankisches Problemturnier,
1933

The key is the delightful **1 ♕h8!**, waiting. In much the same vein as Loyd's problem, White has a single second move which serves against all Black's responses: **2 ♕d8!**. Yet this point seems more obscure – and therefore the key move is deeper – than that of Loyd's problem. One reason for this might be optical – the queen is even further from the black king than in the Loyd. Another possible reason is that, in the line **1...♔xc5 2 ♕d8**, Black finds himself

in zugzwang a second time, that is, although there is no threat, anything Black does leads to immediate mate (in problemist's parlance, the problem is a 'waiter' within a 'waiter').

It is also worth observing that, as we have seen in most of our examples, paradox and depth often go hand-in-hand. This is to be expected, since a move with an obscure point carries a fair probability that it will at least be surprising, and vice versa. Consider the next problem:

3.7   #5

Fritz Giegold & Herbert Engel
Schach-Echo 1973

It is no accident that it, too bears the cachet of Fritz Giegold, a master of depth among problemists. The black king is completely hemmed in, but how does White get at him? In such positions, the obligation to move can be relied upon to contribute to Black's downfall, but even so, White has to deploy plenty of ingenuity, as evidenced by the spectacular key:

1 ♗g1!!

Now let us look at the first of Black's two possible moves: **1...cxb4**. The continuation is **2 ♗xb6 b3 3 ♗c5 e6**. Note that Black's last two moves could have been played in either order. Now comes the *coup de grâce*: **4 ♘f6+! ♚xh6 5 ♗f8#**. As the reader has no doubt noticed, this does not explain the key; as far as 1...cxb4 is concerned, White could have done equally well with 1 ♗f2.

But this variation was merely the *hors d'oeuvre*; after

1 ... e6

we get the main course:

2 ♗h2!

All is now explained, no?

2 ... cxb4
3 ♘g8!

Threatening 4 ♘(either)f6#.

3 ... ♚xg4
4 ♘f6+ ♚f5
5 g4#

The depth of the key move in this work speaks for itself, but wherein lies the paradox? We are sure that the reader will agree that it is the apparently pointless deactivation of the bishop.

So far we have skirted around an issue which is fundamental to our experience of depth – indeed it is fundamental to chess in all its forms: difficulty. There is no doubt that the difficulty of a position raises the

suspense, and the revelation of the solution then releases it, leading to a wonderful 'kick', a unique explosion of intellect and emotion.

Depth and difficulty are very closely related, but they are not the same thing: depth does not have to be accompanied by difficulty, nor difficulty by depth, even though they often travel together. The difference between the two is that there is nothing lasting about difficulty; once you have seen the solution, you have had your high, never to be repeated by the same position (as long as you remember it!). But a deep move will always be a delicacy to be prized, like a choice quotation or a pretty tune. Mastering a difficult position is an intellectual achievement, but not necessarily an aesthetic experience.

Another well-known aspect of difficulty is its subjective component. Of course, we have discussed the subjective aspect of beauty as well, but what makes a chess position difficult is notoriously hard to define; not only individual differences, but also circumstances can play a role. At least we can define what makes something paradoxical or deep, even if these effects are not equally enjoyed by all spectators. Shall we just say that difficulty is strongly influenced by depth and leave it at that?

An interesting tale of the alliance between depth and difficulty occurred in the British Solving Championship final of 1993. The following study had to be solved in thirty-five minutes:

3.8 Win

Emilian Dobrescu, 3rd Prize
L'Italia Schacchistica 1965

1 d7 ♖f4!

1...♔xb6 2 ♔e8 ♖xd7 3 ♔xd7 and White wins. After 1...♖f4 White has the strong attempt 2 ♔c8!? (but not 2 ♔c7? ♖xd4 3 b7 ♖xd7+). The line continues: 2...♖xd4 3 b7 ♖c4+! (not 3...♖xd7 intending 4 b8♕? ♖d8+! forcing stalemate, because White has the decisive reply 4 b8♘+!) 4 ♔b8 ♖b4!! which forces a draw, because 5 d8♕ is met by 5...♖xb7+ followed by 6...♖b8+!. Instead, if 5 d8♘, it is White who is hard-pressed to draw after the straightforward 5...♖xa4. The win can be forced by a little finesse on the second move:

2 d5!

If now 2...♔xb6, 3 ♔e7 ♖e4+ 4 ♔d6 wins, so Black must stick to the plan of eliminating white pawns:

2 ... ♖d4
3 ♔c8

3 ♔c7? ♖xd5 4 b7 ♖xd7+.

3 ... ♖xd5
4 b7 ♖c5+
5 ♔b8

Now we see the crucial difference brought about by White's inter-mezzo on move two: Black's rook does not have the square b5 at its disposal to force the draw by analogy with the 'false trail' line. Instead, he must resort to:

5 ... ♖d5
6 ♔a8! ♖xd7
7 b8♘+!

Avoiding the stalemate after 7 b8♕? ♖d8! once more.

7 ... ♔b6
8 ♘xd7+ ♔c6
9 ♘e5+ ♔c5
10 ♘d3+ ♔c4
11 ♘b2+ ♔b3
12 ♔a/b7 ♔xb2
13 ♔a/b6

and wins.

The strange point of the tale is that three grandmasters, Nunn, Mestel and McNab, failed to solve the study in the allotted time. Now, although difficulty is to some extent subjec-tive, we can still say with utter con-viction that these gentlemen – particularly the first two, who have solved with success at the highest international level – have certainly coped perfectly well with problems many orders of magnitude more difficult than this one. But what it does show is that depth can sometimes prove very difficult!

Our final example shows, if readers will forgive our use of language, the true heights to which depth can ascend!

3.9   Draw

N. Elkies
Internet 1994

After **1 f6! ♕b3** it seems not to matter whether White continues **2 f7! ♕d1+ 3 ♔h6!** or **2 ♔h6? ♕d1 3 f7**. In fact, you have to see no less than 50 moves deep to grasp the subtle difference! Black threatens to drive the white king to f8 and thereby gain a move to bring his king round towards the action via the path a5-a4-b3-b2-c1-d1-e2, etc. White cannot prevent this plan but...

3...♕f3 4 ♔g7 ♕g4+ 5 ♔h8 ♕f5

6 ♔g7 ♕g5+ 7 ♔h7 ♕f6 8 ♔g8 ♕g6+ 9 ♔f8

The stalemate try **9 ♔h8?** fails against 9...♕xf7 when 10 ♘c2 is ready, available and unwanted.

9...♔a4! 10 ♔e7! ♕g7 11 ♔e8 ♕e5+ 12 ♔d7 ♕f6 13 ♔e8 ♕e6+ 14 ♔f8 ♔b3 15 ♔g7 ♕e7 16 ♔g8 ♕g5+ 17 ♔h8 ♕f6+ 18 ♔g8 ♕g6+ 19 ♔f8 ♔b2 20 ♔e7 ♕g7 21 ♔e8 ♕e5+ 22 ♔d8 ♕f6+ 23 ♔e8 ♕e6+ 24 ♔f8 ♔c1 25 ♔g7 ♕e7 26 ♔g8 ♕g5+ 27 ♔h8 ♕h6+ 28 ♔g8 ♕g6+ 29 ♔f8 ♔d1 30 ♔e7 ♕g7 31 ♔e8 ♕e5+ 32 ♔d7 ♕f6 33 ♔e8 ♕e6+ 34 ♔f8 ♔e2 35 ♔g7 ♕e7 36 ♔g8 ♕g5+ 37 ♔h8 ♕f6+ 38 ♔g8 ♕g6+ 39 ♔f8 ♔f3 40 ♔e7 ♕g7 41 ♔e8 ♕e5+ 42 ♔d7 ♕f6 43 ♔e8 ♕e6+ 44 ♔f8 ♔f4 45 ♔g7 ♕e7 (45...♕d7 46 ♔f6!) 46 ♔g8 ♕g5+ 47 ♔h7 ♕f6 48 ♔g8 ♕g6+ 49 ♔f8 ♔e5 50 ♔e7! ♕g7

50...♕e6+ 51 ♔f8 ♔f6 52 ♔g8 leads to the same result.

51 ♔e8 ♔e6 52 ♔d8!

With not a tempo to spare, White claims the draw as there has not been a pawn move or a capture since move two (2 ♔h6? and 3 f7 would have allowed 52...♕xf7! breaking the sequence).

The genius of the composer shines through in this study: the smallest of changes – a mere transposition of moves – proves crucial all of 50 moves later. This is a record that will be hard to beat!

4 Geometry

'In any particular theory there is only as much real science as there is mathematics.'
Immanuel Kant

Our third element deals with chess as a visual art. The term 'geometry' is used in a very loose sense and refers to the appeal of the physical effects of moves and positions to the chess mind's eye. We are not only concerned with the arrangement of chessmen in pretty shapes and symbols (part of what we shall call 'graphic' geometry), but also with the subtle, yet visible relationships among squares, lines and the pieces which occupy and control them ('optical logic' geometry).

For many people starting out on their journey into chess, it is this geometrical appeal which first seduces them and keeps them going. Enjoying the other elements can only come later, but a partial appreciation of chess geometry is possible quite early. Just as well, really, since otherwise many would simply give up!

A fuller understanding of chess geometry is only possible after exposure to a wide range of ideas and motifs. We want to give you a fair sample of geometrical effects in this chapter. For that reason, and not because we regard geometry as more important than any of our other elements, this chapter is a little longer than the introductory chapters on Paradox and Depth.

We will be putting these assorted effects into three broad categories: *graphic*, *optical logic* and *extended geometry*. This is mainly to ease communication and it is not crucial to understand precisely how these are defined. The following overview should be sufficient to illustrate our purpose.

Graphic geometry covers the least abstract patterns. A straight line of pieces, a corner-to-corner move, the switchback of a piece, the moving of a whole configuration of pieces one rank up the board would all be graphic. They are the sort of thing that might conceivably be noticed by a talented chimpanzee! To illustrate what we mean, we have 'composed' the following position:

(see diagram on following page)

Although our chimpanzee would have to be unbelievably talented to know it is stalemate, it might notice that the pieces are in a straight line! In fact, graphic effects are often coincidental. If you move the knight to

4.1   B

JL & DF

a4 and add a white pawn on f2, it is still stalemate, but the graphic effect is lost. In other words, the graphic effect does not arise out of the logic of the position.

'Optical logic', on the other hand, has everything to do with the logic of the position – it would be well beyond even the most brilliant monkey. It is more abstract than graphic geometry and deals with relationships between pieces and the squares they control. Noticing, for example, that a knight on d1 is dominated by an enemy bishop on d4 since the bishop controls all the squares the knight can go to (b2, c3, e3 and f2), is the sort of instant perception that a stronger player would have. Move the knight to e1 and our optical logic is lost. The visual input is similar in both cases, but in the first version the developed chess mind picks out the pattern. We will be showing many

examples of optical logic, including incarcerations, forks and Novotnys. It is probably the most common form of geometry in chess.

With a broad enough definition of geometry, everything could be considered 'geometrical'. We won't go quite that far, but at the end of this chapter we will be extending the meaning of geometry to cover a range of even more abstract ideas. For the moment, it is enough to think of it as a form of conceptual geometry designed to take account of various special effects and patterns. A pawn underpromoting in all three possible ways, as in the following study by Herbstman, would be the sort of conceptual pattern we are talking about:

4.2   Win

A. O. Herbstman, 2nd Prize
Tyovaen Shakki 1934

After **1 ♗h7+! ♔xh7 2 exf8♘+**, White wins, but on **1...♔g7** what happens? The obvious 2 exf8♛+? fails to 2...♚xh7! 3 ♜xd7 stalemate. However, **2 exf8♗+!!** wins. Similarly, **1...♚h8** is met by **2 exf8♜+!!**. A single underpromotion is unusual, but in this position we get all three! They form a pattern, since after the first two underpromotions you are almost expecting the third.

Graphic Effects

Exploring the graphic effects first, we may note that they consist of positions as well as move-sets. An extreme case of position-graphic is the so-called letter problem, an entertaining example of which can be seen in Diagram 4.3:

4.3   #2

G. Hume (after J. Bunting) 1924
Western Morning News & Mercury

In the diagram, the pieces form the letter 'K', but after the key **1 ♜b8** (waiting), it is transformed into an 'R'. Furthermore, after **1...♜xa5** we have a 'P' – albeit with a full-stop on d4 – and after the reply **2 c8♛#** we have an 'F'! But the composer's ingenuity does not stop there: in the variation **1...♜c4 2 ♗b4#** we have the letter 'D' underlined! In the lines **1...♗xb8 2 cxb8♘#** and **1...♗xb6 2 ♜xb6#** there is no graphic effect, but you can't have everything.

One of the simplest graphic effects is the long move, yet it is remarkable how much it can delight the eye. A special case is the move of the bishop from corner to corner, which has attracted the attention of many composers. No. 4.4 is short and sweet with a rather special twist:

4.4   Win

J. Fritz, 1st Prize
Svobodne Slovo 1961

1	♗h1!	♜xh1
2	a8♛	♜d1!

Black fights back well, preventing the queen checks on d5 and d8 and

threatening to queen with check. If 3
a7?, then 3...h1♛+ 4 ♛xh1 ♖xh1+ 5
♔g6 ♖h8.

3 ♛h1!!

The queen follows in the footsteps
of the bishop.

3 ... ♖xh1
4 a7

In a simple and almost symmetrical position, Black's extra rook
proves, paradoxically, to be a decisive disadvantage! White wins after
4...♖g1 5 a8♛+ ♔b5 6 ♛b8+ followed by the capture of the pawn,
leaving a technically won ♛ v ♖
ending.

An eye-catching little work, but
nevertheless rather undeserving of
its First Prize. Unbeknownst to the
tourney judge, the study was antici-
pated by P. Heuäcker a quarter of a
century earlier:

White wins with 1 ♗g7 a2 2
♗xh8 ♖e1 3 ♗a1!, etc. We slightly
prefer the neater 'version' by Fritz.

Switchback

A comparatively rare phenomenon
in actual play is the *switchback*.
'Switchback' is a composer's term
for the return of a piece to a square
which it occupied earlier in a sequence. It is classified under graphic
effects because it is generally an accident arising in the play, although
one could argue that this is not always so. It also possesses a slightly
paradoxical character, pointed up by
the question: if the original move of
the piece improved the player's position, surely its return had the opposite effect?

Take a look at Diagram 4.6:

4.5   Win

P. Heuäcker
Deutsche Schachblätter, 1937

4.6   Win

Leonid Kubbel, 1st Prize
Magyar Sakkvilag, 1934

White appears to have a painful choice between allowing a perpetual check or refraining from making a new queen:

> 1 ♘e4   ♛f3
> 2 f8♛!

This can truly be called a queen sacrifice! Its purpose is to decoy Black's queen, but from what?

> 2 ...   ♛xf8
> 3 ♘f6!!

This is the switchback move. The knight has operated like a gate, first letting the queen through, then shutting it off. Now White has the pleasingly 'quiet' threat of 4 f4 followed by 5 c3#. Black cannot escape by 3...♚xe5 because 4 ♘d7+ forks the queen; the lady herself is strangely helpless and even the resolute 3...♛xf6 4 exf6 gxf6 5 f4 doesn't help. A last attempt, apart from the text, is 3...♛h8 which is neatly met by 4 ♘g4! – now that Black no longer has 4...♛f4+ – threatening 5 c3# while also stopping 5...♛h6+.

> 3 ...   ♛b8

Hoping for 4...♛b4+.

> 4 c3+   ♚xe5
> 5 ♘d7+

and wins the queen and the game.

As you would expect, problem composers have performed many wonders with the switchback. Take but one example (4.7):

The key of this exceedingly clever problem is **1 ♖d7**. This threatens 2

4.7   #4

Valentin Rudenko, 1st Prize
Suomen Shakki, 1983

♖e7+ ♚xd6 3 ♖d7+ (Switchback No. 1) **3...♚e5 4 ♖e4#** (a slight flaw is that after 3...♚c5 four moves of the ♖d4 give mate; this is uneconomical). Black can defend with **1...b3** which arranges a little surprise after 2 ♖e7+? ♚xd6 3 ♖d7+ ♚e5+!. The down-side of this defence is that it interferes with the ♗a2: **2 ♖e4+ ♚xd5 3 ♖d4+** (Switchback No. 2) **3...♚e5 4 ♖e7#** – for now the ♗a2 can no longer interpose on e6. Black can clearly interfere with the threat by **1...♗xd5**, but this self-blocks, as one would expect: **2 ♗f4+! ♚xd4 3 ♗e3+** (Switchback No. 3) **3...♚e5 4 d4#**. Finally, what mistake does **1...♛xd3** make? **2 ♘xf3+! ♚xf5 3 ♘h4+** (Switchback No. 4) **3...♚e5 4 f4#**.

Of course, switchbacks are not the only idea of this problem by an eminent composer. They are integrally interwoven with the clearance of lines and squares by capture (what problemists call *annihilation*): three are executed by the black king and one by the white knight.

An interesting example of switch-backs occurring in an over-the-board game is Karpov-Kamsky; see the games selection at the end of Chapter 6.

Rundlauf

Before we leave the topic of switch-back, we should take a look at a special case called the *Rundlauf* in German. The most suitable English equivalent is probably 'round-trip' and it describes the return of a piece to its initial square in the diagram position by a circuitous route. The piece usually describes a geometrical figure, such as a rectangle, in the course of its travels. This effect rarely occurs in games or even studies, with the notable exception of some endgame situations, particularly *triangulation*. The play in Diagram 4.8, a theoretical position, illustrates this.

With Black to play, the white king must be allowed into b6, winning the a6 pawn and the game. With White to play, the diagram position must be repeated with the obligation to move passed to Black:

1 ♔d5   ♔c8

Black prepares to answer 2 ♔d6

4.8   Win

with 2...♔d8, else the c6 pawn will be ushered through to queen.

2 ♔d4 (c4)   ♔d8 (b8)

White manoeuvres within reach of c5 and d5, obliging Black to remain in touch with the 'corresponding squares' c7 and c8. The reason White wins this position is that he has two adjacent squares, c4 and d4, from which to eye c5 and d5 while he waits, whereas Black's corresponding two squares, b8 and d8, are not adjacent.

3 ♔c4 (d4)!   ♔c8

If Black could play to b8 or d8 he would not lose.

4 ♔d5!   ♔c7

If 4...♔d8(b8) 5 ♔d6 forces the pawn through, although White must remember either to underpromote after 5...♔c8 6 c7 ♔b7 7 ♔d7 ♔a7 or mate in three by 8 ♔c6!.

5 ♔c5

White's Rundlauf is complete and he wins.

4.9   #12

A. Shuriakov & V. Syzonenko
Chervony Girnik, 1985

This is a marvellous example of what can be achieved with slender force. If you were faced with this position as White in a game, would you be thinking about swindling a draw or forcing mate in 12?

1 ♘e8!
Threatening 2 ♘f6#.

1 ...   ♔e4
2 ♘f6+   ♔f5
3 ♘h5   ♔e4

The only other defence to the threat of 4 ♘g3# is 3...h1♘, which fails to 4 f3! followed by 5 ♘g7#.

4 ♘g3+   ♔d5
5 ♘xe2   ♔e4

Now the threat was 6 ♘c3#.

6 ♘c3+   ♔f5
7 ♘b5   ♔e4

Black's moves are forced; again this is the only defence against the threatened 8 ♘d6#.

8 ♘d6+

The knight completes the Rundlauf, but to what end?

8 ...   ♔d5

The diagram position has been repeated, with the exception that there is no longer a black pawn on e2.

9 ♘d3!

The second knight springs into action with the threat of 10 ♘b4#. This did not work on the first move because of 1...e1♕!.

9 ...   ♔c6
10 d5+!   ♔c7

If 10...♔xd5, 11 ♘b4+ ♔e5 12 f4#!

11 ♘b4!

Finally, a threat against which Black has no defence.

11 ...   ♔b8
12 ♘a6#

Echo

We now come to examples of graphic effects which involve entire configurations of pieces. In an **echo**, a configuration occurs in a different location on the board in two or more lines of play. A classic example is Diagram 4.10:

White's difficulty in this position is that the bishops appear to be able to defend against his threats whilst at the same time controlling the victorious advance of the d-pawn. For example, 1 ♖xb2? ♔b7!. A better attempt is 1 ♔c7, but this can be dealt with by Black as follows: 1...♗g3+

4.10   Draw

M. S. Libiurkin, 1st Prize
'64', 1932

2 ♔c8 ♗d1! 3 b7+ (3 ♖xb2 ♗g4+ 4
♔d8 ♗f4 beats off the attack and
prepares the inexorable advance of
the pawn) 3...♔a7 4 b8♕+ ♗xb8 5
♖xb8 ♗b3! 6 ♖xb3 d2 7 ♔c7 ♔a6 8
♔c6 ♔a5 9 ♔c5 and now both
9...♔a4 and 9...d1♕ win.

       1   ♔c8!

White's threats are now very serious, but Black can deal with them in
two ways:

A: 1   ...   ♗g4+
       2   ♖xg4   ♗xb6

Black appears to have neutralized
the threats and maintained every
prospect of winning, since the rook
cannot cope with both pawns: 3 ♖b4
(3 ♖g1 is not on because the bishop
controls this square) 3...d2 4 ♖xb6
♔a7!.

       3   ♖a4+   ♗a7
       4   ♖b4!   d2
       5   ♖xb2   d1♕

       6   ♖b8+!   ♗xb8
Stalemate

B: 1   ...   ♗xb6
       2   ♖xb6   d2
       3   ♖xb2   ♗a6+
       4   ♔c7   d1♕
       5   ♖b8+   ♔a7
       6   ♖b7+!   ♗xb7
Stalemate

The configuration of black king,
black bishop, white king has been repeated, but compared with Variation
A, the second occurrence has the
configuration shifted one rank down.
Because the echoed configuration is
located on squares of the opposite
colour, it is known by composers under the picturesque classification of
chameleon echo.

Echoes are a favourite theme
among problemists.

4.11   #4

Y. Vladimirov
Sovietsky Sport 1985

This position is a particularly clear example.

The move 1...♔e3 is clearly difficult for White to cope with in the diagram position, yet the key **1 ♖a2!!**, conceding two more flights, still comes as a delightful surprise. There is no threat; the white army merely waits for the enemy king to march to his execution. **1...♔c3 2 ♔f4! ♔d4** (**2...♔xd3** receives the same reply) **3 ♗b4 ♔xd3 4 ♖d2#**. If **1...♔xd3**, then **2 ♗g7! ♔e4** (again, **2...♔e3** is met in the same way as the text) **3 ♗c4 ♔e3 4 ♖e2#**.

Comparing the two mates, the arrangement of the pieces in relation to the black king is virtually identical, except for the reversal of the colours. Again, we have an example of a chameleon echo. In spite of the fact that Black has but a lone king, the play is not trivial, and the remaining two variations, while not integral to the echo theme, maintain this standard: **1...♔e3** transposes into the **1...♔c3** variation as follows: **2 ♗b4! ♔d4/ ♔xd3 3 ♔f4 ♔xd3/♔d4 4 ♖d2#**. After **1...♔e5** we see a different thought entirely, and one which makes excellent further use of the white pawn: **2 ♖a4! ♔f6 3 ♖f4+ ♔e5 4 d4#**.

Systematic Manoeuvre

A very similar effect to that of echoes is the **systematic manoeuvre**, in which a piece configuration is repeated at different locations of the board, but in a single line of play. As a solver, it is a particularly enjoyable experience to discover such a pattern moving across the board, especially if these moves represent best play. Look at Diagram 4.12:

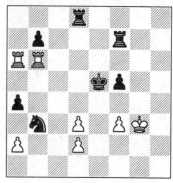

4.12   Draw

V. A. Korolkov and L. Mitrofanov, 1st Prize, 1st FIDE Tourney 1958

White is a piece down and, because the ♖a6 is attacked, it appears that he must lose time moving it and thus enable Black to rescue his knight.

    1 ♖b5+!

This puts Black on the spot, since 1...♔d4 is answered by **2 ♖xa4+**, and 1...♖d5 is even worse because of 2 f4+.

    1 ...   ♘c5!
    2 ♖xc5+   ♔d4

Black now attacks both rooks: White's next is forced.

3 罝aa5   罝g7+!

Black deftly avoids the temptation to fork the rooks immediately by 3...b6, for then White will escape with 4 罝xf5, attacking Black's rook, and if 4...罝g7+, 5 罝g5 when Black's last attempt, 5...罝dg8, is brushed aside by 6 罝xa4+.

4 ✿f4!

White chooses his square carefully; the reason will reveal itself at the end of the solution.

4 ...   b6
5 罝c4+   ✿xd3

Again, the two white rooks are attacked.

6 罝aa4   b5

For the second time, the two rooks are forked by the b-pawn.

7 罝c3+   ✿xd2
8 罝aa3   b4

The third and last fork.

9 罝c5!   bxa3
10 罝d5+!   罝xd5

Stalemate

A delightful study in which the composers, not content with 'just' a clever systematic manoeuvre (geometry), have added depth (4 ✿f4!), flow, and a paradoxical finish.

Loshinsky Magnet

Our last example in this brief survey of graphic effects is one of the great combinations of chess and creative imagination.

The key of 4.13 is the rather good:

4.13   #3

L. I. Loshinsky, 1st Place
1st USSR Championship 1947

1 ♛b1!

with the threat **2 ♘h5+ ✿xe4 3 罝e3#**.

Looking at the mating position, we can see that Black can defeat the threat by vacating d4, and indeed it turns out that the moves of the 罝d4 initiate the main variations of the problem: **1...罝d5 2 罝d4!**. The essence of White's procedure is to create an unanswerable double-threat; in this case **3 ♘h5#** and **3 exd5#**, the latter having been made possible by Black's first move.

Now try **1...罝d6.** White's continuation is **2 罝d5!** with the double threat of **3 ♘h5#** and **3 ♗xe5#**; this time the additional threat is made possible because of the interference by the 罝d6 with the black queen's control of e5.

The third defence, **1...罝d7**, interferes this time with the ♗c8, so that after – yes, you guessed it – **2 ♖d6!**, the threats are **3 ♘h5#** and **3 ♖f6#**.

By most standards, these three lines would be sufficient to win a prize. The idea, which has come to be known as the 'Loshinsky magnet' shows the white rook following its black counterpart at a distance of one square, taking advantage of a variety of tactical features of the position: line-opening of b1-e4, setting up a battery with the ♖d4 and ♗e4, and preparing mates which utilize the interference of the black rook with the ♛b8 and the ♗c8.

Yet Loshinsky has more to show: **1...♖c4**. What error does this move commit? It might take a while to realize that, unlike the first three variations, this move loses control of d3. This means that a move of the ♖d3 threatening 3 ♘h5# no longer has to create a second threat, because 2...♘d3, cutting off the queen's protection of e4, can now be answered by 3 ♘xd3#. The only provisos are that the white rook retains control of e3 and g3, so as to answer 2...♖xg3 with 3 fxg3#, and that the black rook is not allowed to throw a spanner in the works with 2...♖xc1 (or 2...♖c2). By this reasoning, therefore, we arrive at (**1...♖c4**) **2 ♖c3!**.

Similarly, **1...♖b4** and **1...♖a4** are met by **2 ♖b3** and **2 ♖a3** respectively.

The first three variations are graphic effects: the white rook's pursuit of the black is not, in itself, necessary to force checkmate (in other words, it is purely coincidental that the white rook chases its counterpart). In the second group of variations, however, the juxtaposition of the rooks is necessary to White's purpose, because the black rook must be prevented from crossing his plans. Such a set of variations, in which a white piece is obliged by the logic of the position to maintain a geometrical correspondence with a black one, is termed a **duel** by composers. Such duels have both graphic and optical logic geometry.

Finally, we should account for the last two black defences: **1...♖/♘xd3 2 ♛xd3!** and **1...♖xe4 2 ♖f3+!**.

Optical Logic

Optical logic happens all the time in chess and the next study should give you a clearer idea of exactly what we mean by it.

(see diagram on following page)

Black is material ahead, but requires great ingenuity to avoid losing immediately to the advancing pawn.

>**1 a7   ♖g3+!**

Not 1...♔d8? 2 ♖b7. Now White must capture, otherwise the black rook would stop the Great White Hope by 2...♖a3. But what is the purpose of the sacrifice?

>**2 ♔xg3   h4+!**

4.14   Win

B. Gusev & O. Pervakov
The Problemist, 1991

Black continues accurately. If 2...♘f5+, 3 ♔h3 0-0 4 ♖b7 forces the pawn through.

3 ♔xh4

If White refuses the second offer, Black will be able to escape loss by giving up his rook for the pawn: 3 ♔h3 0-0 4 ♖b7 ♖f3+ followed by 5...♖a3. Alternatively, playing to the f-file loses a tempo, e.g. 3 ♔f4 0-0+ 4 ♔e4 h3 5 ♖b7 h2 and it is Black who wins. But after the text move Black cannot continue 3...0-0? 4 ♖b7 ♖f4+ 5 ♔g5! and White will win first the knight and then the rook.

3 ...   ♘f5++!
4 ♔g4!

A deep move. White avoids 4 ♔g5 because after 4...0-0 5 ♖b7 ♘d4 (threatening to draw by 6...♘c6) 6 ♖b8, Black has a tempo-gaining check: 6...♘e6+ 7 ♔h6 ♘c7 8 ♔g6

♘a8 and draws. Now Black faces multiple threats. If he tries another check by 4...♘h6+ (4...♘e3+? is worse because of 5 ♔f3 and there is no defence to all the threats), 5 ♔g5 ♘f7+ 6 ♔g6! ♖h6+ (6...♘e5+ 7 ♔g7) 7 ♔g7 ♖a6 8 ♖xf7 wins.

4 ...   0-0!

This is the point of Black's play and another illustration of graphic geometry. Castling is an odd move, being the only one involving two pieces of the same colour; this gives it a special visual appeal, particularly in an endgame setting, which adds a pinch of paradox.

5 ♖b7   ♘e3+
6 ♔h5!

Another deep move. White avoids 6 ♔g5 (or 6 ♔g3) because after 6...♘d5! we reach a position of reciprocal zugzwang with White to play. This is analysed in detail after White's next move.

6 ...   ♘d5
7 ♔g5!

Now it is Black to move and White wins: either 7...♔h8, or rook anywhere along the rank, allows 8 ♖b8, leaving Black no time for 8...♘c7 because his rook would be unprotected, whilst if the knight moves, 8 ♖b8 and there is no stopping the pawn. Only one move is possible, but it allows White to force a second and final reciprocal zugzwang:

7 ...   ♘f4

8   ♔g4 (h4)!

Again avoiding 8 ♖b8 ♘e6+ and 9...♘c7.

8   ...   ♘d5

9   ♔g3!

At last Black has run out of constructive or waiting moves, so White wins.

Now consider what would happen if it were White to move in the reciprocal zugzwang position (after White's seventh move).

If 8 ♖b8, Black draws by 8...♘c7. Any other rook move along the file also allows 8...♘c7.

8 ♖d7 allows 8...♘b6 (but not 8...♖a8 9 ♔h6!).

If 8 ♔g6/g4, then 8...♖f6/f4+ followed by 9...♖a6/a4 draws; Black is content to give up the rook if necessary and to draw with knight against rook.

Finally, 8 ♔h5 ♖f5+ forces the king to the sixth or the fourth rank whereupon 9...♖f6/f4+ follows.

With White to play in the reciprocal zugzwang position, two geometrical relationships can be seen. Firstly, there is a relationship between the ♖b7 and the ♘d5, in which the rook must guard c7 and b6. This relationship is visually represented by the diagonal axis drawn between the two pieces. The second relationship is more subtle but just as clear to the chess-player's eye: the white king dare not move to the sixth or fourth ranks because the ♘d5 will support the black rook's checks on f6 or f4; again there is an axis between the knight and the king, and this time it is a horizontal one.

Although this study is especially notable for its paradoxical and deep reciprocal zugzwangs, it also serves to illustrate the difference between two of our categories. The castling move is a purely visual entertainment; its attraction lies in the physical nature of the move, and not to any significant degree in the logic of the situation on the board. It is therefore 'graphic'. On the other hand, the juxtaposition of the ♘d5 and the ♖b7, and also that of the ♘d5, ♔g5 together with the lurking ♖f8, derive their interest almost entirely from the situation on the board: it just so happens, for example, that the squares c7 and b6 about the d5-b7 axis are critical in the play. Such geometric phenomena are so embedded in the experienced player's subconscious that they require some intellectual effort to separate from the underlying rationale of the positions in which they occur. We are calling such phenomena 'optical logic'.

There are other cases of optical logic in this rich and economical study. White's last move – and indeed the final position – demonstrate a subtle, yet thrilling tension, which arises because of the enormous precision demanded of the players owing to geometrical forces. White must prevent the rook from checking on the rank and then switching to the a-file, whilst also avoiding repetition of position. And the whole point of Black's rook sacrifice was geometrical: it gained a tempo *to clear the line* between the black king and rook so as to make castling possible.

Let us now turn to look at some of the leading ideas in optical logic. If we were to organize a survey of geometric effects, we could do worse than start off with two basic categories: square effects and line effects. This distinction is not intended as a systematic concept: it is more a question of emphasis. Thus, in an effect of the square type, our focus is on one or more particular squares, whilst in an effect of the line category, our concentration is more upon the lateral and diagonal control of the line-moving pieces. We have already covered many examples of both types informally. To take just one example of each, No. 3.5 featured multiple self-blocks – a square effect; No. 1.6 showed a number of *interferences* – a line effect. (Note that this problem also contained a lovely graphic effect, the black rooks and bishops being arranged as 'organ pipes'.)

Paralysis or Incarceration

Diagram 4.15 is a study by a former

World Champion and shows an unusual square effect.

But first, what does White do about the unstoppable a-pawn?

4.15   Draw

V. V. Smyslov
5th HM, Shakhmaty v SSSR 1937

1 ♘h8+   ♚g8!

Black avoids 1...♚f8 2 ♘g6+ ♚g8 (2...♚e8 3 fxg7, or 2...♚f7 3 ♘h8+ repeating the position) 3 ♘e7+ ♚f7 4 fxg7 ♚xg7 5 ♘f5+ followed by 6 ♘xd4 and the counterattack has resulted in the a-pawn being caught after all.

2 f7+   ♚f8
3 ♚g6!

White now blithely sets about an apparently hare-brained and irrelevant manoeuvre.

3 ...   a2

Black is powerless to upset White's plan (whatever it is). Black only loses time with 3...♘e5+ 4 ♚h7 and the knight must return in view

of the twin threats 5 ♗b4+ and 5
b8♕+.

    4 ♔h7!   **a1♕**
    5 g6!

Threatening self-stalemate with
5 ♗b4 and 6 b8♕+.

    5 ...   **♕h1**
    6 ♗h6   **♗f4**
    7 b8♕+   **♗xb8**

Stalemate

How did White engineer this
amazing coup? Apart from getting
his king securely locked up, his
pawns blocked and his bishop
pinned, the secret of the stalemate
lies in the *incarceration* of White's
knight. The pawns on g6 and f7 occupy the available squares, paralys-
ing the noble steed; the knight itself
performs the vital role of blocking a
flight square.

In this study, paralysis of a white
piece was exploited by White. In No.
4.16 Black's downfall is caused by
the cleverly induced paralysis of his
rook.

Surveying White's possibilities,
we note that 1 c6? is met by 1...♖h6!
and 1 ♔f8? gets nowhere against
1...♗h6!.

The accurate move is **1 ♔f7!**.
Now **1...♗h6** allows **2 c6** leaving
Black helpless against the simple
advance of the pawn. Therefore,
Black must play **1...♖h7**. Now that
the rook is where White wants it,
he continues with **2 ♔f8!** threatening **3 ♕f7** and **4 ♕g8#**. Black's only

4.16   #4

A. Kraemer 3rd HM in Ring
Tourney, Die Schwalbe
Die Welt 1949

defence is **2...♗h6**, preparing a discovered check should White attempt
to carry out this plan. But the black
pieces have been neatly corralled,
enabling the gentle, yet lethal manoeuvre to be completed with **3
♔e7!** and Black cannot stop **4 ♕e8#**
because the rook is incarcerated and
unable to vacate the h7 square.

A problem with a very special
touch. Not only is the paralysis idea
shown in a most satisfyingly clear
form, but the white king gives the
impression of bringing off the entire
coup by a kind of remote control,
performing a lovely little Rundlauf
all the while.

It is often interesting to speculate
upon the frequency of occurrence of
a geometrical effect in the various
genres, game, study or problem. For
example, paralysis is not very often

exploited by composers, but crops up – usually unnoticed – with surprising frequency in the game. Consider the typical schema in Diagram 4.17:

Because of the incarceration of

4.17   B

the ♖f8, Black's superior force is helpless against the threat of ♕h7# and he can only try 1...♔g7 after which 2 ♕g5+ forces mate in a further two moves. If the rook could move, it would be able to vacate f8 and create a flight square which might well turn the position into a win for Black.

Fork

One of the game's most important tactical elements is the fork, or double attack, illustrated so delightfully by No. 4.12 (by Korolkov and Mitrofanov). This square effect features as the point of a problem comparatively

rarely. A charming exception is No. 4.18:

4.18   #4

Yakov Vladimirov
Die Schwalbe 1963

After the key,
    1 ♕h4!
Black is in zugzwang and we have the following five variations:

A: 1 ...   ♖g8
        2 ♕h2+   ♔a8

The variation 2...♔c8 3 ♕c7 is a 'short mate', so called because it occurs before the full solution length of the problem; if 2...♖g3, then 3 ♕xg3+ followed by mate on c7 or g8.

        3 ♕a2+!

An elementary fork: the queen hits the king and rook simultaneously, and **4 ♕xg8#** follows.

B: 1 ...   ♖f8
        2 ♕g3+   ♔a8
        3 ♕a3+!   ♔b8
        4 ♕xf8#

C: 1   ...   ♜e8
     2   ♛f4+   ♚a8
     3   ♛a4+!   ♚b8
     4   ♛xe8#

These variations constitute a threefold echo. A further fork occurs after:

D: 1   ...   ♚c8
     2   ♛e7!

Threatening 3 ♛c7#.

     2   ...   ♚b8
     3   ♛e5+!   ♚a8
     4   ♛xh8#

The last, and intriguingly game-like variation is:

E: 1   ...   ♚a8
     2   ♚g7!

Threatening simply 3 ♚xh8 and 4 ♛d8#. If now 2...♜e8 (2...♜b8 and 2...♜d8 allow short mates), we have a repeat of the 3 ♛a4+ fork.

     2   ...   ♜c8
     3   ♛a4+   ♚b8
     4   ♛a7#

Thus 2...♜c8 turns out to be a prospective selfblock and the variation provides a pleasing pinch of variety.

Focal Play

A very popular idea amongst problem composers is the *focal theme*, which is, in a sense, the opposite of a fork and is, incidentally, a very clear illustration of what is meant by optical logic. Consider Diagram 4.19:

The black knights are tied down to preventing mates on c1 and d3,

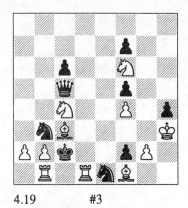

4.19   #3

*R. C. O. Matthews, 1st Prize
The Problemist 1951*

and the queen is in a 'focus', having to keep an eye on a3 and e3 simultaneously. If it were Black to move, **1...♛xc4** would be met by **2 ♗xc4**, threatening 3 ♗xb3# and if the ♘b3 moves, one of the rooks would give mate on c1. Black can, however, set up a new focus by playing **1...♛a7!** which still keeps control of the ♘c4's mating squares. To this White has the deliciously delicate riposte **2 ♗b4!** which places Black in zugzwang: the knights are still tied down, and, because of White's last move, the queen cannot return to her original focus on c5 because the bishop now interrupts the line from c5 to a3. The only remaining move, **2...c5**, results in an interference, whereby the queen's guard of e3 is cut, allowing **3 ♘e3#**. Note the very important feature that, had White attempted **2 ♗d4?** instead, the queen would be able to cope by resorting to a third focus with **2...♕e7!**. And, speaking of the move ...♕e7, what would happen if Black were to play this on the first move? Yes, you've spotted it, after **1...♕e7**, White has a crusher which is analogous to the first variation, namely **2 ♗d4!** and again Black is unable to retain the focus. This time **2 ♗b4?** would not succeed because of **2...♕a7!**.

So far, all we have seen is the purely hypothetical situation if it were Black to play in the diagram. In fact, as you probably suspected, there is no means by which White can maintain the status quo, and the key move is the radical **1 ♘d7!** threatening the brutal capture of the queen. Since **1...♕xc4** still fails to **2 ♗xc4**, Black must defend by moving the queen to a7 or e7, keeping control of a3 and e3: **1...♕a7 2 ♗d4!**. White's key move has turned the situation upside-down, because **2 ♗b4?** instead fails to **2...f6!**, a waiting move which Black did not have before. On the other hand, after **2 ♗d4!**, Black does not have any way of preventing the threatened **3 ♘e3#** whilst at the same time maintaining the guard on a3: the ♘d7 prevents the queen from moving to the alternative focus on e7. And by applying the same logic, it is easy to see that the reply to **1...♕e7** is **2 ♗b4!**.

There are two further geometrical features of this brilliant problem

which we must mention before passing on. The first one is the **symmetry** of the position and the play. The c-file is the central axis and all the important squares are paired off on either side of it: a3 and e3; b4 and d4; a7 and e7. Symmetry is often an attractive feature in a composition, but sometimes it can make the play seem too mechanical. Because Matthews' work contains just two symmetrical variations, they complement each other ideally; a further pair of this kind would probably have been over the top.

The second interesting feature of the problem lies in the relationship between the **set play** – the variations which would be possible were it Black to play in the initial position – and the **actual play**. In the set play, 1...♕a7 and 1...♕e7 were answered by 2 ♗b4 and 2 ♗d4 respectively; in the actual play, the same two defences are answered by 2 ♗d4 and 2 ♗b4 respectively. In other words, the white continuations have been switched round, leading to the theme of **reciprocal change**. Such formal relationships among moves will be further discussed under Extended Geometry at the end of this section.

The idea of focal play will be recognized by players as related to the 'overloaded piece', a recurrent tactical motif.

Diagram 4.20 is a neat illustration in a study.

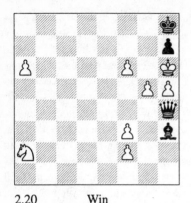

2.20   Win

L. A. Isaev & S. S. Levman,
1st Prize, Magyar Sakkvilag 1926

1   a7

Not 1 f7?? ♛f4 and White is embarrassed for a defence against 2...♛d6+ 3 g6 ♛f4#.

1   ...   ♛a4
2   f7   ♛a3

This is the only spot from which to control both pawns' promotion squares, since 2...♛c6+ 3 g6 ♛c8 4 g7 is mate. The queen is now in a focus and White proceeds to overload it.

3   ♘b4!

Did you notice that Black was threatening mate in one?

3   ...   ♛xf3

Again the queen finds the one adequate defensive square.

4   ♘d5!   ♛a3

If 4...♗c8!?, then 5 ♘f6! (not 5 a8♛?? ♛f6+! drawing) 5...♛a3 6 ♘xh7 wins.

5   ♘e7!   ♛f3

The queen has been thoroughly humiliated by the knight, but to what purpose?

6   ♘g6+   hxg6
7   hxg6

And the pawns triumph over the queen as the threat of **8 g7#** is added to the promotion threats, and this is too much. Unfortunately, this otherwise delightful little work has an unwanted *dual*. The equally thematic 6 ♘f5 also wins, as discovered by Fritz 3! A number of studies will doubtless be 'cooked' by computer analysis; we hope not too many of those in this book will suffer such a fate! In our opinion, a dual such as 6 ♘f5 does rather spoil the aesthetic value of the above study, but does not completely ruin it.

Interference

We move on now to look at one of the many line effects catalogued by problemists, that of *interference*. This term refers to the closing of a line of one piece by another piece of the same colour, creating a weakness which can be exploited by the opponent. The organ-pipe problem, No. 1.6, was a fine example in a two-mover. Let us have a look at a pretty miniature:

(see diagram on following page)

White begins with 1 ♘e3 threatening 2 ♘d5, which in turn threatens 3 ♘f4#. If Black prevents this with

4.21   #3

James Quah, Kipping Prize
The Problemist 1992

2...e5 then this allows **3 ♞f6#**. Therefore, Black has to concentrate on preventing **2 ♞d5**. If he tries **1...e6**, then **2 ♞g4!** followed inevitably by **3 ♞f6#**; the interference of the pawn with the ♝c8 allowed the knight to occupy g4 with impunity. If Black tries **1...♝e6**, there comes **2 ♞g2!**. This shows Black's first move to be a more subtle interference – its effect is not seen immediately, but rather on the next move, in that the ♝e6 prevents 2...e5 and Black is therefore unable to prevent **3 ♞f4#**.

This problem shows one of the most famous problem themes, the *Grimshaw*, in which two line-moving pieces mutually interfere on the same square, in this case e6. And yes, the pawn is a 'line-moving piece' when, as here, it is on its initial square and therefore capable of making its 'double-move'.

Novotny

Have you heard of a Novotny? If not, you will certainly find it useful, whether as player or composer. A Novotny is the sacrifice of a piece on the intersection square of two enemy line-pieces, often leading to a double-threat. It is a blend of line effect and square effect. No. 4.22 is an elegant example.

4.22   #2

M. Lipton, 2nd Prize
B. C. P. S. Ring Tourney 1966

If we look first at the ♝c3 and the ♜e2, their intersection square is e5, so we can try **1 ♝e5?** threatening **2 ♞g7#/♜e7#**. Black manages to refute this with **1...♞xh7!** removing White's control of f8. The intersection square of the ♝c3 and the ♜d1 is d4, which looks very promising. Let us try **1 ♞d4?** threatening **2 ♞f6#/♜d8#**. Again Black finds a saving resource, this time **1...♜e7!**

shutting off the control of f7 by the ♖b7. How about **1 ♖d4?** instead? This threatens **2 ♘d6#/♘f6#**. Black can prevent both these threats with **1...♘e4**, but this interferes with the ♖e2 and allows **2 ♖e7#**. Nevertheless, Black can escape with the simple fork **1...♖e6!** which protects both mating squares without incurring any weakness. Finally, we try **1 ♗d4!** and this has the one double-threat that is irresistible: **2 ♘g7#/♖d8#**.

This problem is a typically modern work, showing a great deal of interesting strategy in the tries and their refutation, but a negligible amount of play after the key. It is also an impressively economical work, with the distinction of being completely devoid of pawns; problemists call such compositions 'aristocrats'.

Craig Pritchett overlooked a Novotny to his cost when both players were in time trouble:

32	**...**	**♗xc3?**
33	**♕xf7+**	**♔h8??**

33...♔h7! would have led to an unclear position after 34 ♗e5! ♕xd7! 35 ♕xd7 ♗xe5!.

34 ♗e5!!   Resigns

There is nothing to be done against the threats of 35 ♕xg7# and 35 ♕xe8+ followed by mate. If 34...♖g8, then 35 ♗xc3 wins a piece. With the king on h8, 34...♕xd7 does not help either: 35 ♕xd7 ♗xe5 36 ♕xe8 is check.

4.23   B

A. J. Miles – C. Pritchett
London, Lloyds Bank Masters 1982

In the diagram position, Black can win with **32...♕c2!** 35 ♖b1 (White must resist the temptation of 35 ♕xf7+? ♔h8 36 ♖b1 ♗xc3 37 ♗e5 ♕xb2+! followed by mate, because the queen can no longer interpose on d1 after 38...♖e1+) 35...♗xc3 36 ♗e5 and now simply 36...♗xe5 wins as after 37 ♕xf7+ ♔h7! the ♕c2 controls g6 whilst White cannot capture on e8 because of the mate on b2.

The Novotny has been used in so many different ways by problem and study composers that a hefty and very enjoyable tome could be written on the subject. Diagram 4.24 is a study in which sharp and accurate introductory play brings the forces into position for the Novotny:

1 ♘e3

1 ♘d2? would not succeed in stopping the black pawn because of the reply 1...♖d4.

4.24　　　　Win

T. B. Gorgiev, 1st Prize
Schakend Nederland 1959

1 ...　　　　f1♕+

If 1...♖b4, 2 ♘d7 and White will
be able to guarantee the promotion
of a pawn. 1...♗h2 is another attempt, after which White wins by 2
b8♕ ♖d4+ 3 ♔e2 ♗xb8 4 ♘e6! ♖e4
5 f7 ♖xe3+ 6 ♔xf2 ♖xe6 7 f8♕.

2 ♘xf1　　　　♖xf1+
3 ♔e2!

It is important to ensure, by attacking the rook, that Black is unable
to stop the b-pawn with the bishop;
thus if 3 ♔c2? ♗h2 4 ♘d7 ♔b5 it is
now White who has to fight for a
draw.

3 ...　　　　♖f2+!

A clever manoeuvre which, as
will be seen, ensures that Black
achieves the desirable set-up of rook
on f-file and bishop on h2-b8 diagonal after all, albeit at the price of
some loss of time.

4 ♔e1!

White's king continues to monitor
the rook so as to deter ...♗h2.

4 ...　　　　♖b2
5 ♘e6!

White must protect the △c5, but
the reason for the choice of e6 over
d7 will soon be seen.

5 ...　　　　♗f2+

Here or on the next move, stopping the f-pawn with the bishop
would lead to a prosaic loss: 5...♗e3
6 f7 ♗h6 7 f8♕ ♗xf8 8 ♘xf8 ♔a7 9
♘d7. Black is in zugzwang and
must release the white king, which
marches up the board to assist the
knight and pawns. Note that 5...♗h2
6 f7 ♗g3+ 7 ♔d1 transposes back to
the main line.

6 ♔d1

6 ♔f1? ♗g3 and the ensuing
7...♖f2 comes with check.

6 ...　　　　♗g3
7 f7　　　　♖f2

Black's clever play has borne fruit
and it seems that White can do no
better than 8 f8♕ ♖xf8 9 ♘xf8 ♔b5
with a draw.

8 ♘f4!!

Now White's fifth move is explained; the Novotny ensures the
promotion of one of the pawns. Nevertheless, the fight has not gone out
of Black, and it is one of the great
merits of this study that it does not
come to a sudden halt at this point,
but ends in style.

8 ...　　　　♖xf4!
9 b8♕　　　　♖f1+

Not 9...♖d4+? 10 ♔e2 ♗xb8 11 f8♛.

10 ♔e2   ♖f2+!

An unusual repetition of the check on move three. Black lures the king into a fiendish trap.

11 ♔e3   ♗xb8
12 c7!!

A most surprising move. The immediate 12 ♔xf2? does not win – Black replies with 12...♗a7! so that 13 f8♛? can be met by 13...♗xc5+! 14 ♛xc5 forcing stalemate, explaining Black's 10th move. If White tries to avoid the trap with the ingenious 13 f8♗! Black still caps this with 13...♗b6!! threatening to win the c6 pawn by 14...♔b5. White plays 14 ♗d6, to answer 14...♔b5? by 15 cxb6, but Black coolly replies 14...♗a5!, renewing the threat of 15...♔b5. White can now only try 15 c7, but after 15...♔b7 Black will capture the ♙c7 and whether White chooses a ♗+♙ or just a ♙ ending, it is a draw. A study within a study!

12 ...   ♗xc7
13 ♔xf2

and White wins.

Critical Play

Another blend of square and line effects is *critical play*. A *critical move* is executed by a line-moving piece passing over a *critical square*, which is later occupied by another piece, thereby blocking the return path.

This might sound a little complicated, but it is actually a problemist's expression of an important tactical motif, which is so 'optically logical' that players probably take it for granted. Diagram 4.25 is an elegant example.

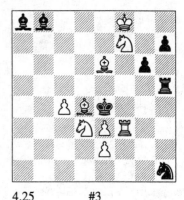

4.25   #3

*Alfred Sutter, 1st Hon. Men.
Parallèle 50, 1950*

The key is **1 ♔g8!** threatening the Novotny **2 ♘fe5**, with the threats **3 ♘c5#** and **3 ♖f4#**. If White were to try 1 ♘fe5?, 1...♗d6+! gains time to defend c5 and, after the king has moved, Black can easily prevent the other threatened mate. After the key move, however, Black cannot play 1...♗d6 as this would allow immediate mate. Black can defend against the threat by getting the rook or bishop beyond e5, so as to leave only one threat to cope with on the second move: **1...♖a5** defeats the threat of **2 ♘fe5** because then there would be only one threat, **3 ♖f4#** which would be prevented by **2...♗xe5**. The drawback of **1...♖a5** is that White too can exploit the fact that the rook is now west of e5 by selecting a different Novotny: **2 ♘de5!** with the decisive double-threat of **3 ♖f4#** and **3 ♘g5#**. Similarly, Black can defeat the threat by **1...♗h2**, so that after **2 ♘fe5?** ♖xe5! there is no mate. Again, White can also capitalize on the fact that the bishop has moved to the near side of e5 with a third Novotny: **2 ♗e5!** with the threats **3 ♘c5#** and **3 ♘d6#**. The only other variations are **1...♖f5(d5)** which are straightforwardly met by **2 ♗xf5(d5)+** followed by **3 ♘c5#**. The whole affair is like a beautiful piece of Swiss clockwork.

In this problem, Black's defences **1...♖a5** and **1...♗h2** were critical moves with respect to e5 because the white pieces were able to shut the rook and bishop off by playing a piece to that critical square, threatening a mate on the other side of it. The intriguing thing about the problem is that these black defences were also *anti-critical* with respect to e5, because they *countered* a shut-off which White threatened on that square.

The concept of critical play has been very fertile ground for composers. The original use of the idea was in the Indian theme, where White plays a critical move followed by a self-interference to relieve stalemate,

followed by a discovered mate. This recipe should enable you to solve No. 4.26 quickly :

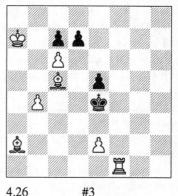

4.26   #3

D. G. McIntyre
Natal Mercury 1917

1 ♗g8! dxc6 2 ♖f7! ♚d5 3 ♖f4#. The bishop passes over the critical square f7, allowing the rook to interfere with it, luring the king onto a square where he can be mated. There is a pleasing side variation after **1...d6 2 ♗g1!** (the only safe square for the bishop on the g1-a7 diagonal) **2...d5 3 ♗h7#**.

This is not all that the problem has to show. If you move the entire position two files to the right, so that the white king is on c7 and the black on g4 and so on, a new problem, also a mate in three, is produced. Now we see a very interesting demonstration of chessboard geometry, because there is insufficient space for the former key (**1 ♗i8??**). On the other hand, the black king is now much nearer to the board edge and this means that the king can be mated on a different square with another Indian manoeuvre: **1 ♖h8! fxe6 2 ♗h7! ♔h5(4) 3 ♗f5#**. In this line the rook and bishop exchange roles. There is a bonus in this setting, because not only is the key critical with respect to h7, it is also anti-critical with respect to h2, as is seen in the variation **1...f6 2 ♗h2 f5 3 ♗d1#**.

A useful tactic to bear in mind is the decoying of a piece over a critical square so as to shut it off, as is neatly demonstrated in No. 4.27:

4.27   Win

H. Rinck
2nd Prize, Sydsvenska
Dagbladet Snällposten 1911

White appears to have insufficient material advantage to win. 1 exd7, with the idea of 1...♘xd7 2 ♗f5+ forking the knight, fails to the in-between move 1...♔g4+!. The attempt

to improve by 1 ♗f5+ ♔h4 2 e7 (or 2 exd7 ♔g5+ 3 ♔g2 ♖d6 and the ♙d7 is lost) 2...♔g5+ 3 ♔g2 ♖h8 4 ♖e2 (or 4 ♗h3 ♘c8 5 ♖a8 ♔f6 6 ♗xd7 ♖g8+ followed by 7...♘xe7) 4...♖e8 and the attack on the bishop gives Black enough time to surround and win the ♗e7.

1 e7!

By leaving the bishop on h7, White keeps the black rook's route to h8 closed.

1 ...   ♔g4+

Black must again prepare ...♖e6 by cancelling the fork on f5.

2 ♔g2   ♖e6
3 ♖e2!!

This is the decoy move: Black must take, and in doing so the rook passes over the critical square e4.

3 ...   ♖xe2
4 ♗e4!

And this is the shut-off. In this case, it has the charming feature that the bishop is only indirectly defended.

4 ...   ♖xe4

There are no improvements. The attempt to maintain rough material parity by 4...♔f4 5 e8♕ ♖xe4 fails to 6 ♕b8+ winning the knight. In this line, 5...♘d5 (there is no other hiding place for the knight – 5...♘c4 6 ♕f7+) is met by 6 ♕h5! ♘e3+ 7 ♔h3!

5 f3+

and White captures the rook and queens the pawn.

Bristol

Invented by a problem composer, the Bristol manoeuvre is a device well worth bearing in mind by all players.

4.28   Win

A. P. Guliaev,
3rd HM, A. Troitsky Tourney,
Zadachi i Etiudi 1929

The idea is clearly demonstrated in No. 4.28, which kicks off with:

  1 ♖h8!

The first part of the Bristol. It is obvious that the rook has to make room for the pawn to promote, but the reason for choosing the most distant square will soon be seen.

  1 ...   **g1♕**
  2 a8♕+   **♗a3**
  3 ♕g8+

Here it is. The new-born queen follows in the rook's tracks; if the rook had played to any other square on the eighth rank, it would have prevented the queen from reaching the

g8 square. This effect, where a piece clears a line for another piece by moving to the end of that line, is called the Bristol Theme. It bears this name because of a three-mover by Frank Healey which first showed the idea, winning the First Prize in the Bristol Tourney of 1861. It has remained one of the most popular geometric themes ever since.

  3 ...   **♔a1**
  4 ♖h1!

Sacrificing the rook to decoy Black's queen. A forced mate now ensues, brought about by the white queen performing yet another geometric motif, the staircase. Other examples of this charming effect are No. 5.1, showing a king descending the stairs, and No. 9.14, in which a rook does the honours.

  4 ...   **♕xh1**
  5 ♕xg7+   **♔a2**

The rest of the solution runs: **6 ♕f7+ ♔a1 7 ♕f6+ ♔a2 8 ♕e6+ ♔a1 9 ♕e5+ ♔a2 10 ♕d5+ ♔a1 11 ♕d4+ ♔a2 12 ♕c4+ ♔a1 13 ♕c3+ ♔a2 14 ♕b3+ ♔a1 15 ♕xa3#**

The synthesis of the two geometric devices of Bristol and staircase has yielded an enjoyable, if rather easy study. One negative note might be sounded by purists of the Logical School of composition (which we describe in Chapter 8): the purpose of the rook's move to h8 was not only to allow the queen to move to g8, but also to go to h1 afterwards.

According to the tenets of this school, there should be 'purity of aim' in the white manoeuvre, implying that the rook should play no further part after the Bristol has been executed. To most chess players this criticism would be baffling, particularly in the context of a study rather than a problem; we tend to slave over our chessboards searching precisely for those moves which have as many advantages as the position will endow. This is one of the few areas where a particular artistic viewpoint does not coincide with the intuition of the player.

The Extended Meaning of Chess Geometry

At the beginning of this section, we described chess as a visual art. We have reviewed a selection of geometric ideas which support this conception by the manner in which they establish pleasing relationships among squares, lines and the pieces which occupy and move along them. Extended geometry is about conceptual patterns, generally fairly abstract ones. Let us look again at one of the most popular of these – the full set of underpromotions. In Diagram 4.2 (Herbstman) we saw three underpromotions in separate variations. In our next position, 4.29 they come one after the other in a single line of play.

4.29   Win

E. L. Pogosiants
(after M. S. Liburkin), 1st HM
Schakend Nederland 1975

White has two extra pieces and a selection of pawns on the seventh rank. His king, however, is in serious trouble.

1 ♗b2+   ♚d2

The whole b-file is mined on account of 2 b8♕+. 1...♚c4 allows 2 ♘e3+ with tempo (e.g. 2...♚c5 3 ♘f3 ♗e4 4 ♗a3+ followed by queening with check). So 1...♚d2 is forced.

2 ♘f3+   ♚d3

The only move avoiding both the e-file and 3 ♘e3+.

3 ♘e5+   ♚e2

After 3...♚d2, the continuation 4 ♘c4+ ♚d3 5 ♘ce3 ♗xf5, 6 e8♕ is safe enough.

4 ♘g3+   ♚d1

Clearly the best square, since 4...♚e3 and 4...♚d2 allow destructive knight checks. The text prepares

5 e8♕?? ♗e4+! 6 ♘xe4 f1♕#, as well as a cunning stalemate trap.

5 ♘g6   ♗xg6

The scene is set for an astounding series of underpromotions. The point is that White must avoid 6 e8♕? ♗e4+ 7 ♕xe4 f1♕+ 8 ♘xf1 with a surprise stalemate.

6 e8♖!!   ♗xe8
7 b8♘!

To cover the c6 square. Black now prepares the same stalemate as before, only to be thwarted by yet another underpromotion.

7 ...   ♗g6
8 a8♗!!

White wins on material.

The sort of patterns we are classifying under extended geometry are extremely rare in over-the-board chess. They are even unusual in studies, but such abstract ideas have become the very stuff of which problems are made. Problemists never seem satisfied. Just as opening variations become high fashion in tournament chess for a time, so are new themes and ideas heavily exploited, until enthusiasm wanes and the fashion changes. So it was one day when the interest of composers of two-movers subtly shifted from visual to abstract art. This was not just a new theme, however, but a whole complex of ideas; the change was to a new epoch, paralleled in the game perhaps by the advent of the Hypermodern School.

The abstractions which were the subject matter of this new age focus essentially on the relationships between move-sets, rather than upon the physical relationships we have been looking at hitherto. Let us look at two of the leading ideas.

Correction Play

4.30   #2

M. Parthasarathy, 1st Prize
The Problemist 1963,
Brian Harley Award

Diagram 4.30 is solved by **1 ♕c2!** placing Black in zugzwang. If the ♗c3 moves **randomly**, denoted by **1...♗~**, it opens a line for the queen to mate by **2 ♕c5#**. The bishop can **correct** this error by **1...♗d4!** which, though it still commits the error of the random move, avoids the original punishment by protecting c5. However, it commits another error, which is to interfere with the ♖f4, allowing **2 ♕c4#**. If we now turn our attention to the ♘b5, **1...♘b~** un-guards d6 allowing **2 ♖(x)d6#**. By playing **1...♘bd4!** instead, this mate is prevented because the control of c5 by the ♗f2 is cut. Again, the correction interferes with the ♖f4, this time permitting **2 ♗c4#**. Looking now at the ♘e2, if **1...♘e~**, the line of the ♖e1 to e6 is opened, allowing the ♖c6 to release its hold on this square and to play **2 ♖c5#**. Black's knight can correct this error by cutting off the ♗f2 from c5 with **1...♘ed4!**, but this time there is an interference with the ♗c3 allowing **2 ♖e5#**. Finally, we consider the ♖f4. All its moves lead to **2 ♕(x)e4#** except **1...♖c4 2 bxc4#**, and **1...♖d4**, which again interferes with the ♗c3 leading this time to **2 ♕f5#**. The rook moves are a small blemish to the purist, because 1...♖d4 is not strictly a correction as it does not commit the error of unguarding e4 in the first place. Nevertheless, this is a superb problem, showing four random and correction pairs leading to eight distinct mates, where the correction moves are all interferences on d4. **1...♗d4** and **1...♖d4** also conform to the Grimshaw theme, defined above.

Patterns

The three-move problem, No. 4.19, discussed under focal play showed the theme of reciprocal change, in which, after black moves **1...x** and **1...y**, White replies **2 A** and **2 B** respectively in the set play, and **2 B** and **2 A** respectively after the key. We have expressed the structure of the theme symbolically so as to emphasize the abstract pattern expressed by the relationship between the two white mating moves. Indeed, every theme in the rich complex of pattern themes is defined in much this way, expressing the move-relationships symbolically.

As can be seen from the definition of reciprocal change, it is a *two-phase* theme: the first phase occurs before the key in the *set play* and the second is the *actual play*. Some pattern themes are entirely contained in the actual play, as in No. 4.31:

4.31   #2

C. J. Morse, 2nd Prize
British Chess Magazine, 1962

The good key is **1 ♕f8!** and, just as in the preceding problem, Black is in zugzwang. Again, the story is one of random and correction moves, but there is a difference as you will soon notice. 1...♘e7~ opens the queen's line to c5 allowing 2 ♗c3# (let us call this Mate A). The correction is 1...♘d5! protecting c3, but interfering with the ♗b3 to allow 2 ♘xe6# (Mate B). If we move the ♗b3 randomly off the a2-e6 diagonal, 2 ♘xe6# (Mate B) again results. Black can correct the error of unguarding e6 by 1...♗d1+! but this loses control of d1 for 2 ♖xd1# (Mate C). If instead we move the ♗b3 randomly along the a2-e6 diagonal, control of d1 is again lost and 2 ♖d1# (Mate C again) results. The bishop can correct this error with 1...♗c4! preparing to interpose on d3, but this blocks a potential flight square enabling White to release it with 2 ♘f3# (Mate D). The ♘e6 moving randomly opens the line of the ♗g8 to c4, again allowing 2 ♘f3# (giving Mate D again). The knight corrects by 1...♘xc5 ruling out 2 ♘f3 because d3 would become a flight; however, c5 is now blocked, enabling the

♗b4 to release it for 2 ♗c3#, and we are back at Mate A.

Let us step back a little and review what is going on in this problem. There are four pairs of random and correction moves, much as in the Parthasarathy work, but here there are only four distinct mates, instead of the full complement of eight. Each of the four mates occurs twice, once after a random move and once after a correction move from a different pair. If you wrote down the mates in their paired sequence, the following pattern emerges: **A-B, B-C, C-D, D-A**. Because of the cyclic nature of this pattern, the theme is known as **cyclic black correction**. Sir Jeremy Morse was the first to extend the cycle from three to four mates with this pioneering problem.

It is strange to reflect that this very formal, mathematical kind of beauty is being wrought with chess pieces. Indeed, it is too remote from the game for the taste of many a player, but the realm of chess art is very broad, and there is plenty to offer those who prefer realism.

5 Flow

'All things arise and pass away.'
Buddha
'Go with the flow'
Popular saying

We come to last of our four elements – 'flow', probably the hardest to define rigorously. As was indicated in the introduction, flow relates to dynamic movement in chess, and is usually exhibited by a series of moves rather than a single one. The longer the sequence of moves for which the tension is maintained, the greater the flow. More generally 'flow' could be regarded as the major aesthetic component of a sport/art such as ice skating. A series of dominoes knocking each other over would also exhibit flow.

The main characteristic of flowing chess is crispness. Long and difficult side variations, clouding the clarity of the main line, get in the way of appreciating aesthetic flow. This does not mean all the moves have to be trivial, it is simply that flow is independent of depth. The degree of tension created by a sequence of moves may be seen as the flow 'multiplied' by the depth of the sequence. The greater the tension, the stronger the aesthetic effect.

Smooth and Turbulent Flow

Only two types of flow will be distinguished. The more common form is 'smooth flow' where, typically, one side dominates the other and controls the play over a lengthy sequence of moves. The rarer form is 'turbulent flow' or 'passage at arms' where, for a series of moves (not necessarily so long) the play is very violent. High dramatic content, twists, cuts and thrusts and paradoxical moves characterize the play. The tension is maintained, but changes its form rapidly as both sides hit the other with powerful moves. Which type of flow you find more pleasing may very well depend on your character.

Most top class games of chess have an element of flow in them. In this section we will look at just two games but further examples will be found later in the book. There is little flow in short problems such as mate in two or three, but there can be flow (usually of the smooth variety) in longer problems. The section ends with an extraordinary problem by Markus Ott, in which the flow lasts for over a hundred and fifty moves. Further long problems can be found in the problem chapters towards the end of the book. However we start off by illustrating flow with the help of five wonderful studies. The first three show 'smooth' flow and the other two have phases of 'turbulent' flow. Further examples of studies with both forms of flow will be found in the studies section in part two.

I (J.L.) memorized the following study (by the brilliant Georgian grandmaster of composition, Gia Nadareishvili) after coming across it as a junior. I still remember it even today, more than fifteen years later.

5.1   Win

G. Nadareishvili, 1949
Source unknown

White, with his extra bishop, must maintain complete control since the advanced black pawn on b2 is threatening to queen.

1	♗e3+	♚b1
2	♗h6!	

Blockades the pawn. Black now tries for a stalemate, which he threatens in three moves. White must bring his king down the board and this is achieved with the help of a 'ladder':

2	...	b5
3	♔e7!	b4
4	♔f6	b5
5	♔g5!	

Blocking the bishop just in time, releasing the stalemate. The white king now 'ladders' down the board. He has a choice of squares to achieve this effect but the basic idea is the same. The repeated pattern of the ladder is both geometrical and flowing.

5	...	♚c1
6	♔f5+	♚b1
7	♔f4!	♚c1
8	♔f3+	♚b1
9	♔e3	♚c1
10	♔e2+	♚b1

Now the only way to make progress is to release the h-pawn.

11	♗d2	h5
12	♔d1	h4
13	♗xb4	h3
14	♔d2	h2
15	♗d5	

White's last two moves could have been in either order, a minor flaw in a study of this length. Black must now promote; it does not matter what to.

15	...	h1♛
16	♗xh1	♚a2
17	♗d5+	♚b1

Now it is mate in four, but precise play is needed first of all:

18	♗a3!	b4
19	♗b3!	bxa3
20	♗g8	a2
21	♗h7#	

Again the bishop had a choice of squares on move 20.

At the time, I felt the wonderful flow and the snap, paradoxical finish (a smothered mate effect) more than made up for the minor defects. One can only dream of finishing a real game off with a sequence like that! The tension is maintained for a large number of moves. The flow is smooth since White completely controls the play, Black simply doing what he has to do. Nowadays, jaundiced by experience, I find the defects more significant, but quite forgivable on a good day.

Long, flowing sequences are achieved with extreme economy in the next two positions. Kasparian, necessarily laconic as he squeezed 2545 domination studies into one book, described the first position as a 'gem of endgame composition'.

To win this position White must prevent Black from sacrificing his knight for the pawn. Further than this he must also win the knight since the pawn cannot otherwise be forced past the g7 square. An assortment of domination and zugzwang ideas are used to achieve these ends, but first (paradoxically) the knight

5.2   Win

G. Zakhodiakin
1st prize, '64' 1931

is forced over to the kingside, in order to obstruct Black's king.

1   ♔c5

Threatens 2 ♔c6 trapping and winning the knight. Black must escape:

| 1 | ... | ♘c7 |
| 2 | ♔d6 | ♘e8+ |

Forced in view of 2...♘a8 3 ♔c6!.

| 3 | ♔e7 | ♘g7 |

Necessary since 3...♘c7? allows 4 ♔f7! when the g-pawn decides the issue immediately.

4   ♗g6!

Trapping the knight. Black's options are limited but one deep move is still necessary to seal his fate.

| 4 | ... | ♔g8 |
| 5 | ♗f7+ | ♔h7 |

5...♔h8 leaves White with an easier task: 6 ♔f6 ♔h7 7 ♔e5 ♔h8 8 ♔f4 ♔h7 9 ♔g4 ♔h8 10 g6 wins. After 5...♔h7 White must aim for the same position by losing a tempo. His king must stay in contact with the f5 square to stop the knight escaping, and so there is only one convenient place to 'triangulate' – around the e5, e4 and f4 squares. Meanwhile Black can only oscillate with his king.

6	♔f6	♔h8
7	♔e5	♔h7
8	♔e4!	

The deep move, subtly losing a tempo on his path to g4.

8	...	♔h8
9	♔f4	♔h7
10	♔g4	♔h8
11	g6	

Wins the knight (and then the game) by means of zugzwang. It is very surprising that White can force a win from the start – most top players would simply assume it was a draw. The final zugzwang is also 'paradox'. There is a deep idea of triangulating (8 ♔e4!) and also a pleasing appearance to the initial set-up with both black pieces in the corners. But the flow of the play, chasing the knight from one side to the other with a series of delicate moves, is the dominant aesthetic element. The extreme economy with which all this fine play is achieved ranks this study very high indeed. It is a very pure piece of chess, for the connoisseur, with less immediate appeal.

Similar considerations apply to the next, much more recent study.

The smooth flow of the play, a whole series of domination ideas and the striking economy make a powerful impression. Nothing remarkably deep or paradoxical about any single move, so it really is the flow (and to some extent the 'geometry' of domination) that is responsible for the effect.

2.3   Win

J. Lerch
1st Prize, Magyar Sakkélet 1988

White wins if he can promote his d-pawn.

1	d6	♗e8

1...♗e6 2 ♘c5+ ♔b5 3 ♘xe6 ♔c6 4 ♔e5 wins.

2	♘f6	♗c6!

After 2...♗b5? 3 ♔c5! zugzwang decides the game at once.

3	♔c5	♗b5
4	♔b6	♔b4
5	♘d5+	♔c4
6	♘e3+	♔b4
7	♘c2+	♔a4

Black is always restricted to just one move as the knight pirouettes across the board.

8   ♔c7   ♗e8

Moving the king runs into yet another knight fork.

9   ♔d8   ♗h5

After 9...♗b5 10 ♔e7 ♗c6 11 ♘d4 White can force through the pawn, while 9...♗g6 fails to 10 ♘d4 ♗h5 11 ♔e7 ♗g4 12 ♘e6.

10 ♘e3   ♗e2

Moving the bishop to f3 instead loses immediately to 11 ♔c7.

11 ♔e7   ♗b5
12 ♘c2!

and 13 ♘d4 winning.

Think twice in future before swapping that knight off for the bishop! Right through the play it is clear White is better with his further advanced pawn and the badly placed black king. Better, but only just winning after a superbly balanced battle for supremacy of the key squares. Without the black pawn on a5 the lack of zugzwang would leave the position completely drawn. Playing over this study can have quite a hypnotic effect.

The following study by the great Kasparian shows turbulent flow and features an astonishingly resourceful defensive idea by Black.

White is a rook down but has two dangerous passed pawns on the sixth rank. There is a violent start as both sides make forceful, obvious

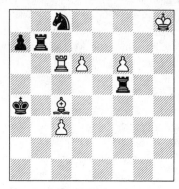

5.4   Win
Kasparian
Shakhmatny Listok 1930

moves that any self-respecting family player could relate to.

1   ♖a6+   ♖a5
2   f7

Threatening to queen, so Black gives up his rook.

2   ...   ♖xf7
3   ♗xf7!

Exchanging rooks first would only draw. White has left his rook on a6 *en prise* so as to capitalize on the passed d-pawn. Black must take the rook since 3...♘xd6? 4 ♖xd6 leaves him lost 'on material'.

3   ...   ♖xa6
4   ♗e8+!

After the direct 4 d7? ♘d6! Black defends since 5 ♗e8 is met by ♘f7+! (5...♘b7? 6 d8♕+) 6 ♗xf7 ♖d6 with a drawn position. Hence White gives the bishop check first expecting to simply win by queening the pawn. So far the play has had a heavy, 'Thump! Thump!' nature to it (turbulent flow) but now Black uncorks an astounding stalemate trap, the central idea of the study.

| 4 | ... | ♔a5! |
| 5 | d7 | ♘b6!! |

So that 6 d8♕? is a surprise stalemate, the point of Black's last two paradoxical moves – notice the self-incarceration of Black's rook. White counters this by underpromoting to a rook, not so surprising in itself (Black threatened 6...♘xd7) but placing Black in an unexpected zugzwang!

| 6 | d8♖!! | ♘c4 |

If 6...♘a4, 7 ♖d5+ ♔b6 8 ♖d6+ ♔b7 9 ♖xa6 ♔xa6 10 ♗xa4 wins easily enough.

7	♖d5+	♔b6
8	♖b5+	♔c7
9	♖c5+	♔d8

The last three moves of smooth (forced) play set up a final, brief passage at arms. White attacks the knight so Black has countered by attacking the ♗e8.

| 10 | ♗b5 | |

Attacks the rook on a6 too. No good now is 10...♖h6+ 11 ♔g7 ♖h3 12 ♖xc4 winning since the c-pawn is defended. Black instead counters with a pin:

| 10 | ... | ♖a5 |
| 11 | ♖d5+ | |

Unpins with check. White wins after 12 ♗xc4, e.g. 11...♔c7 12 ♗xc4 ♖a3 13 ♖d3.

The central paradoxical idea is the stalemate defence by Black (6 d8♕? stalemate). The play leading to that crescendo is turbulent but there is an unusual amount of smooth flow in the fading out phase (moves 6 to 12). It is always harder to solve studies where both sides make brilliant moves, but it should be no harder simply to appreciate the play. In our final illustrative study by the friendly Israeli composer, Yochanan Afek, you will again witness powerful counter-punching from both White and Black. Of course, White lands the final punch, and it is a knockout blow!

5.5   Win

Yochanan Afek
2nd Prize, Tidskrift för Schack 1972

White is a piece up but has to deal with the threat to his knight.

| 1 | ♖xb5+ | |

The natural move 1 ♘e5? fails to 1...♔xb6 2 ♘d7+ ♔c6 3 ♘xf8

♗xg4 with sufficient counterplay for the draw (the threat is 4...♗d1 followed by 5...b4 and also 4...♗f5 dominating the knight). White's solution is more violent.

1 ... ♔xb5

Otherwise Black is losing on material.

2 ♘e5+ ♔a4

No choice as alternative squares fail to 3 ♘d7+ and 4 ♘xf8 winning (this time Black is without the b5 pawn). Almost dominated, the black king is forced to the side.

3 ♘d7!

Threatening two sudden mates and seemingly decisive. There now follows a violent 'passage at arms' as Black hits back with a sacrificial 'stalemate attack'.

3 ... ♗e2!
4 ♗xe2 ♖b8+!
5 ♗b5+!!

Not 5 ♘xb8 stalemate. If now 5...♔xb5, then 6 ♘xb8 wins, so Black must take the bishop with his rook.

5 ... ♖xb5+
6 ♔a2!

Zugzwang! This final paradoxical twist, as an apparently mobile rook is dominated by a mere knight, decides the issue.

Competitive Chess

Somewhat different criteria apply to games than to studies. In a forty move game you could hardly expect all the winning side's moves to be unique, only moves to win, while all the losing side's moves were demonstrably forced! Given the starting position is probably drawn this would be logically impossible anyway. The criteria for a sound study have to be relaxed when applied to the game. For a phase of a game to be described as flowing, the moves need not be forced but should be logical, or, at the very least, plausible.

Even blunders need not totally ruin a game. Unsound play is not necessarily unaesthetic, although it is a fairly serious detraction. A beautiful move should be a correct move, ideally, although earlier incorrect moves may be forgiven in the overall context of the game.

Flow and Technique

Good technique, or the winning of won positions, is often characterized by smooth flow. Often there is no need for deep, subtle moves or tricky tactical nuances, although being alert to such possibilities is the best approach, since the game might be wrapped up more efficiently. Winning by the steady implementation of a twenty-move plan is very impressive, but far less so if you overlook an instant tactical win.

The first game is a famous miniature played in London, 1912.

Ed. Lasker – Sir George Thomas
London blitz 1912

1 d4 f5 2 ♘f3 e6 3 ♘c3 ♘f6 4 ♗g5
♗e7 5 ♗xf6 ♗xf6 6 e4 fxe4 7 ♘xe4
b6

Although not obviously wrong,
this move seems to lead to trouble.
Earlier, 3...d5! might have been best,
and now 7...0-0 8 ♗d3 ♘c6 was to
be preferred. One of the striking
things about this game is that Black's
play seems reasonable and yet he is
mated in eighteen moves.

8　♗d3　　　♗b7
9　♘e5　　　0-0?!

After this Black is in mortal danger.

10　♕h5　　　♕e7?

Looks best, preparing to meet 11
♘xf6+ with 11...gxf6! defending h7.
However it leads to a brilliancy by
White. More stubborn was 10...g6
11 ♘xg6 hxg6 (11...♕e8 12 ♘xf8!
♕xh5 13 ♘xf6+) 12 ♕xg6+ ♗g7 13
h4 (13 ♘g5 ♖f6!) with a dangerous
attack, probably winning once the
king's rook gets in on the act. The
next move is both deep and paradoxical, but it is not just this move
that makes the game stand out. The
king is hunted from g8 to g1 in a
wonderful flowing sequence. The
stakes are high, White having sacrificed a whole queen, and only the
final mate resolves the tension which
hangs in the air for a full eight
moves.

11　♕xh7+!!　♔xh7　12　♘xf6++
♔h6 (12...♔h8 13 ♘g6#) 13 ♘eg4+
♔g5 14 h4+ ♔f4 15 g3+ ♔f3 16
♗e2+ ♔g2 17 ♖h2+ ♔g1 18 ♔d2#.

Some might have preferred 18
0-0-0#! A beautiful game, even if
rather brief.

The second game shows less forcing play and has a completely different sort of appeal. It is a long game,
smoothly played by Karpov in all its
phases. The endgame is especially
attractive. This quickplay game decided the Tilburg knockout tournament of 1993, with a great deal of
prize money resting on the result.

V. Ivanchuk – A. Karpov
Tilburg 1993

1　e4　　　c6
2　d4　　　d5
3　e5　　　♗f5
4　h4　　　h5

A standard error here would have
been 4...e6?? 5 g4 ♗e4 6 f3 ♗g6 7
h5 trapping the bishop.

5　c4　　　e6
6　♘c3　　　♘d7
7　cxd5　　　cxd5
8　♗d3　　　♗xd3
9　♕xd3　　　♘e7
10　♗g5　　　f6

Karpov has judged that White
cannot exploit the slight weakening
created by this move.

11　exf6　　　gxf6
12　♗d2　　　♔f7!

Good judgement again. Disregarding the orthodox principles about castling into safety, Karpov simply places his king on what is probably its safest square.

13	♘ge2	♘g6!
14	g3?!	

Perhaps White should interpret the position more aggressively with a double-edged move such as 14 0-0-0!?. In the next few moves he drifts into a passive endgame.

14	...	♗d6
15	♘b5	♗b8
16	♗b4	a6
17	♘d6+	♗xd6
18	♗xd6	♕b6
19	♗a3	♕a5+
20	♕d2	♕xd2+
21	♔xd2	♖ac8

At first glance it appears that White has a weak isolated d-pawn, but in fact Black cannot get at it (so it should not be described as weak). Instead Black exchanges it off in order to gain space and advance his centre pawns. At this stage it is not clear that Black has anything more than a slight edge.

22	♖hc1	e5!
23	b3	♔e6
24	dxe5	fxe5
25	♖xc8	♖xc8
26	♖c1	♖xc1
27	♗xc1	

Neither side could cede the c-file, so all the rooks have come off. Now Black cramps White further.

27	...	d4!
28	f3	♔d5
29	♗a3	a5
30	♔d3	b5

Threatening ...b4 followed by ...♘c5+. White decides to keep control of the c5 square, but to do this he has to obstruct his own bishop and weaken the c4 square. Over the last few moves, without doing anything violent and probably without needing to calculate any variations, Black has smoothly increased the size of his advantage. Smooth, flowing, positional play – always cramping and restricting his opponent – vintage Karpov! Unlike Kasparov, whose play often involves deep/complex or dynamic/tactical ideas, Karpov's moves often seem deceptively easy to understand. Both of the great Ks play aesthetic chess, but in different ways: Karpov's play has more flow, while Kasparov makes more use of violent, paradoxical moves. Kasparov is often the more spectacular player but we certainly enjoy Karpov's games just as much.

31	b4	a4!

Increasing his winning chances by keeping pawns on the board.

32	♗c1	♘f6
33	♗g5	e4+! *(5.6)*

A beautiful, geometrical knight pirouette is about to follow. The sacrifice of the d-pawn is only temporary. In fact White's last chance was not to take it.

5.6   W

34 fxe4+   ♘xe4
35 ♘xd4?

A controversial error. Karpov, annotating this game for *New In Chess* magazine, claims simply that 'All other moves are bad, e.g. 35 ♗f4 ♘f2+ 36 ♔d2 ♔e4'. However Van der Wiel claims a draw for White with 35 ♘f4+ ♘xf4+ 36 gxf4! (36 ♗xf4 ♘f2+ 37 ♔e2 ♘g4 38 ♔d3 ♘e5+ and White must give ground since the pawn ending is lost). The critical line seems to be 36...♘c3, when 37 f5! (37 a3? ♘b1 38 f5 ♘xa3 39 f6 ♘c4 40 f7 ♘e5+!) 37...♘xa2 38 ♗d2! ♘c3 39 f6 ♔e6 40 ♔xd4 ♘e2+ 41 ♔e3 ♘g3 42 ♔f4 should hold. Brilliant play by Karpov, but not such impressive notes! Aesthetically it does not detract from the game that, at this stage, a series of 'only' moves could save White. Karpov outplayed his opponent and got the advantage – but not yet a decisive one. Unless the current analysis is

overturned, one must conclude that the position only becomes lost after 35 ♘xd4?. In studies everything should be 'black and white', but in games you get almost the whole spectrum.

35 ...   ♘e5+
36 ♔e3   ♘g4+
37 ♔d3   ♘gf2+
38 ♔e3

Black wins after 38 ♔e2 ♔xd4 39 ♗e3+ ♔c3 40 ♗xf2 ♔xb4.

38 ...   ♘d1+
39 ♔e2

White must give ground. 39 ♔d3? ♘ef2+ 40 ♔e2 ♔xd4 41 g4 hxg4 42 h5 ♘e4! is hopeless.

39 ...   ♔xd4
40 ♔xd1   ♘c3+!

In the final phase Karpov calculates accurately. 40...♘xg3? gives a pleasant advantage but maybe no forced win.

41 ♔c2   ♘xa2
42 ♗d2   ♔c4
43 g4

The best chance; waiting just makes it worse: 43 ♗e1 a3 44 ♗d2 ♘xb4+ 45 ♗xb4 ♔xb4 46 g4 hxg4 leaves Black with an easy win.

43 ...   hxg4
44 ♔b2 (5.7)

A critical variation, which Karpov must have seen before playing 40...♘c3+, runs 44 h5 g3 (one cute pitfall runs 44...♘xb4+? 45 ♗xb4 ♔xb4 46 h6 g3 47 h7 g2 48 h8♕ g1♕ 49 ♕c3#) 45 h6 g2 46 ♗e3

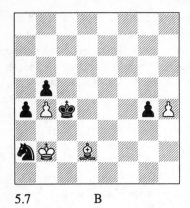

5.7   B

♘xb4+ 47 ♔d2 ♘d5 48 h7 (48 ♗f2 ♘f6) 48...♘xe3 49 h8♕ g1♕.

44	...	♘xb4
45	h5	♘d3+
46	♔a2	g3

Apparently falling into a trap, but probably Karpov had seen the finish and decided to wrap up in style rather than simply retreating the knight to cover the h-pawn (46...♘e5 wins easily enough).

47	h6	♘e5
48	♗f4	g2
49	♗xe5	g1♕
50	h7	

Remarkably enough, the queen cannot stop the h-pawn. The bishop controls h2 and 50...♕g2+ 51 ♗b2 forces Black to play 51...a3! if he wants to win. Karpov chooses a more sparkling finish.

50	...	b4!
51	h8♕	b3+
52	♔a3	♕c5+

                    0-1

Mate is forced. A truly marvellous game by Karpov, and even more impressive when one bears in mind the competitive significance and the speed of play (although these do not affect the 'objective beauty' of the moves). Ivanchuk joined the audience to applaud his opponent's victory!

Now we move from the high profile, big money world of top-class grandmaster chess, to the pure and relatively obscure world of the series helpstalemate! We hope you are not put off by the definition of the problem, since it is a personal favourite (of JL). A classic of modern chess composition, it is in many ways a perfect problem.

5.8   SH=153
            Markus Ott
    Prize, Feenschach 1980

The stipulation is 'series help-stalemate in 153'. What, exactly, does this mean?

You have to find a sequence of 153 black moves in a row (without giving or walking into check; White not moving) so as to reach a position where White can make one move, stalemating Black.

Since Black is making all the moves, his pieces will remain on the board. So in order to be stalemated, Black must immobilize his own men. This is in fact quite easy. Play the moves 1...♜g4, 2...♜h3, 3...♚h2, 4...h5 and 5...h4 and you have almost done it. The knight on g2 is pinned and so the only move available to Black in this position would be 6...♚g1. All White needs to do is control g1 and we are home. Presently no single move will do this; however if you imagine that White no longer has the pawn on d4, the move 1 ♗c5 will do the trick.

But how can we get rid of the pawn on d4? It seems Black can do nothing since he is not allowed to check White. The knight must stay on g2, the bishop on h1 and the only black pawn that can move is the h-pawn (which can go no further than h4 for the final stalemate). This means the rooks cannot get out of the 'box' on the kingside. Only the black king remains for active service. However after 1...♚f1 and 2...♚e1 you can go no further.

At this stage you either give up or discover the mechanism by which the black king gets in and out of the

kingside noose. We are now ready for the actual solution:

1...♜g4	2...♜h6	3...♚h2
4...♚h3	5...♚h4	6...♚h5
7...♜h4	8...♜h2	9...♚h4
10...♚h3	11...♜h4	12...♜g4
13...♚h4	14...♚h5	15...♚h6
16...♚g7		

The king has escaped to the open country. What is the plan? Ultimately to capture the d4-pawn. Black must never capture the bishop on e7 or the rook on a2 since these pieces are needed for the final stalemate. First he must capture the rook on d3, then come back and take the bishop on d1, then the knight on b3, then the knight on b1 and finally he can get the pawn on c3 followed by his real target – the pawn on d4!

17...♚f7	18...♚e8	19...♚d7
20...♚c7	21...♚b6	22...♚b5
23...♚c4	24...♚xd3	

Notice that at every stage, Black has only one move in order to achieve his purpose in the shortest possible time. There are never two ways to do it. For example, to get from e8 to c7 his majesty must go via d7, d8 being controlled by the bishop. This absence of 'duals' throughout the 153-move solution represents a phenomenal achievement by the composer. Now the rook on d3 is gone, Black must return for the bishop on d1 which is no longer protected. The king travels through the 'mechanism' in reverse gear:

The next moves are:

25...♚c4	26...♚b5	27...♚b6
28...♚c7	29...♚d7	30...♚e8
31...♚f7	32...♚g7	33...♚h6
34...♚h5	35...♚h4	36...♚h3
37...♜h4	38...♜h6	39...♚h4
40...♚h5	41...♜h4	42...♜g4
43...♚h4	44...♚h3	45...♚h2
46...♚g1	47...♚f1	48...♚e1
49...♚xd1		

Black would like to continue to gobble up the knight on b1 as well but first he must go back for the path protector on b3 (which prevents access to the c1 square). The knight on b3 is no longer defended by the now deceased bishop on d1.

50...♚e1	51...♚f1	52...♚g1
53...♚h2	54...♚h3	55...♚h4
56...♚h5	57...♜h4	58...♜h2
59...♚h4	60...♚h3	61...♜h4
62...♜g4	63...♚h4	64...♚h5
65...♚h6	66...♚g7	67...♚f7
68...♚e8	69...♚d7	70...♚c7
71...♚b6	72...♚b5	73...♚c4
74...♚xb3		

And back again:

75...♚c4	76...♚b5	77...♚b6
78...♚c7	79...♚d7	80...♚e8
81...♚f7	82...♚g7	83...♚h6
84...♚h5	85...♚h4	86...♚h3
87...♜h4	88...♜h6	89...♚h4
90...♚h5	91...♜h4	92...♜g4
93...♚h4	94...♚h3	95...♚h2
96...♚g1	97...♚f1	98...♚e1
99...♚d1	100...♚c1	

Not even Geoffrey Boycott reached a hundred as systematically as that. After taking the knight on b1, the c3-pawn loses its defence and then the d4-pawn can finally be taken.

101...♚xb1	102...♚c1	103...♚d1
104...♚e1	105...♚f1	106...♚g1
107...♚h2	108...♚h3	109...♚h4
110...♚h5	111...♜h4	112...♜h2
113...♚h4	114...♚h3	115...♜h4
116...♜g4	117...♚h4	118...♚h5
119...♚h6	120...♚g7	121...♚f7
122...♚e8	123...♚d7	124...♚c7
125...♚b6	126...♚b5	127...♚c4
128...♚xc3	129...♚xd4	

At last! Even now the road home is precise. After 130...♚e5? you have to retreat again, losing two moves. The final twenty five moves should come as no surprise:

130...♚c4	131...♚b5	132...♚b6
133...♚c7	134...♚d7	135...♚e8
136...♚f7	137...♚g7	138...♚h6
139...♚h5	140...♚h4	141...♚h3
142...♜h4	143...♜h6	144...♚h4
145...♚h5	146...♜h4	147...♜g4
148...♚h4	149...♚h3	150...♚h2
151...♜h3	152...h5	153...h4

White now plays ♗c5 and it is all over bar the counting!

There is some paradox in this problem (the way the mechanism works; at first it seems impossible) and some geometry in the back and forth repetitions (as well as in the working of the mechanism itself). Of course, the whole concept is deep – 153 moves deep – but there is no single move in the sequence which could be described as subtle or deep according to our meaning of the term. What is truly astonishing about the problem is the flow of the solution. 153 'only' moves following a clear plan without a single side variation! The tension created is large because the solution is so long, even if the depth at any moment is not that great ('area of tension' = length × depth). Notice the economy: the a2-rook, e7-bishop and the pawns on e4 and d5 force a precise, dual-free, route of the black king. The start position is striking, with the black and white forces unusually separated. The systematic, stage-by-stage progress of the solution also pleases. All in all a fantastic achievement by the Swiss composer. Perhaps series problems are an acquired taste, but even so, most people who see this position seem to know instinctively that it is something very special.

Part Three: Sampling the Spectacular

We have now finished introducing our four elements. Each has received its own chapter and we hope the reader already has a good, intuitive, understanding of what we mean by them.

In the final part of the book, we are going to survey the aesthetic sides of chess one by one; starting with the game, moving on to the study and concluding with problems. Each field, or genre, has its own distinctive flavour, but, as we will demonstrate, the four basic elements can be usefully applied to all of them.

6 The Poetry of War: the aesthetics of practical play

'War is the father of all.'
Heraclitus
'Competitions are for horses, not artists.'
Béla Bartók
'Unfortunately – and this is part of the tragedy of the genuine chess artist – it takes two players to create one chess masterpiece.'
Alexander Alekhine

It is well known that many players do not have much time for studies and problems. It is less well known that there are some problemists who do not have much time for the practical game! They argue that the game is over-competitive and lacks the purity and beauty found in composition. Why bother playing chess when the prettiest ideas are found in studies?

For competitive players it is impractical to approach the game positively trying, or expecting, to play beautiful chess. The objective is to win, and beauty – if there is any – is merely a side product. Judging only by artistic criteria, it is difficult to argue with our 'game-hostile' problemist friends. However, in order to appreciate chess (the game) fully, one has to see it in a sporting context. It is just plain unrealistic to expect the same artistic standards from both the competitive game and composition. Anything achieved under the strain of over-the-board conditions, in the midst of the 'fog of war' is that much more impressive. Naturally, in purely chess terms, greater things can be done in the privacy of one's study (no pun intended). Just think of the advantages: all the time in the world, moving pieces around while analysing, putting them wherever you like to begin with, removing any piece you want to... To criticize the game 'because the pawn on h2 played no relevant part' is absurd. It is almost like expecting a great painter to produce a masterpiece while simultaneously warding off an angry Mike Tyson!

Once you make allowance for such limitations, there is a great deal to appreciate, aesthetically, in competitive chess. Our four elements (paradox, geometry, depth and flow) apply mainly to 'episodes' – pieces of chess action. But a whole game can consist of several phases, each comprising one or more such episodes. Complete games can be symphonic in nature, and this can lead to much disagreement over the beauty involved. While there might be agreement over the aesthetic quality of a single episode, once you put several of these together players start to disagree about the value of the whole.

For example, should 'brilliancy' (usually a relatively crisp, short game involving spectacular sacrificial play) be emphasized or should prizes go to 'best games' (usually longer, quality games not necessarily involving any brilliancy)? Returning to the flow chapter, do you prefer Lasker-Thomas (a brilliancy) or Ivanchuk-Karpov (a best game)? To some extent it is a question of temperament and whether you prefer paradox to depth and flow.

In recent years *Informator* has regularly had a panel of leading players trying to decide which game was the best of the preceding volume. Disagreement is typical and rife. Usually several players give zero to the winning game and several give '10'. This is not so surprising since the criteria for judging games are not well developed. In chess, unlike in art, correctness – and the ability to perceive it – comes before any further commentary. This means any serious critic must be a strong player, but strong players rarely make good critics! Usually they are competitive, somewhat secretive about their taste, with strong egos to protect and a tendency to look mainly at their own games rather than those of others. For all of these reasons the art of chess criticism has not really come a long way.

So different players like different aspects of beautiful games. It is limiting to give absolute criteria, and players often cannot say in advance what appeals to them most about a game of chess. Maybe a single tactical move, or a new strategic plan, or a psychological aspect or simply the good timing of moves. What is clear though, is that players do find certain games very attractive. Julian Hodgson once related that games he liked had a certain 'something' about them, a quality he could not really specify. Typically, players have an holistic approach: looking at the whole game as an entity before making any judgement.

Our four elements are designed to help us discuss the beauty of the moves themselves; but competitive chess involves several other factors which can affect aesthetic judgement. Among these more 'subjective' factors are:

1) Originality.
2) Intentionality. For example, how aesthetic is it if a player blunders a rook, but it subsequently turns out to be a brilliant move, winning

despite the oversight. Such unintentional brilliancies occur more frequently than one might imagine. The reaction of players to such instances is more typically 'My word! That was lucky' rather than 'How beautiful.'

3) Strength of opponent, and competitive significance. According to Kasparov, 'The value of any brilliantly won game increases in accordance with the strength of the opponent.'

4) How much of it was opening preparation? Brilliant play at the board (in the midst of the fog of war), is generally considered more impressive than clever preparation, however brilliant.

5) Blunders. Is a fabulous game, full of originality, profound conceptions and stunning ideas, but which is slightly ruined by a blunder near the end (which might reverse the result), to be considered less aesthetic than an unspoilt game of lesser brilliance?

It is difficult to be definitive on any of these issues. Even in the world of composition, the moves alone are not the sole determinants of aesthetic quality (originality is an important consideration there, too); but in the game as played, as indicated above, 'other factors' are very important. Still, the objective chess content (the moves alone) should remain the primary consideration!

In this chapter we will survey the potential for beauty in the three phases of the game (opening, middlegame, ending). There will be some exercises for readers to test their own ability and eye for the spectacular and finally there will be a selection of complete games. We make no claim that these are the best or most brilliant masterpieces ever played, but they will all be terrific games with which, hopefully, the reader will not be over-familiar. Anderssen-Kieseritzky will not be there, and that's a promise!

Beauty in the Opening

Just before civil war and strife erupted in Sarajevo, Jan Timman played a Candidates Match there against Robert Hübner. The highlight of the match was the following game where Timman wins due to his original and unorthodox handling of the opening:

J. Timman – R. Hübner
Sarajevo Ct (3) 1991

1	e4	e5
2	♘f3	♘c6
3	d4	exd4
4	♘xd4	♗c5
5	♘f5	

Kasparov continued with 5 ♘xc6 ♛f6 6 ♛d2 twice against Nigel Short during their 1993 PCA World

Championship Match. Instead, Timman breaks an old rule about not moving the same piece more often than is strictly necessary in the opening. He spends four moves sending it from g1 to e3.

5	...	♕f6
6	♘c3	♘ge7
7	♘e3	0-0
8	♗d3	

A new move. Despite Black's development lead, White's grip on d5 probably secures the better prospects.

8	...	♘e5
9	♗e2	♘5g6
10	g3	d6
11	h4!	♖e8
12	h5	♘f8 (6.1)

6.1   W

13   ♖h4!

An unorthodox deployment of the rook so early in the game. From h4 it controls important central squares and cannot easily be attacked.

13	...	c6?!

Better was 13...a6. Still not bothering to develop his bishop on c1, White now decentralizes his knight. White is breaking a lot of rules, advancing on the flank, leaving his king in the centre and yet he already has a serious advantage!

14	♘a4!	♕d4
15	♘xc5	♕xc5?

The best chance was 15...dxc5 16 ♘c4 when White has a clear advantage. Black is now lost since his queen is about to be trapped.

16	♘c4	♖d8
17	♗e3	♕b5
18	a4!	♕a6
19	b4!	

Controlling a5 and thus threatening 20 ♘b6. If 19...b5, then 20 ♘xd6 with axb5 to come.

19	...	d5
20	♘b6	♕xb6
21	♗xb6	axb6
22	exd5	♘f5
23	♖f4	♖xd5

With two knights against the queen, Black is materially lost. The knights seem to hold the balance for a while, but the end result is inevitable:

24 ♗d3 g6 25 hxg6 hxg6 26 ♖e4 ♗e6 27 ♕d2 ♘d4 28 ♕c3 c5 29 bxc5 bxc5 30 ♗c4 ♖h5 31 ♗xe6 ♘fxe6 32 ♖h4 ♖f5 33 ♔f1 ♖f3 34 ♕b2 ♖e8 35 ♖e1 ♖e7 36 a5 ♖d7 37 ♔g2 ♖f5 38 ♖eh1 ♘g5 39 a6 b5 40 c3 ♘df3 41 ♖f4 1-0

The game would probably be better known if Hübner had resigned on move twenty. Very striking and effective play by Timman. Hübner's moves were plausible enough, which is important aesthetically to the effect of the game. We particularly like the way White flouts one principle after another and yet wins effortlessly. Essentially, this is paradox at work, since preconception and instinct are being shown up. The queen domination is pleasant enough but poor compared to what can be seen in studies.

The necessity to develop one's pieces makes it harder to find strongly paradoxical moves in the opening. When they do come, the effect can be all the stronger if they come as novelties in known positions.

The move 11...♔e7 played by Karpov against Kamsky (Dortmund 1993) – see the Paradox chapter – is a good instance of this. Paradox and novelty together create an exciting stir.

A curious 'double novelty' was recently unearthed by correspondence players. After the moves 1 e4 e5 2 ♘f3 ♘f6 3 ♘xe5 d6 4 ♘f3 ♘xe4 5 d4 d5 6 ♗d3 ♘c6 7 0-0 ♗g4 8 c4 ♘f6 9 ♘c3 ♗xf3 10 ♕xf3 ♘xd4 11 ♕h3 (in the fifteenth game of their world championship match in Moscow 1985, Kasparov played 11 ♖e1+ against Karpov) 11...♘e6

12 cxd5 ♘xd5 *(6.2)* we arrive at the point of departure.

6.2   W

James Howell played the normal enough 13 ♖e1 against Van Kemenade in 1991 (see *Informator 52*, Game 301). White got nothing and lost the game. The two new moves are both paradoxical; the bishop on d3 can strike out in either direction:

a) **13 ♗b5+!!** looks rather pointless at first sight but Pletánek-Dufek, corr. 1992 showed the point: 13...c6 14 ♖d1! cxb5 15 ♖xd5 with a dangerous attack.

b) **13 ♗g6!!** is a stunning move, which actually seems to work! Nadanian-Sarbatov, corr. 1992 continued 13...♕d7 14 ♖e1 0-0-0 15 ♘xd5 hxg6 16 ♕xh8 ♗b4 17 ♕xd8+ ♕xd8 18 ♘xb4 a5 19 ♘c2 ♕d3 20 ♘a3 b5 21 ♗e3 b4 22 ♖ed1 ♕a6 23 ♘c2 and Black resigned. Detailed analysis of the two games, suggesting that White has a clear advantage after either novelty, can be found in *Informator 58*, Game 336.

The following example, (shown to J.L. by Julian Hodgson) is quite sensational in its own way:

After the moves 1 d4 g6 2 c4 d6 3 ♘f3 ♘d7 4 ♘c3 e5 *(6.3)*,

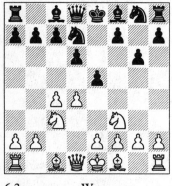

6.3   W

the move 5 c5!! is unusually effective. Such a move goes strongly against instinct. It seems premature, non-developmental and the sort of move that ought to be no good at all. Julian Hodgson and I (J.L.) spent quite a while convincing ourselves that it really is a good move, since neither of us could believe it at first. Paradox is the aesthetic factor at work here.

How does Black respond? If 5...♗g7 (ignoring it), then 6 cxd6 cxd6 7 e4, and d6 is a weak point. 5...dxc5 6 dxe5 ♗g7 7 ♗g5 ♘e7? fails against 8 ♘d5. After 5...exd4 6 ♕xd4 ♕f6 7 ♘d5 ♕xd4 8 ♘xd4,

White is better. A grandmaster game continued 5...♘gf6 6 cxd6 ♗xd6 7 e4, when White should be better due to the weakening of g7 and h6.

Having been impressed by this last idea, it was probably easier for Julian to find the stunning move 6 c5! in the opening of his game with Lev Psakhis from Metz 1994: 1 c4 e5 2 ♘c3 ♗b4 3 g3 d6 4 ♗g2 ♗xc3 5 bxc3 f5 6 c5!. After 6...dxc5 7 ♗a3 ♕d6 8 d4 White went on to win a fine game in twenty more moves.

Some openings have been analysed extensively and deep moves involving a great deal of subtlety and refinement have been unearthed. In some of the sharper openings there are flowing tactical sequences, but impressive geometrical ideas are rare. (Geometry is generally more prominent in composition than in practical play.) Many players regard opening theory as a necessary evil, but there are those who seem to love it for its own sake. The former British Correspondence Champion, Peter Millican, probably knows as much about the Double Muzio as anybody else on the planet! He has studied it exhaustively and he singled out the following line as being especially beautiful, adding that he got the impression the rules of chess had been invented specially so as to make this line just work! Incidentally, to those assuming there is nothing of practical use in a book about aesthetics, we should point out that the final moves overturn an assessment in *ECO* given by Korchnoi (line C37), and it's not in the book *ECO Busted* either!

1 e4 e5 2 f4 exf4 3 ♘f3 g5 4 ♗c4 g4 5 0-0 gxf3 6 ♕xf3 ♕f6 7 e5 ♕xe5 8 ♗xf7+ ♔xf7 9 d4 ♕xd4+ 10 ♗e3 ♕f6 11 ♗xf4 ♘e7 12 ♘c3 ♘f5 13 ♘e4 ♕g6 14 g4 ♗e7 15 ♔h1 ♘h4 16 ♕e3 ♔g8

At this point *ECO* gives 17 ♗e5 b6!, but Millican gives the simple

17 ♗h6!

threatening 18 ♘f6+. The game Millican-N.Down, corr. continued 17...♕e6 18 ♖f2 b6 19 ♖af1 ♘g6 20 ♕d4 and White forces mate. Another try for Black is:

17 ...   ♘c6
18 ♘f6+   ♔f7 *(6.4)*

6.4   W

Now 19 ♘d5+ ♔e8! is not so clear, but the elegant **19 ♘g8+!!** wins at once. To use an old air force

expression, I wouldn't touch either side of the Double Muzio with yours, but 19 ♘g8+ is still a lovely move. After 19...♔xg8 (19...♔e8 20 ♖f8#), 20 ♕xe7! wraps up.

Beauty in the Middlegame

The middlegame is the richest and most complex phase of the game where, unlike the opening, players are dependent entirely on their own resources and imagination. Hitting upon the right plan, finding your way in this maze of complexity can be enormously satisfying. To play a beautiful game usually means playing a beautiful middlegame, and all the games at the end of this chapter involve such beauty. GM Jan Smejkal, asked what he valued most in chess, replied 'the depth of a strategic idea'. Typically such ideas occur in the opening or middlegame (but not in the endgame, when the strategy is usually clear). Answering the same question GM Ivan Radulov replied 'the beauty of a sacrifice' – and that's what we will look at in this section. Sacrifices can occur in any phase of the game from gambits in the opening to the pure tactics of some endgames, but for practical players a talent for middlegame combinations is essential.

An intriguing episode took place in game seventeen of the 1993 PCA World Championship. Kasparov

(White) is about to make his twenty-third move:

6.5   W

G. Kasparov – N. Short
London PCA Wch (17) 1993

23 ♔g2?!   hxg3
24 fxg3

Missing Black's reply. Better was 24 ♗xg3 with a small advantage. After the game the World Champion was angry about this oversight since he had seen that Black was threatening 23...hxg3 and 24...♗xf2+ in the diagram position, but thought that 23 ♔g2 had prevented it. It is more difficult to see sacrifices on empty squares!

24 ...   ♗f2!!

A beautiful, paradoxical move. Black wins a pawn by force. Short wrote that he was 'delighted with this move'. The combination is four moves deep, but it was trapping Kasparov with such an aesthetic blow

that so pleased Nigel.

25 ♔xf2   ♖xh2+
26 ♔f1   ♖exe2!
27 ♖xe2   ♖h1+
28 ♔f2   ♖xd1

Unfortunately Black's advantage proved insufficient – Kasparov defended tenaciously to draw. Going back to the diagram position, is there no way White can defend against the combination? Of course, he can play 23 ♔g2 hxg3 24 ♗xg3 but White would like to maintain his pawn structure. The best way to do this seems to be the deep and paradoxical:

23 ♖c1!!

An extraordinary move, deactivating the rook. Neither the players nor any of the commentators have pointed out this possibility. The point is that after 23...hxg3 24 hxg3 ♗xf2+? 25 ♔xf2 ♖h2+ 26 ♔f1 ♖exe2 (26...♖h1+ 27 ♔g2 ♖xe2+ 28 ♔xh1) 27 ♖xe2 ♖h1+ 28 ♔g2 the rook on c1 is defended by the bishop. If instead 23...♖e8, 24 ♔f1! and Black has no useful attacking moves (e.g. 24...♖a5 25 c3 ♗b6 26 f3 ♖a4 27 a3 when Black has too many pawn weaknesses and no activity to compensate). 23 ♖c1 prepares 24 ♔g2 and 25 f3, and we see no good move for Black in reply. Had Kasparov played 23 ♖c1, he might have enjoyed it since the commentators would have been more than slightly baffled.

Another strongly paradoxical tactical blow was missed by Ivanchuk in his game against Rozentalis (Manila OL 1992).

6.6   W

Ivanchuk played 16 ♕d1 but after 16...♘xd4 17 ♗b1 ♗g4 18 f3 ♗f5 Black had excellent compensation for the exchange and won in good style. Rozentalis, who annotated the game for *Informator*, failed to mention the brilliant possibility (pointed out by Icelandic GM Petursson):

16 ♗xg6!!

After which Black does not get adequate play for the exchange in any of these lines:

a) 16...♘xd4 17 ♕h5.

b) 16...fxg6 17 c6!:

b1) not 17...bxc6 18 ♕a6+ ♔b8 19 ♖b3+ and White mates.

b2) 17...♗xc6 18 ♕xe6+ ♔b8 19 ♕xg6.

b3) 17...♘xd4 18 cxd7+ ♔xd7 19 ♕d1.

The unexpected nature of the move 16 ♗xg6!! makes it very hard to see.

The next three tactical combinations are left as exercises for the reader; the solutions are at the back of the book.

6.7   W

J. Levitt – A. Kveinys
Augsburg 1994

This game was played on New Year's Day 1994. Instead of offering seasonal greetings I set the friendly Lithuanian grandmaster a trap:

27 ♖c3! ♖xc3+?! (the best continuation was to 'copy' White with 27...♖c6!, which should hold) **28 ♘xc3 ♔e6 29 ♖c1 ♖c8?** (and now only the surprising 29...♘b8! hangs on)

Exercise 6.7: What should White play next?

The second position, allegedly from a friendly game between two people named Schmidt, is a win for

6.8   W

P. F. Schmidt – P. R. Schmidt
Heidelberg 1946

White after a brilliant sacrificial finish in the traditional style.

Exercise 6.8: Try to calculate (to forced mate) how White concludes his attack.

6.9   W

M. Tal – A. Koblents
USSR 1976

Exercise 6.9: Tal (White, to play) was one of the great masters of the paradoxical tactical blow. Here his knight is attacked, but still he engineers a spectacular breakthrough. How?

Beauty in the Endgame

Although less complex, the purity and economy of form found in the endgame make it, in many ways, the most elegant and attractive phase of the game. The simplified material balance also gives rise far more often to long forcing sequences (flow). Indeed, the worlds of practical chess and composition merge in the endgame. The next chapter, on studies, will feature several endgame-like positions which might just as well have come from practical play (many endgame studies are based on real games). However, the necessity for a study to have a unique solution does exclude a number of real endings, full of twists and turns, such as the following:

(see diagram on following page)

White should force an immediate draw with 1 g5! hxg5 2 ♔g4! since 2...gxf4 3 h6! gxh6 4 ♔xf4 leaves Black with bishop and rook pawn of the wrong colour. Instead he played the casual:

  1 ♔e3?   ♗a3!
  2 ♔f3   ♗c1

Now Julian sank into thought and found a very deep idea: **3 g5 hxg5 4 fxg5 ♗xg5 5 ♔g4** when:

6.10   W

J. Hodgson – A. Baburin
Neuchâtel 1993

a) **5...♗h6 6 ♔f5** draws (a position of mutual zugzwang; if 6...♔c6, 7 ♔e6 or 6...♗c1 7 ♔g6 ♗h6 8 ♔f5. White to move would lose)

b) **5...♗c1** is answered by 6 h6!!, a beautiful, deep and paradoxical move. The point is that 6 ♔f5? ♗h6! gets to the mutual zugzwang above, only this time with White to play. Surprisingly White does not need his h-pawn. After 6 h6!! ♗xh6 7 ♔f5 it is still mutual zugzwang: 7...♗c1 8 ♔g6 ♗h6 9 ♔f5 ♔c6 10 ♔g6! or 7...g5 8 e6! ♔d6 9 ♔f6 g4 10 e7 ♗g5+! 11 ♔xg5 ♔xe7 12 ♔xg4.

A gorgeous variation. Life, however, can be full of disappointments; the game continued:

3	g5	hxg5
4	fxg5	♗b2!

and Black is winning since 5 h6 g6 6 h7 ♗xe5 is no good at all. Also 5 g6 ♗c1 wins easily enough. A very

interesting endgame. To make a study out of it one would have to start with the position after 4...♗xg5 5 ♔g4 ♗c1?.

6.11   Draw
J.Hodgson, 1993

Solution: 1 h6! ♗xh6 2 ♔f5 g5 (sidelines as given above) 3 e6 ♔d6 4 ♔f6 g4 5 e7 ♗g5+ 6 ♔xg5 ♔xe7 7 ♔xg4. All of White's moves in this sequence are unique. Essentially this study was composed by Julian Hodgson in his analysis at the board! It is a worthy study with paradox, depth and flow.

We move now on to our selection of complete games.

Selected Games

The gulf between commonly held opinions and reality is sometimes quite astounding. Many people seem to regard Karpov as a boring player and it is easy to find examples of adverse comments: Timman in 1979 wrote: 'We must learn to live with Karpov as World Champion ... [although] ... his games have even begun to show a little more colour'. Agur, while praising Fischer's aesthetic eye, describes Karpov as a player 'whom no one could possibly accuse of being aesthetically biased!' English grandmaster Danny King mischievously went so far as to call Karpov's style 'turgid' and 'ditch-water dull' in a recent article in *Chess Monthly* magazine (May 1994).

In reality Karpov plays beautiful chess. In your authors' opinion he has played a higher number of aesthetic games in the last five years than any other player! There are a couple of reasons why this is so; firstly, there is a correlation between beauty and truth in chess, which, more simply, means that strong moves are often beautiful. Secondly, the only player demonstrably stronger than Karpov in recent years, Garry Kasparov, has played far fewer games over the same period.

Apart from the fact he is very strong, why is Karpov's style aesthetic? Probably since his advantage over other top players is not based on calculation. His games often exhibit smooth flow with tension being created and released in a controlled fashion. His antithesis, Kasparov, is strong at all aspects of the game, but especially powerful as a calculator and logician (leading to disruptive paradoxical moves being the chief aesthetic element at work in his games). Karpov's strength is based on his superb strategic handling as well as his early and subtle perceptions. In terms of our elements it can be said generally that positional players exhibit more flow, whereas tacticians generate more paradox (often of a sacrificial nature).

Earlier we saw a typical flowing Karpov game (against Ivanchuk). The next game was judged to be the best game of *Informator 56*:

A. Karpov – G. Kamsky
Moscow 1992

1	d4	♘f6
2	c4	g6
3	♘f3	♗g7
4	g3	c6
5	♗g2	d5
6	cxd5	

A further 'secret' of spectacular chess is that you are more likely to play a brilliant game if you pick a sharp, aggressive opening. Paradoxically enough, many of Karpov's most beautiful games come from a relatively quiet choice of opening!

6	...	cxd5
7	♘c3	0-0
8	♘e5	e6
9	0-0	♘fd7

10 f4

A genuinely 'turgid' player would be more likely to relish the 'ditch-water dull' 10 ♘xd7.

10	...	♘c6
11	♗e3	♘b6
12	♗f2	♗d7
13	e4	♘e7
14	♘xd7	♕xd7
15	e5	♖ac8

A new move deviating from a game between the two 'K's. Kasparov played 15...♖fc8 against Karpov in Seville 1987. It is too complex to tell whether Kamsky, yet another 'K' (it is well known that a ridiculous number of top players' names begin with K), has actually improved with this move or not. Since he is about to double rooks, it may not make that much difference anyhow.

| 16 | ♖c1 | a6 |
| 17 | b3 | |

Weakens a3, but strengthens c4. The knight on b6 is being restricted. Karpov often finds ways to misplace his opponents' pieces, and unlike certain blitz hustlers, he does it legally!

17	...	♖c7
18	♕d2	♖fc8
19	g4	♗f8
20	♕e3!	

A strong move based on one of those subtle Karpov perceptions. Rather than simplifying with a tiny edge (20 ♘e2) he uses the fact that his opponent has only one constructive move, and that has a drawback.

| 20 | ... | ♘c6 |
| 21 | f5 *(6.12)* | |

6.12 B

In moving to c6 the knight has 'come off' f5, allowing White this important pawn break. However, Black has the opportunity to take the f5 pawn and, given he is worse the way the game actually went, he probably should. After **21...exf5 22 gxf5 ♕xf5** White has the skewer **23 ♗h3**.

Annotating for *ChessBase Magazine*, Anand simply ended here, implying White was winning. Karpov himself, annotating for *Informator*, goes further since Black can arrange an attractive reciprocal skewer against White's queen and rook: **23...♕h5! 24 ♗xc8 ♗h6 25 ♕h3 ♗xc1 26 ♕xh5 gxh5 27 ♗xb7** and Karpov assessed this as clearly better for White. However Karpov is a better player than writer and he too has stopped short (rather strangely in a position that has not yet reached quiescence). After 27...♗b2!, Black has no problems since the white bishop is dominated: 28 ♗xc6 (28 ♘d1 ♗xd4 29 ♗xc6 ♗xf2+) 28...♗xc3 29 ♗e8 ♔f8!.

Putting Fritz to work, it was discovered that White also has (after 21...exf5 22 gxf5 ♕xf5 23 ♗h3 ♕h5 24 ♗xc8 ♗h6) **25 ♕g3!** with some advantage after 25...♗xc1 26 ♗xb7 ♕g5. Another idea is to sacrifice a pawn for the initiative with **23 ♘e2**, which offers good chances for White. Despite Karpov's error in analysis, there is nothing wrong with 21 f5 and the game maintains its 'correctness' from White's point of view. Quite where Black goes wrong remains a mystery.

	21	...	♗a3
	22	♖cd1	♘b4
	23	♕h6!	

Threatening mate in two by 24 f6.

	23	...	♕e8
	24	♘b1!	

Earlier in the book we discussed the geometrical and paradoxical properties of the 'switchback'. This game features an extraordinarily large number of white switchbacks. This paradoxical undevelopment of the knight is to inconvenience the black bishop on a3.

	24	...	♗b2
	25	♕d2	

Switchback number two. Black finds the right defence to the double attack, avoiding the trappy 25...a5? 26 a3! (26 ♕xb2?? ♖c2 27 ♕a3 ♖xa2 nets the queen) when 26...♘c2 allows 27 ♕xa5 and 26...♖c2 27 ♕e1 ♕b5 28 axb4! ♖e2 29 ♕xe2 ♕xe2 30 bxa5 ♘d7 31 ♖d2 shows White's queen 'offer' has been none too generous (rook and two bishops). Two attractive queen traps are hidden beneath the surface of the game here, one good and one bad for White.

	25	...	♘c2
	26	♔h1	♕e7
	27	♗g1	♘d7
	28	♖f3	♕b4
	29	♕h6	

Switchback number three, designed to pacify the black queen.

	29	...	♕f8
	30	♕g5	

Threatening 31 fxe6 when the black f-pawn is pinned. The black queen now gets bottled up on the kingside, but otherwise the white attack would be too dangerous.

	30	...	♕g7
	31	♕d2!	

Number four! Hypnotic and bewitching play. Black now advances on the queenside, mainly to control the b4-square and prepare an exit for the c2-knight.

	31	...	b6
	32	♖df1	a5
	33	h4	♘b4

Not sacrificing the bishop, since the same queen trap as before is still operative. Kamsky defends imaginatively throughout the game, but nothing saves him.

34	a3	♖c2
35	♛f4	♞c6
36	♗h3	

Eyes the weakness on e6, which Black promptly defends.

36	...	♞d8
37	♗e3!	

Yet another switchback. Number five in fact and we are only counting Karpov's! White is about to make a strategic switch as well: from the kingside to the queenside. With the black queen passive and the bishop on b2 a target, this sets Black insoluble problems. Black has defended too well and now finds himself vulnerable where he was previously attacking!

37	...	b5
38	♖3f2!	

A move displaying his deep strategic grasp. White penetrates the queenside instead of the f-file. The bishop on b2 is threatened.

38	...	b4
39	axb4	axb4
40	♖xc2	♖xc2
41	♖f2!	♖xf2
42	♛xf2	♗a3

After 42...♗c3 White plays 43 f6 ♛f8 44 ♛c2 ♗e1 45 h5. On a3 the bishop is defended securely, but stranded.

43	♛c2	♞xe5

43...♛f8 44 ♛c7 leaves Black completely tied down. Karpov is not a man you want sitting on you, so Black gets desperate in a bid to randomize the game. 43...gxf5 loses to 44 ♛c8!.

44	dxe5	♛xe5

It is important for White to punch home his advantage incisively, and not to go passive with his extra piece. Karpov finishes energetically:

45	♛c8!	♛e4+
46	♗g2!	

Switchback number six, but who's counting?

46	...	♛xb1+
47	♔h2	♗b2
48	♛xd8+	♔g7
49	f6+!	♗xf6
50	♗h6+!	♔xh6
51	♛xf6	♛c2
52	g5+	♔h5
53	♔g3!	

Another secret of spectacular chess is not to mess it up right at the end. This neat little side-step avoids 53 ♔h3? ♛f5+ and wraps up a flowing final stage.

53	...	♛c7+
54	♔h3	1-0

A great achievement by Karpov. This game is strong on geometry (the second stage of each switchback may be seen as a reflection of the first stage in an appropriately placed mirror). There is also paradox in the back and forth movements involved. With strategic depth as well as a number of subtle touches (20 ♛e3!,

24 ♘b1!, 38 ♖3f2!, 49 f6+! and 53 ♔g3!) and also a little flow towards the end, this game seems very complete. It will perhaps become known as the 'Switchback Game'.

B. Spassky – T. Petrosian
Moscow Wch (7) 1966

In the year that England won the World Cup, Petrosian successfully defended his world title against Spassky. A key victory in that tight match was the flowing positional masterpiece that follows.

1	d4	♘f6
2	♘f3	e6
3	♗g5	d5
4	♘bd2	♗e7
5	e3	♘bd7
6	♗d3	c5
7	c3	b6

Carefully keeping options open for his king. 7...0-0 would be less accurate.

8	0-0	♗b7
9	♘e5	

After playing a relatively quiet opening, Spassky now seeks more complex play. However Black's chances are already at least even.

9	...	♘xe5!
10	dxe5	♘d7
11	♗f4	

11 ♗xe7 ♕xe7 12 f4 0-0 13 e4 was objectively preferable here, with equality, but this would be admitting that the opening has not been a

success. But in a match one is supposed to win with White...

11	...	♕c7
12	♘f3	

12 ♕g4? runs into 12...g5!. Black now decides on the aggressive plan of advancing his kingside pawns and castling queenside. Timing is important; castling at once would allow 13 h4 h6 14 h5, so Black expands on the kingside first (12...h6 13 h4 g5 14 hxg5 hxg5 and the h-file is too dangerous).

12	...	h6!
13	b4!?	

An imaginative riposte. It is tempting for Black to accept the sacrifice, since after 13...cxb4 14 cxb4 ♗xb4 15 ♖c1 ♗c5 the c5-square is very solid. However, 15 ♘d4 gives reasonable play since after 15...a6 16 ♕g4 g5 17 ♗g3 White has tricks against the loose bishop on b4 as well as the f4 pawn break. Instead of this, Black carries on with his original plan.

13	...	g5
14	♗g3	h5!
15	h4	gxh4

15...g4 16 ♘g5 ♘xe5 17 ♗b5+ ♔f8 wins a pawn, but gives White chances to develop active play. Petrosian again prefers not to be distracted by such possibilities. Grabbing the b-pawn with 16...cxb4 17 cxb4 ♗xb4 allows White to open the f-file with 18 f3!.

16	♗f4	0-0-0

17 a4? *(6.13)*

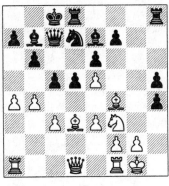

6.13   B

A move which has been strongly criticized. Spassky probably did not expect the following deep move which paradoxically shuts in the bishop on b7 and gives White the square d4. The purpose is to close off the queenside completely so as to concentrate on the other wing without having to worry about counterplay. In view of this 17 bxc5 bxc5 18 ♖b1 would have been stronger.

17 ...   c4!

18 ♗e2?!

Spassky saw, but rejected, the stronger 18 ♗f5!, an elegant as well as paradoxical way to get the bishop to h3 (18...exf5 19 e6! ♗d6 20 ♗xd6 ♕xd6 21 exd7+ ♖xd7 22 ♘d4 with excellent compensation for the pawns). He decided that the bishop on h3 was too passive, hitting only the stonewall on f7 and e6. However, such a set-up was necessary, since

now he never gets back into the game as Black starts a general advance.

18 ...   a6!

Sealing up the queenside, for example if 19 a5 b5!, or alternatively 19 b5 a5!.

19 ♔h1   ♖dg8

20 ♖g1   ♖g4!

An aesthetically motivated move, preparing a future exchange sacrifice to liven up the kingside pawns. Such judgements, not based on calculation, are sometimes very easy for top-class players.

21 ♕d2   ♖hg8

22 a5   b5

23 ♖ad1   ♗f8

Preparing to round up the e5-pawn. White feels compelled to do something.

24 ♘h2   ♘xe5!

25 ♘xg4   hxg4

With two pawns and an attacking space advantage for the exchange one cannot really speak of a sacrifice or paradox of material. Black starts a wave-like advance of all his central pawns. It creates a strange geometrical effect since the far-advanced pawns stretch from one side of the board to the other. White struggles hard to keep his chances alive but Petrosian punches home his advantage dynamically.

26 e4   ♗d6

27 ♕e3   ♘d7

28 ♗xd6   ♕xd6

29 ♖d4?!

As before, Spassky should accept a totally passive position in order to improve his holding chances. 29 f4 f5 30 e5 ♕c7 gives Black all the time he could want to organize his attack, but perhaps not enough scope to force a win. Such positions are extremely uncomfortable, psychologically, for the defending side, so Spassky seeks complications instead.

29 ...   e5
30 ♖d2

Giving back the exchange with 30 ♖xd5 ♗xd5 31 ♖d1 ♘f6 32 exd5 also leaves Black in control.

30 ...   f5 *(6.14)*

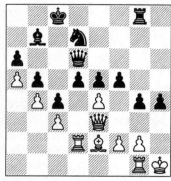

6.14   W

31 exd5

After 31 exf5 Petrosian intended 31...♘f6 32 ♕h6 ♕d8 followed by 33...♖h8.

31 ...   f4
32 ♕e4   ♘f6
33 ♕f5+   ♔b8

34 f3

No good is 34 ♕e6? ♕xe6 35 dxe6 ♘e4 hitting the rook on d2 as well as threatening surprise mate by 36...♘xf2+ 37 ♔h2 g3#!

34 ...   ♗c8
35 ♕b1   g3

The flowing wave of black pawns continues its advance. White is being crushed.

36 ♖e1   h3
37 ♗f1   ♖h8
38 gxh3   ♗xh3
39 ♔g1   ♗xf1
40 ♔xf1

If 40 ♖xf1, then 40...♕d7! threatening ...♕a7+ and ...♕h3. The king tries to run but cannot escape the pawns.

40 ...   e4!
41 ♕d1 *(6.15)*

6.15   B

After 41 fxe4 f3! no further tactical brilliance will be necessary.

41 ...   ♘g4!

Incisively wrapping it up. This sacrifice would have been calculated to a finish. Still, nice to see a touch of paradox of material added to the brew.

42	fxg4	f3
43	♖g2	fxg2+

A pity to spoil the pawns, but perhaps good enough since **White** now **resigned** (44 ♔xg2 ♛f4 wins). More elegant would have been 43...♖h1+! 44 ♖g1 ♛h6 with mate soon to follow, for example 45 ♛c2 ♛h3+ 46 ♛g2 ♛xg2#.

A very powerful display of positional chess from Petrosian. The main aesthetic feature was flow, in particular the across-the-board advance of the whole army of black pawns. There were a number of other nice touches too, such as 18...a6!, 20...♖g4! and 41...♞g4!. Some of the ideas that did not materialize on the board were also attractive (18 ♗f5!, the mate after 34 ♛e6). Petrosian timed everything right in this game and won one of the smoothest and most emphatic victories ever recorded in a World Championship match. There were no major tactical thunderbolts but nevertheless, in its own way, it is a very spectacular game.

In our next presentation, English Grandmaster Tony Kosten uncorks a vintage game in the style of Morphy. His opponent, the usually solid Hungarian GM Farago, admirably complements this by playing in the true style of 'the allies'.

A. Kosten – I. Farago
Amantea 1992

1	c4	♞f6
2	♞c3	e5
3	♞f3	♞c6
4	e4	

True, the opening is not very 'Morphyesque'. The self-inflicted weakness on d4 is 'positionally paradoxical' but difficult to exploit. 4...♗c5 allows 5 ♞xe5! with advantage to White. Co-author D.F. has played this system (as White) and considers Black's best to be 4...d6 5 d4 ♗g4, but Farago follows the example of Karpov – 'mysteriously' losing a tempo getting the bishop to c5 (so as to avoid the fork trick).

4	...	♗b4
5	d3	d6
6	g3	♗c5
7	♗g2	♞d4
8	♞xd4	♗xd4
9	h3	♗e6

The immediate 9...c6 is preferable, with a balanced position.

10	f4	c6

Deviating from Gulko-Karpov, Reykjavik 1991 where Black chose 10...a6 instead, aiming for a later ...b5. Kosten's early f4 has caused his king a slight problem, which he solves in the next few moves with an imaginative manoeuvre. In that he breaks a rule about not moving the king around in the centre, these moves may be seen as paradoxical, but the logic is clear: White moves his king to a safer position. First he gains time by hitting the bishop.

11	♘e2	♗c5
12	♗f3	♕b6
13	♔f1!	♗e3?!

This does not work out well. Black has, seemingly, not done much wrong but is soon in serious trouble. However, it was difficult to perceive at this stage the energy which White is about to unleash.

| 14 | ♔g2 | exf4 |
| 15 | gxf4 | ♗xc1 |

After the game, Farago showed that his queen would have been dominated if he had played 15...d5 16 cxd5 cxd5 17 ♗xe3 ♕xe3 18 e5 ♘g8 19 d4!. Black would get a lousy ending after 19...♖c8! 20 ♖c1 ♖xc1 21 ♕xc1 ♕xc1 22 ♖xc1 due to the weakness of the d5-pawn as well as his deficit in development.

| 16 | ♕xc1 | d5? *(6.16)* |

Black is consistent, but, surprisingly, he seems to be just lost after this. Castling one way or the other, with 'only' a strategic disadvantage (poor central control) was objectively better. White now charges forward in the centre, opening up the game with a devastating sacrificial advance. Further paradox is involved here: giving up a pawn and ruining his main asset (the pawn centre) at a

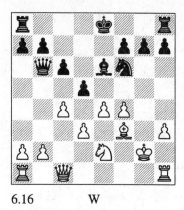

6.16   W

time when his rooks do not seem ready for it. However, Black is pushed back into a state of even greater unreadiness.

17	f5!	dxe4
18	dxe4	♗d7
19	e5	♘g8
20	c5!	

As in Spassky-Petrosian earlier, the pawns all go forward together. This advance is to enable the move 23 ♘d4! later.

20	...	♕c7
21	e6!	fxe6
22	fxe6	♗xe6
23	♘d4!	♗d7

The bishop keeps an eye on the f5 square, hoping to chop off the white knight should it venture there. White's rooks now take up their posts with a dangerous attack. However, the white minor pieces are not yet threatening anything serious, so Black has, it seems, fair chances to hold on. Any chances he might have had are destroyed by a series of tactical blows.

24 ♕g5!	♘f6
25 ♖ae1+	♔f8!

Another 'secret' of playing spectacular chess is for your opponent to play just badly enough to let it all happen, but not so badly as to make it too easy. 25...♔f7 allows 26 ♖e7+! ♔xe7 27 ♕xg7+ when Black falls apart 'with check'. After 25...♔f8, 26 ♖e7? fails to the counter-tactic 26...♗xh3+!. The alternative 25...♔d8 26 ♖d1 ♔c8 27 ♖he1 is also bad for Black due to his boxed-in a8-rook.

26 ♖hf1	h5 *(6.17)*

A defensive resource preparing to buttress the sensitive f6 point and bring the h8-rook into play with ...♖h6. The immediate 26...♕d8 is no better since after 27 ♗g4! ♗xg4 28 ♕xg4 one need only compare the two sides' rooks to conclude the case in favour of the prosecution.

6.17　　　　W

27 ♗d5!?

27 ♖e6! (Nunn) is a simpler win, e.g. 27...♕d8 28 ♗xh5 ♖h6 29 ♘f5. This alternative removes a chunk of aesthetic integrity from the game. However, 27 ♗d5!? is more spectacular, and after 27...♕d8 comes the strongly paradoxical 28 ♖e8+!!, winning. The rook is *en prise* several times; however, 28...♘xe8 is illegal, 28...♔xe8 allows 29 ♕g6+ and 30 ♕f7#, 28...♗xe8 29 ♘e6+ wins material and, lastly, 28...♕xe8 29 ♖xf6+ ♔e7 30 ♖f7#. Black plays the other natural defence only to run into an elegant queen sacrifice.

27 ...	♖h6
28 ♕xh6!	gxh6
29 ♖xf6+	♔g7
30 ♖f7+	♔g6

If 30...♔h8, then 31 ♖ee7 ♖g8+ (31...cxd5 32 ♖h7+ ♔g8 33 ♖eg7+ ♔f8 34 ♘e6+ ♗xe6 35 ♖xc7 winning) 32 ♔h1! ♖g1+ 33 ♔xg1 ♕g3+ 34 ♗g2 wins.

31 ♗b3

In time trouble Tony fails to play the more straightforward 31 ♘e6! winning (e.g. 31...♔xf7 32 ♘xc7+, or 31...♗xe6 32 ♖xe6+ ♔xf7 33 ♖xc6+). However, the situation is not critical and 31 ♗b3 maintains the win. That there is this luxury of choice is an aesthetic fault, but in games you cannot have everything. In fact, 31 ♗b3 leads to a more elegant, flowing finish with a pretty final mate.

31 ...   ♛a5

Attacks the rook, but White deals with this easily enough. 31...♛c8 32 ♖ee7 ♗xh3+ 33 ♔h2 ♗g4 (nothing else helps) 34 ♗c2+ ♔g5 35 ♖e5+ ♔h4 36 ♖f4 with 37 ♘f3 mate is no better. There is no defence.

32 ♘f3!   ♖e8
33 ♖xe8   ♗xe8 *(6.18)*

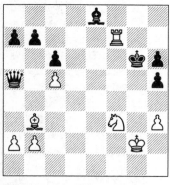

6.18   W

Can you see the mate in four? With very little time on his clock, Kosten finds the only path:

34 ♘e5+   ♔g5
35 h4+!   ♔xh4
36 ♘f3+

and **Black resigned** in view of 36...♔g4 37 ♗e6 mate!

One of your co-authors was present at the tournament where this game was played and can vouch as to how satisfying this performance was to the winner. The poolside demonstration on a warm Italian evening left several slightly drunk

and envious players wishing they had produced such a game! It is quite lightweight (no long difficult variations) but has a flowing finish, a fine opportunistic pawn charge early on and some excellent paradoxical touches (21 e6!; 27 ♗d5!?; 28 ♛xh6! and, best of all, 28 ♖e8+!! if Black had played 27...♛d8).

P. Vučinić – Durović
Yugoslavia 1984

1 e4   ♘f6
2 ♘c3   d5
3 exd5   ♘xd5
4 ♗c4   ♘b6

Safe enough is 4...♘xc3 5 ♛f3! e6 6 ♛xc3 ♛f6.

5 ♗b3   e5?!

Loosening. Black should not be so ambitious.

6 d3   ♘c6
7 ♘f3   ♗g4
8 h3   ♗h5?

The losing move, although it has been seen in several games. Necessary is 8...♗xf3 9 ♛xf3, when White is better.

9 ♘xe5!!

Rather deeper than Legall's mate (e.g. 1 e4 e5 2 ♗c4 d6 3 ♘f3 ♗g4 4 ♘c3 g6? 5 ♘xe5 ♗xd1 6 ♗xf7+ ♔e7 7 ♘d5#), but the same basic idea.

9 ...   ♗xd1
10 ♗xf7+   ♔e7
11 ♗g5+   ♔d6

12 ♘e4+ ♚xe5
13 f4+ ♚d4
14 ♖xd1! (6.19)

6.19   B

The end of the flowing sequence. Black now has a number of alternatives but they all lose. Rozentalis-A. Mikenas, Vilnius 1981 continued 14...♘b4 15 c3+ ♚e3 16 0-0 (and not the spectacular 16 ♖f1?? ♘c2 mate!) 16...♘xd3 17 ♘g3 1-0. Instead Black tries to give back the queen:

14 ... ♛xg5
15 c3+ ♚e3
16 0-0

Pleasingly ignoring the queen although 16 fxg5 also leads to mate after 16...♚f4 17 0-0+ ♚e5 18 d4+! ♚xe4 19 ♖f3! ♘xd4 20 ♖e1+ ♘e2+ 21 ♖xe2#. If Black tries 16...♗c5, 17 0-0 will transpose to the next note.

16 ... ♛h4

After 16...♗c5 17 fxg5 ♘a4 (to prevent a simple win on material), 18

♘g3 threatens mate. One elegant win: 18...♛d4 19 ♖f2! (threatening 20 ♘f1 mate) 19...♘e2+ 20 ♚f1! ♘xg3+ 21 ♚e1 ♘xc3 22 bxc3 when Black cannot prevent 23 ♖f3 mate. There is plenty of paradox in this line since White first castles and then allows Black to drive his king back to e1 (with check). Fritz 3, who discovered this variation, probably enjoyed it greatly.

17 ♖f3+ ♚e2
18 ♖d2+ 1-0

18...♚e1 allows 19 ♖f1 mate.

A sparkling miniature with sacrificial paradox, some depth and an elegant flowing king-hunt (with a geometrical across-the-board effect as in Lasker-Thomas seen earlier). The central idea (9 ♘xe5!!) is not original, however, so stronger players may not rate this game as high as they would otherwise. Still, it has a naïve charm which balances some of the more sophisticated stuff seen in the other games of this section.

We finish with two games by the strongest player of our age, Kasparov. His games are almost always dynamic and packed with life. Maybe because he plays less than Karpov he is able to play consistently with such creativity and energy. As has already been pointed out, his style (based on power and calculation) tends to be disruptive and violent rather than smooth – perhaps this is a reflection of the true nature of chess when played correctly by only one of the two sides.

The first game is relatively lightweight. The eighteen-year-old genius crushes the usually reliable Andersson in sparking style:

G. Kasparov – U. Andersson
Tilburg 1981

1	d4	♘f6
2	c4	e6
3	♘f3	b6
4	a3	♗b7
5	♘c3	♘e4
6	♘xe4	♗xe4
7	♘d2!	

Gaining time against the bishop. After 7...♗b7 8 e4 White gains the advantage due to his pawn centre. Andersson goes the other way, allowing White to seize the long h1-a8 diagonal.

7	...	♗g6
8	g3	♘c6?!

Several of Andersson's moves in this game are a little provocative (9...a6 and 12...♘a7 fall into this category). Better would be the solid 8...c6, with just a slight disadvantage for Black.

9	e3	a6
10	b4!	

More accurate than 10 ♗g2 b5 11 cxb5 axb5. By leaving the bishop on f1 temporarily, White attacks b5 for a little longer.

10	...	b5

11	cxb5	axb5
12	♗b2	

Not 12 ♗xb5? ♘xb4! with a comfortable position for Black. Now Black must defend b5. His next move places the knight on a passive square, but Andersson is hoping to have time for a subsequent ...d5, ...♘c8, ...♘d6, ...♘c4 after which he would be fine. However Kasparov disrupts all this with a very deep pawn sacrifice.

12	...	♘a7
13	h4	h6?! *(6.20)*

13...h5 was better. Later on White makes good use of the g4 square.

6.20   W

14   d5!!

A deep and genuine sacrifice of a pawn. White opens the diagonal for his bishop on b2 and causes its opposite number on f8 some developmental problems. Clear compensation perhaps, but it is a 'big' central pawn that he is giving away in original fashion. The sacrifice is based on dynamic considerations such as the weak knight on a7 and the ease with which White's pieces flow into dangerous attacking positions over the course of the next ten moves. Kasparov later described this game as being one of his favourites. Although the finish is most attractive, it may well be the paradoxical and nonchalant 14 d5 which really appealed to him.

14	...	exd5
15	♗g2	c6
16	0-0!	

Calmly completing his development. White is looking to open it up with e4 but first extracts the maximum from the position. If Black tries to prevent e4 with 16...f5 then White elegantly switches plans with 17 ♘f3 ♕e7 (stopping 18 ♘e5 with 17...d6 weakens e6 and c6, and after 18 ♘d4 ♕d7 19 a4 Black cannot cope with his problems) 18 ♘e5 ♕e6 19 a4. Black must try to develop: 19...♗d6 (19...♗xb4 20 ♘d3 ♗f8 21 axb5) 20 ♘xg6 ♕xg6 21 axb5 0-0 22 b6 ♘b5 23 ♖xa8 ♖xa8 24 ♗xd5+! illustrates White's advantage. Instead, Black tries to block the long dark diagonal so as to develop his bishop.

16	...	f6
17	♖e1	♗e7
18	♕g4	

Well timed, only after ...♗e7 has weakened the defence of g7.

18	...	♔f7
19	h5	♗h7
20	e4	dxe4
21	♗xe4	♗xe4
22	♘xe4	♘c8 (6.21)

The alternatives are no better: 22...♖e8 23 ♕g6+ ♔f8 (23...♔g8 24 ♗xf6!) 24 g4 with 25 ♘g3 and 26 ♘f5 to follow, except after 24...♘c8 25 ♘g3 ♘d6 when 26 g5! hxg5 27 h6! gxh6 28 ♘h5 leaves Black a touch cramped. Also 22...♖f8 23 ♖ad1 d5 24 ♘xf6! wins since either capture of the knight allows mate in one. At least ...♘c8 gives Black the lateral defence of d7 by ...♖a7.

6.21   W

23	♖ad1	♖a7
24	♘xf6!	

Destruction; Black has no adequate defence. If 24...♗xf6, then 25 ♕g6+ ♔f8 26 ♗xf6 gxf6 27 ♖e6!.

24	...	gxf6
25	♕g6+	♔f8
26	♗c1!	d5

27 罝d4

Threatening 28 罝g4. Black brings his knight across to deal with this, but only to fall into a deeply prepared final combination. If instead 27...皇d6, 28 罝g4 罝ah7 29 皇xh6+! 罝xh6 30 豐g7#.

27 ...   ♘d6
28 罝g4   ♘f7
29 皇xh6+!!

Despite being defended twice, the pawn is taken anyway. 29...罝xh6 30 豐g8# or 29...♘xh6 30 豐g7+ ♚e8 31 豐xh8+ ♚d7 32 豐xh6 are both terminal for different reasons – mate and massive material advantage.

29 ...   ♚e8
30 皇g7   1-0

Black cannot deal with the h-pawn as well!

Some strong paradoxical blows (14 d5!!, 24 ♘xf6!, 29 皇xh6+!!), a deep pawn sacrifice (14 d5!!) and perfect timing throughout give this game a strong appeal. The game was earlier described as lightweight since all White's moves are easy to understand. Basically, Andersson just got heavily punished, in elegant style, for his faulty opening choices. It is hard to find anything wrong with his play after 13...h6?!.

A. Karpov – G. Kasparov
Moscow Wch (16) 1985

At the time of writing, these two great players have faced one another

more than one hundred and sixty times! Not surprisingly, one could write a whole book on the aesthetic aspects of a number of great games between 'K' and 'K'. However, Kasparov himself is a great annotator and has covered most of these games, including the one below. It is game sixteen of the world championship match in which Kasparov first gained the title. We will restrict ourselves only to the crucial variations so as to concentrate on the aesthetic factors. (Readers who want more details should refer to Kasparov's wonderful notes in his book of the match).

This game is a complete masterpiece. It involves a deep and original strategy, sacrificing a central pawn in order to establish an outpost for a knight behind enemy lines. This piece restricts the opponent totally and Kasparov backs this up with perfect timing and an energetic, powerful finish. Kasparov commented that none of his earlier games compared 'as regards the grandiosity of the overall plan'. Unfortunately the game is a little too 'complete', also including a curious double blunder in the opening (a fact that was not unearthed until a year later) ...

1	e4	c5
2	♘f3	e6
3	d4	cxd4
4	♘xd4	♘c6
5	♘b5	d6

6	c4	♘f6
7	♘1c3	a6
8	♘a3	d5!?
9	cxd5	exd5
10	exd5	♘b4
11	♗e2	

If Black simply recaptures the pawn on d5 now, he is a bit worse in the simplified position that results. Kasparov gives the continuation 11...♘bxd5 (11...♘fxd5 was later recommended) 12 0-0 ♗e7 13 ♘xd5 ♘xd5 14 ♗f3 ♗e6 15 ♘c2 as a sample line. However, Kasparov prepared the game continuation up to move twenty, missing (even in his notes after the game) the key improvement for White (12 ♗e3!) altogether. This move only came to light in the game Karpov-Van der Wiel, Brussels 1986, so presumably none of the world championship match commentators saw it either!

11	...	♗c5? (6.22)

6.22　　　　W

12 0-0?

This move was innocently passed over without comment by all the annotators until the improvement 12 ♗e3! was played in the above-mentioned game. After 12 ♗e3! ♗xe3 13 ♕a4+! ♘d7 14 ♕xb4 ♗c5 15 ♕e4+ White had a big advantage, as indeed he would have done with 14 fxe3 too. The final verdict has to be that 11...♗c5 is a blunder since the brilliant conception that follows here can be side-stepped by White with a clear advantage. Despite this major aesthetic flaw, the game still ranks high because of its compensating virtues.

12	...	0-0!
13	♗f3	

White is now a clear pawn up, but Black's conception is deep: despite the lack of white weaknesses, Black is able to 'play round' the d5 pawn and get dynamic activity for all his pieces.

13	...	♗f5
14	♗g5	♖e8!

Keeping control of e4. Timing is so important in chess. Often the secret is to do what you want to do, but to make sure your opponent cannot do the same. 14...b5? 15 ♗e4! would leave White better.

15	♕d2	b5
16	♖ad1	♘d3

From its outpost behind enemy lines, the knight seriously cramps the white rooks. Karpov should react dynamically now with 17 d6 when the position is unclear. He prefers to hang solidly on to his extra pawn, but Kasparov regards the next move as his opponent's fatal error.

17 &ab1?   h6
18 &h4   b4!

From b4 the black pawn dominates the knight on b1. White is being slowly constricted. Apparently Kasparov's preparation went as far as the next move!

19 &a4   &d6
20 &g3   &c8
21 b3   g5!! *(6.23)*

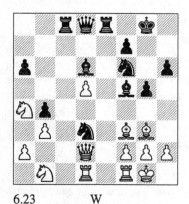

6.23   W

A move players often enjoy making, since they derive pleasure from the paradox of breaking the rule about not charging pawns forward in front of their own castled king. Here it is designed to constrict White still further, the natural 22 &b2? failing to 22...&xb2 23 &xb2 g4 24 &e2 &c2.

22 &xd6   &xd6
23 g3   &d7!
24 &g2

After 24 &b2, one beautiful variation is 24...&f6!! 25 &xd3 &xd3 26 &xd3 &e5, with a paradoxical queen-trap in the middle of the board. Black's next move prevents the freeing 25 &b2 by White.

24 ...   &f6!
25 a3   a5!

Simply keeping control.

26 axb4   axb4
27 &a2   &g6
28 d6

Hoping for 28...&xd6 29 &d2 &e2 30 &c4! with some chances. Instead Black keeps White totally hemmed in.

28 ...   g4!
29 &d2   &g7
30 f3   &xd6
31 fxg4   &d4+
32 &h1   &f6

Black's powerful centralized forces prove more than ready for the opening up of the game. Kasparov now closes in for the kill with a few more powerful blows.

33 &f4   &e4!
34 &xd3   &f2+!
35 &xf2   &xd3
36 &fd2 *(6.24)*

Now 36...&e3 should win 'on material', but Kasparov finds a more dynamic finish.

36 ...   &e3!
37 &xd3   &c1!

6.24   B

38   ♘b2
After 38 ♖xe3 ♖xd1+ 39 ♗f1
♖xe3 White will lose another piece.
38   ...   ♛f2!

39   ♘d2
Mate follows 39 ♖xc1 ♖e1+ 40
♖xe1 ♛xe1+ 41 ♗f1 ♛xf1#. The
same mating pattern would have occurred if Karpov had not resigned after the next move.
39   ...   ♖xd1+
40   ♘xd1   ♖e1+
                    0-1

A great game, not just because of
what Kasparov did, but also because
of who he did it to. The master of
constriction (Karpov) is himself bottled up and disposed of. A game well
prepared, well played and well finished.

7 Tactical Fantasies; the charm of Studies

'The beautiful rests on the foundations of the necessary.'
Ralph Waldo Emerson

'There are no positional assessments in studies.'
Mikhail Botvinnik

To many people studies are the highest form of chess art. Closer to the game than problems, but distant enough to maintain elevated aesthetic criteria, endgame studies should be pure and perfect – sound, yet with no extras and no waste. The word 'study' (from the French word 'étude') is off-putting to some, and, with its connotation of academic heaviness, fails to capture the essence of what it denotes. Studies are essentially pure tactics – often crisp and dazzling, always precise. Botvinnik expressed the real difference between the game and the study very succinctly: 'There are no positional assessments in studies.' Games are played for competitive reasons. Studies are composed mainly for aesthetic beauty. Good studies should never be boring.

Readers have already come across a number of studies earlier in the book. There they were chosen partly for their beauty and partly to illustrate our 'theory'. In this chapter you are in for a treat, and the studies are chosen purely to delight you! To illustrate the power of the endgame study, we will start with a masterpiece by the consistently spectacular Korolkov. Firstly we look at the logic of the moves, saving the aesthetic judgement until afterwards:

7.1   Win
V. Korolkov
1st Prize, Lelo 1951

1 f7

A natural opening move, threatening to promote. If 1...♖f6?, then 2

♗b2 wins at once. All else fails, so Black must give a check.

1 ... ♖a6+!

2 ♗a3!

Not 2 ♔b2? ♖f6! when 3 ♗b2 is not available.

2 ... ♖xa3+

3 ♔b2 ♖a2+

If 3...♖b3+?, then 4 ♔a2 and the checks run out. The rook cannot be taken in either case, since ...♗e6+ draws, but how does White avoid endless desperado checks from Black's rook? White's next move is both precise and deep, the point only becoming clear on White's twelfth. 4 ♔c3? would fail: 4...♖c2+ 5 ♔b4 (5 ♔d4 ♖d2+ and ...♖d8) 5...♖b2+ 6 ♔c5 ♖c2+ 7 ♔b6 ♖b2+ and White cannot make progress since 8 ♔c7 allows 8...♖b7+ and 9...♖xf7.

4 ♔c1!! ♖a1+

Again 4...♖c2+ 5 ♔d1 and Black is helpless. There follows a flowing sequence in which the white king runs across the board in search of shelter.

5 ♔d2 ♖a2+

6 ♔e3 ♖a3+

7 ♔f4 ♖a4+

8 ♔g5 ♖g4+!

Black plays resourcefully too in this study. Now 9 ♔xg4? ♗xf5+ 10 ♔xf5 ♔g7 11 ♔e6 ♔f8 12 ♔f6 is stalemate. Also 9 ♔f6 or 9 ♔h5 both allow 9...♖g8! drawing. Only one move wins:

9 ♔h6! ♖g8!

9...♖g6+ 10 ♔xg6 ♗xf5+ 11 ♔f6! wins. The finish is spectacular and unexpected:

10 ♘e7! ♗e6!

The rook is constrained by the twin possibilities f8♕ and ♘g6 e.g. 10...♖f8 11 ♘g6# or 10...♖g1 11 f8♕+. It appears now that the position is still drawn since 11 ♘g6+ ♖xg6+ 12 ♔xg6 ♗xf7+ reaches king vs. king. However, White can now offer his killer pawn and mate with just the knight.

11 fxg8♕+! ♗xg8

12 ♘g6#

If you have never seen this study before and fail to find it exciting, our only advice is to give up the game straight away. You will have no future in chess!

Why is this study so good? Primarily because of the long forcing sequence leading to the surprise mating finish. There is turbulent flow right across the board (note the geometrical effect created by the white king going from the a-file to the h-file), a paradoxical finish, and depth too (4 ♔c1!). A little bit of everything, but perhaps the most striking element is the economically constructed flow taking the solver from the start position to mate in twelve action-packed moves. A perfectly presented study, although not, in fact, original. The finish had been seen in a slightly weaker study published two years earlier by J. Selman.

Notation

From here until the end of the book we shall be using a new notation involving the four letters P (paradox), G (geometry), D (depth), F (flow). If, for example, the solution to a problem or study involves strong paradox and geometry but no depth or flow, the letters PG would appear below the diagram. The order of the letters is significant and gives our opinion of the order of prominence of the elements shown in the solution. A bracket round a letter indicates that the element in question is only partially present. This notation is not meant to be absolute or definitive; it is just a shorthand to communicate which elements we think are present in the solution. It would be interesting to know whether readers generally agree with our lettering. The Korolkov above would receive the 'valuation' FPGD. The first study in this book (the Gurvich from the introduction) would be simply P(D) suggesting that paradox is the main element, there is little or no geometry or flow, but some depth (the point of 2 ♕f2!! only becoming clear two moves later). It is not necessarily the case that a study with all four letters would be 'better' than one with 'only' three. Exceptional paradox alone might make a study outstanding. Anyway, you should judge for yourself!

Unless otherwise stated, diagram positions in this chapter are with White to play.

Practical player or composer?

Further evidence of the practical value of aesthetic sensitivity is provided by the number of leading grandmasters who have also made an impact on the world of composition. Players such as Duras, Réti, Keres, Smyslov, Benko and Timman stand out. Four of these make it into Keene and Divinsky's controversial list of the 64 top players of all time, as judged in their 1989 book *Warriors of the Mind*. Smyslov is ninth, Keres sixteenth, Timman twenty-eighth and Duras sixty-second.

Several of these players might also make it into an analogous list of top study composers (we are still awaiting the book *Matadors of the Aesthetic* ...). Kasparian would probably occupy one of the top spots, and he is also an International Master of practical play. Other leading contenders would include: Troitsky, Kubbel, Rinck, Korolkov, Liburkin, Grigoriev, Gurvich, Nadareishvili, D.Gurgenidze and Gorgiev to name but two handfuls. Here we will look at some compositions by practical-play grandmasters, starting with ex-World Champion Smyslov. You have already seen an example of 'incarceration' by him earlier; the following shows a positional draw and is exceptionally strong on paradox:

7.2   Draw   PD

V. Smyslov, 4th Prize
Shakhmaty v SSSR 1938 - II

1 ♗f6+!!

Giving away his only piece. 1 f4 ♖a6+ wins for Black.

1 ... exf6
2 f4

White is now threatening simply to move his king and advance the h-pawn. Black prevents this in straightforward fashion.

2 ... ♖h8+
3 ♔g7!

3 ♔g6 would fail after 3...♖xh5 4 ♔g7 ♖g5+ 5 ♔h8 ♔h5 6 ♔h7 ♖g6 7 a3 (7 a4 ♖g5!) 7...♖h6+ 8 ♔g7 a4!. Some subtle zugzwang play is involved here (depth).

3 ... ♖xh5
4 a4! ♖g5+
5 ♔h8!

Not 5 ♔h7? ♔h5! when White is in zugzwang.

5 ... ♖g6
6 ♔h7 ♔h5
7 ♔h8 ♖h6+
8 ♔g7 ♖g6+
9 ♔h8

and Black can make no progress because 9...♔h6 is stalemate. The rook cannot extricate itself. A deep and paradoxical conception with subtle play.

Jan Timman published the next study in his magazine *New in Chess*.

7.3   Win   FP(D)(G)

J. Timman
New in Chess 1994

1 ♗d6+!

White must keep the initiative since his own king is exposed. The immediate 1 ♗e6? would fail after 1...♕e8+ 2 ♔f5 ♕h5+ 3 ♔f4 ♕xh2+ 4 ♔f3 ♕h1+! 5 ♔e2 ♕e4+! when the bishop will also join in the attack. The introduction/foreplay features a series of sacrifices to force the striking position after White's sixth:

1	...	♚xd6
2	♖xd5+	♚e7
3	♗e6!	♚xe6

With the black pawn on d5 gone 3...♕e8+ 4 ♚f5 ♕h5+ 5 ♚f4! allows the king to escape to the queenside, winning for White. If the first three moves did not seem sufficiently clear to you, you will feel happier from here on in – it is all beautifully crisp.

4	♖d8!	♗xd8
5	♖a8!	♕xa8
6	b7!	

A beautiful position, the basic idea of which had been seen earlier in a study by Nadareishvili. The finish of the study (on move sixteen) is also not original and dates back to the sixteenth century. What is original is the brilliant way the two phases have been combined into a flowing whole. Black now has two options: the main line below or 6...♕a6 after which White wins technically with 7 cxd8♕ ♚e5+ 8 ♚g5 ♕xb7 (there are no useful checks) 9 ♕h8+! ♚d6 10 ♕d4+, forcing off the queens.

6	...	♕xb7
7	cxd8♘+	♚d5
8	♘xb7	♚c4

All clever stuff, but isn't Black just drawing now?

9	♚f5	♚xc3

10	♚e4	♚b2
11	♚d3	♚xa2
12	♚c2	

No! We now have the ancient finalé (Stamma's mate).

12	...	♚a1
13	♘c5!	♚a2
14	♘d3	♚a1
15	♘c1	a2
16	♘b3#	

Why does this get the annotation FP(D)(G)? Because the main feature is the wonderful flow from the start position all the way to the final mate sixteen moves later. Plenty of sacrifices in the initial phase contribute to the paradox, as would the finish if it were not so well known. Although the study taken as a whole is deep, no individual move is especially profound. The point of each move is either immediately apparent or rapidly becomes so. The '(G)' is for the graphic geometry of the position after White's sixth. The trapezium of forces on a8, b7, c7 and d8 forms a memorable pattern. Spectacular chess indeed!

Hungarian-American Grandmaster Pal Benko, despite a late start, has become a leading study composer. He is also well known as a commentator and critic, often finding small improvements to previously published studies. Benko's contribution to the following study was simply to start the d-pawn a square further back – everything else is as in the

7.4   Win   GP(F)
J. Ban (version by P. Benko)
1st Prize, Tipografia 1961

original by J. Ban. Clearly he is an aesthetic perfectionist!

1 d5!   ♘f6

If 1...♔xh5?, then 2 d6 ♘f6 3 g7 ♔g6 4 d7 wins.

2 d6   ♔g7!

Not 2...♘d7 3 ♔g4 and the king supports the pawns directly. The next move is paradoxically retrograde, but is the only way to win. 3 ♔h4 ♔h6 4 ♔h3 makes no progress while 3 ♔g2? allows 3...♘xh5! 4 d7 ♘f4+ and 5...♘e6 with a draw.

3 ♔h2!!   ♔h6
4 ♔g1!   ♔g7
5 ♔f1!

5 ♔g2? is no good as explained above, and 5 ♔f2? fails to 5...♘e4+. The square e2 is also 'mined' since if on the next move 6 ♔e2? ♘xh5 7 d7 ♘f4+ and ♘e6. This explains the crawl along the back rank. Once the white king gets round the other side

to support the d-pawn, Black is helpless.

5 ...   ♔h6
6 ♔e1!   ♔g7
7 ♔d1!   ♔h6
8 ♔c2   ♔g7
9 ♔b2!

Avoiding the pitfall 9 ♔b3? ♘e4 10 d7 ♘c5+.

9 ...   ♔h6
10 ♔a3   ♔g7
11 ♔b4!

and White will win the knight once his king supports the d-pawn.

The geometrical march across the first rank is achieved with superb economy. If somebody pulled off a finish like that in a real game it would become legendary. As a study it will become well known at best.

Domination and the paradox of positional draw

The colourful term 'Domination' (introduced by Frenchman Henri Rinck) essentially denotes the trapping of a piece. The trapping of a king (checkmate!) is usually classed separately although it could easily be regarded as a special case of domination. 'Positional draw' denotes positions where one side draws despite an apparently fatal material disadvantage. The following positions illustrate these terms:

In diagram 7.5 (the end of a study by Herbstman, 3rd Prize *Zvezda*

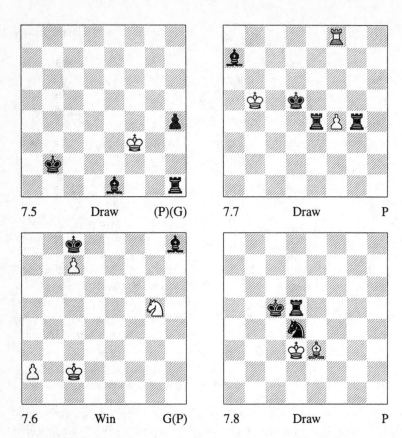

7.5   Draw   (P)(G)   7.7   Draw   P

7.6   Win   G(P)   7.8   Draw   P

1934) White dominates the rook with 1 ♔g2! and obtains the well-known positional draw based on the 'wrong-coloured' rook pawn.

In diagram 7.6 (H. Rinck, *El Escacs a Catalunya*, 1935) White dominates the bishop along the long diagonal: 1 ♘f7! ♗a1 2 ♔b1 wins, e.g. 2...♗c3/d4 3 ♘d6+ ♔xc7 4 ♘b5+ or 2...♗f6/g7 3 ♘d6+ ♔xc7 4 ♘e8+. Surprising how many squares the knight controls!

In diagram 7.7 (the finish of a Korolkov/Mitrofanov co-production, 1st Prize *Trud* 1960) White either gets a perpetual check or wins a rook, reaching a materially drawn endgame: 1 ♖d8+! ♔e6 2 ♖e8+ ♔f5 3 ♖f8+ ♔g6 4 ♖g8+ ♔h5 5 ♖h8+ drawing.

Diagram 7.8 is the sort of thing that can seriously upset your computer! Black cannot make progress despite having a clear extra rook. A simple positional draw. Be warned: one of the exercises at the end of this chapter will finish with this position!

The theme of domination necessarily involves some geometry. The Rinck above has graphic geometry (a long diagonal move) but more often it is of the 'optical logic' type. Sometimes dominations can be very surprising, in which case the final position, or some of the moves leading to it, will involve paradox too. Domination itself does not involve flow, but it is interesting to see the way composers can introduce flow into the 'foreplay'. In the chapter on 'flow' the study by Afek (5.5) ends with a paradoxical domination after a series of moves involving 'turbulent flow'. In the following study by Vitaly Halberstadt there is a little flow plus two deep opening moves.

1 ♗e6!

In general the material balance is already winning for White. However Black has a stalemate trick that helps him to win the white pawn. Why only 1 ♗e6! works will be clear in the final position.

1	**...**	**♖b3!**
2	**♗d6!**	**♖c3+**

Not immediately 2...♖xf3 because of 3 ♗e5+. It is pretty the way all the white pieces move into their positions for the surprising finish.

3	**♔d2**	**♖xf3**
4	**♔e2!**	

and wins the rook.

7.9   Win   GPD(F)

V. Halberstadt
L'Italia Scacchistica 1951

A typical domination in that there is a large dose of 'optical logic' geometry. The bishops control everything: 4...♖c3 5 ♗e5 ♔b2 6 ♔d2 and 4...♖f6 5 ♗e5+ should convince you.

Another way flow can be introduced into a domination study is as follows: White attacks a key black piece and almost dominates it – it is forced to go to its only remaining safe square. White attacks it again and so on until the end. A fine example of this was the Rinck from the introduction (1.5) where the king chases the bishop in this way. Another dramatic example by Troitsky dates from 1910:

(see diagram on following page)

1 ♖b4!

The chase begins. 1...♕xb4 and 1...♕a7 allow 2 ♘c6+.

| **1** | **...** | **♕c8** |

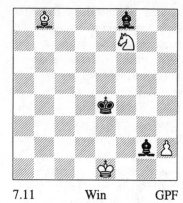

7.10   Win   GPF
A. Troitsky
Deutsche Schachzeitung 1910

7.11   Win   GPF
H. Rinck
First prize, Le Temps 1929

2   ♖b8!   ♕h3
3   ♖h8!   ♘h4
4   ♖xh4!

Now it goes in reverse direction! Fine slapstick. Note the multiple rook offers. Repeated sacrificial paradox, but there is no real depth.

4   ...   ♕c8
5   ♖h8!   ♕b7
6   ♖b8!

Wins the queen and the game. The back-and-forth movement adds to the geometry of a scintillating chase.

The next example shows a type of 'double domination': White attacks one bishop so as to trap the other:

White has an extra h-pawn but must win a bishop to get a decisive advantage.

1   ♔f2   ♗h1

Not 1...♗h3 2 ♘g5+.

2   ♔g1   ♗f3
3   ♘g5+   ♔e3

4   ♗a7+   ♔e2

If 4...♔f4, 5 ♘e6+. So far, Black has had to defend his light-squared bishop. Suddenly White switches his attention to the other one:

5   ♘e6!

Creating a surprise domination. 5...♗a3/b4 6 ♘d4+ ♔e3 7 ♘c2+ or 5...♗h6/d6/e7 6 ♘d4+ ♔e3 7 ♘f5+.

Positional draws typically show paradox. Surprisingly enough, a large material advantage does not suffice to win. Sometimes they can be complex too, requiring a dynamic appreciation of why the position is drawn (depth of the subtlety type). Geometry and flow are not generally involved, although again, good composers can bring them into the background of the study. The exercise leading to position 7.8 (see end of chapter) has both geometry and terrific flow in the play before the surprise 'positional draw' finish. At least it would have come as a surprise had we not told you about it!

One of the first composers to examine positional draws systematically was F. M. Simkhovich (1896-1945). We finish this section with one of his spectacular blockbusters. When GM David Norwood saw this study, he considered it the best he had ever seen.

1 ♘f7

7.12   Draw   PDF

F. Simkhovich
L'Italia Scacchistica 1924

White, a rook down, must attack something! Now 1...♖f8 allows 2 ♖f3+ ♔g6 3 ♘e5+ ♔g7 4 ♖g3+ ♔h7 5 ♖h3+ delivering perpetual check.

1 ...   ♖e8
2 ♘d6+!!

The point of this move only becomes clear about fifteen moves later! Perhaps you can already see

the contours of the forthcoming positional draw?

2 ...   exd6
3 ♖f3+   ♔g6
4 ♖g3+   ♔f7
5 ♖f3+   ♔e7

Black attempts, naturally enough, to win by avoiding the continuous rook checks. To do this he must escape to d8. Now comes a highly paradoxical exchange of rooks, followed by a perfectly timed king march to set up an unassailable 'fortress' (a term introduced by Simkhovich himself).

6 ♖e3+   ♔d8
7 ♖xe8+!!   ♔xe8
8 a3!   ♗b7
9 ♔d1 (d2)   ♔f7
10 ♔e1 (e2)   ♖a8
11 ♔f1   ♖h8
12 ♔g1!

Just in time to keep Black out. Now White cannot be prevented from completing his barricade. The lack of uniqueness on moves nine and ten is a negligible aesthetic drawback.

12 ...   ♔f6
13 g3   ♔f5
14 f3

Again, just in time to keep the king out. Everything 'fits' into place perfectly in this study. You could expect something a bit better than average to make up for the unnatural start position. The last few moves are not forced, but demonstrate the draw.

14	...	♖e8
15	♔f2	♖e7
16	♔f1	♖h7
17	♔g2	♖h8
18	♔g1	

Black can make no progress (18...♖e8 19 ♔f2 ♖e7 20 ♔f1 ♖e3 21 ♔f2 ♖d3 22 ♔e2 with a domination thrown in too). The extraordinary final fortress explains all the earlier sacrifices. The well-timed 8 a3 (preventing Black from playing ...a3) and the white king march help to create a pleasant flow. Heroic and spectacular play, with some good sacrifices and a big 'concept' to end it all.

Before we move on to our final selection of studies and examples, we will take a brief interlude to look at the effect of computers on composition and chess in general...

Beauty, Truth and the Computer

Over the last decade, the influence of the mighty computer has been increasingly felt in all forms of chess. The practical player now has at his disposal a formidable analyst (especially in wild tactical positions), an enormous opening theory database and a strong blitz sparring partner. The composer has a brilliant solver on hand to test the soundness of his problems. Using trial and error he is able to find better piece arrangements to express his ideas; so computers are certainly helping composers to compose better, more aesthetic problems even though they (the computers) have no aesthetic judgement beyond 'sound' and 'unsound'.

Another significant development is the rise of the endgame database. These give definitive results by systematically categorizing all the possible positions. The new results are overturning theoretical judgements of the past, and a large number of endgames studies are being simultaneously cooked every time that happens. For example it was previously held that the material balance of ♔, ♖, ♗ vs. ♔, ♗, ♘, with opposite-coloured bishops was in general a draw and only winning for the exchange-up side in exceptional cases where short-term tactical considerations predominated. Now computer analysis suggests that it is in general a win, and only a draw in exceptional (tactical) cases! Another (semi-) reversal is seen in the case of ♕ vs. 2♘. An example will help illustrate this:

(see diagram on following page)

A great pity that the computer has cast doubt on this, since the idea is very beautiful. Let us have a closer look and then try to 'rescue' it. The composer obviously liked it since the back cover of one of his books consisted of a small diagram of the position, surrounded by black.

6.13   Draw   FGP

G. Nadareishvili
3rd Prize, Thèmes 64 1958

Nadareishvili assumed, along with many others, that, in general a queen wins against two minor pieces, the result only being a draw in exceptional 'tactical' cases (such as the intended finish to this study). However, although this holds for ♕ vs ♗ and ♘, it does not hold for ♕ vs. 2♘s. Many 'normal enough' positions involving ♕ vs. 2♘s are drawn without there being a short-term tactical reason, although the situation is very complex and it is unsafe to assume anything at all! Returning to the study, White has a problem since his minor pieces are all in danger:

1 ♘b4+   ♔a5!

Forced as 1...♔b7? and 1...♔b5? lose to 2 ♘d6+. After 1 ♗e2+ ♔a5 White would indeed be lost (even allowing for the latest computer results) since a piece will drop in an unacceptable way.

2 ♘c6+   ♔a4!
3 ♘b6+!

After 3 ♘8e7 (or 3 ♘6e7) ♕xh5+ a ♕ vs 2♘s position is reached. According to John Nunn and his database this one would be a win for Black (the study is sound so far).

3 ...   ♔a3!
4 ♘c4+

If 4 ♗f3 White loses the knight on b6 (4...♕xf3 5 ♘c4+ is a draw, as in the main line of the intended study) after 4...♕h3+! 5 ♔g7 ♕g3+ 6 ♔h6 ♕h2+ 7 ♔g5 ♕g1+ and 8...♕xb6 winning.

4 ...   ♔a2

Now 5 ♘b4+? fails to 5...♔b3 when White has no way to continue. Unfortunately the computer cook comes here: 5 ♘4e5 is, apparently, a draw, while 5 ♘6e5 loses! It is beyond normal human comprehension why that is, although John Nunn might be able to explain it if you ever get stuck on a desert island with him! Anyhow, rational people seem to have faith that the computer is right. The study loses its unique solution at this point but Nadareishvili's drawing idea is very cute (and by far the easiest way to draw).

5 ♗f3!!

Protects the knight on c6 and threatens to keep all three minor pieces with ♘4e5 (definitely a draw!). Black can pick off either the bishop or the c4-knight, but in either case tactics save White:

a) 5...♕xf3 6 ♘b4+ ♔a1 7 ♘c2+ ♔a2 8 ♘b4+ with repetition, the composer's intended main line.

b) 5...♕f8+ 6 ♔h7 ♕f7+ 7 ♔h8 ♕xc4 8 ♗d5!! ♕xd5 9 ♘b4+ drawing.

Is this study beautiful, despite the computer cook? Some might think so; there is a beautiful flow as the knights chase the black king in a straight line down the a-file (a geometrical aspect here, too). Paradoxical twists end both lines 'a' and 'b'. However, in studies soundness is crucial. The rules for soundness are strict: essentially White should only have one way to achieve the task. The idea may be beautiful but the above study is of no value since it has two solutions. It is possible to rescue the study, but only at some aesthetic cost. Add a black pawn to the diagram position on f3. After that only Nadareishvili's intended solution works – exactly the same moves, but 5 ♗f3 is replaced by the more suggestive 5 ♗xf3 – a loss of paradoxical content as well as economy.

An attempt to remove this blemish would be as follows: turn the diagram position upside down (the white king is now on a1). Place a black pawn on c7. The solution now appears to work properly after 1 ♘g5+ ♔h4 2 ♘f3+ ♔h5 3 ♘g3+ ♔h6, but unfortunately 4 ♗c6 draws as well as the intended continuation

(4 ♘f5+) since the black queen can no longer pick off the g3-knight by 4...♕a6+ 5 ♔b1 ♕b6+ 6 ♔a1 ♕a7+ 7 ♔b1 ♕b8+. Now the new pawn prevents the knight's capture (compare the note to 4 ♘c4+). Maybe readers can find a better fix?

As well as destroying certain studies, the database is helping to create new ones; databases can be searched to reveal surprising reciprocal zugzwangs such as the following pair (7.14 and 7.15):

7.14   =/–   P

computer

In both positions, White to move only draws whereas if Black is to move, White wins. One would never suspect that having the move is such a serious disadvantage for either side in the rook and pawn ending. It is too complex for any easy explanation, but readers can get a better idea why it is a reciprocal zugzwang by consulting diagram 173 in John Nunn's

7.15   =/–   PD

Nunn/computer

Secrets of Rook Endings. The four queen position is easier to understand: Black's king is in danger and the black queens cannot move without weakening the defence. White cannot move without allowing Black a chance to simplify. What is paradoxical about the position is the very existence of a mutual zugzwang with this material balance. It is, in fact, unique.

There is a certain beauty to these positions, in some ways similar to the beauty experienced by mathematicians when they come across surprising but true equations in pure mathematics, e.g.

$$e^{i\pi} + 1 = 0$$

$$\frac{\pi}{4} = 1 - \frac{1}{3} + \frac{1}{5} - \frac{1}{7} + \frac{1}{9} - \frac{1}{11} + \dots$$

In both cases a sense of wonder is evoked that the 'truth' comes in such unexpected and elegant forms.

Assorted Brilliance

Further 'truth in unexpected and elegant form' is provided in the next two studies by Liburkin.

7.16   Win   FPG(D)

M. S. Liburkin, 4th Prize
Shakhmaty v SSSR 1938 - I

The strategic overview is straightforward: White, the exchange up but with no pawns, needs to win a piece. If the ♗e1 is captured, Black gains the knight in return, with a draw. White cannot wait, since Black threatens ...♘f3, coordinating his pieces.

  1 ♘d4+   ♔c3
  2 ♘b5+!   ♔c4!
If 2...♔b4?, 3 ♖b1+ and 4 ♔xe1.
  3 ♘d6+!
Not 3 ♘a3+? ♔b3 4 ♔xe1 ♔b2 5 ♘c2 ♘f3+ 6 ♔d1 g3 7 ♔e2 ♘d4+!.
  3 ...   ♔c5
If 3...♔d5?, 4 ♖d1+!.
  4 ♘b7+!!

Some depth is needed to see why the alternative is no good: 4 ♘e4+? ♚d5! 5 ♘f6+ ♚e5! 6 ♘d7+ ♚e6! and the fun runs out after either 7 ♘f8+ ♚f7! or 7 ♘c5+ ♚d5!.

4	...	♚c6
5	♘d8+	♚c7
6	♘e6+	♚d7
7	♘f8+	♚e7
8	♘g6+	♚f7
9	♘h8+!	♚g7
10	♖xe1	

Only now! The rest is relatively easy: **10...♚xh8 11 ♖h1 g3 12 ♚e3! ♚g7 13 ♚f4 g2 14 ♖g1 ♘f1 15 ♖xg2+ and 16 ♖f2** winning.

Notice the right-angled path of the black king chasing the zigzagging knight in a flowing, systematic manoeuvre.

The next study is difficult to solve, but easy to appreciate!

7.17   Win   PGD
M. S. Liburkin, 1950
1st Prize, USSR All-Union Tourney

White wins if he can both promote the g-pawn and stop Black promoting the a-pawn. The natural 1 ♘e5+? fails since it blocks the a1-h8 diagonal: Black draws after 1...♚e4 2 g7 a2!.

1	♘g5+	♚f4

It is useful to attack the knight, but 1...♚g4 allows 2 ♘h6+ and 3 g7.

2	g7	

Black now has two options, which we shall look at separately:

A)

2	...	♘g6
3	♚b3!	

Stops the black a-pawn, but the deep point is revealed only after White's next move.

3	...	♚xg5
4	♚a2!!	

A very surprising zugzwang! White wants to move his knight and promote the g-pawn, but an immediate 4 ♘h6? fails to 4...♘e7. Black must meet white knight moves with ...♘e7, which is why Black cannot now move the knight. The king appears mobile enough, but this is deceptive. After 4...♚f5, 4...♚h5 or 4...♚g4 White can move the knight with check and then promote. Also 4...♚f4 5 ♘f6! ♘e7 6 ♘d5+! deflects the black knight, as does 4...♚h4 6 ♘h6! ♘e7 6 ♘f5+!. The line-up from g8 to g5 is not only geometrical, it contains a subtle mutual zugzwang. White wins since he has a waiting move on the other side of the board (4 ♚a2).

B)

2	...	♘f7
3	♘e6+	♚e5
4	♚b3!	

As above, necessary to stop the a-pawn. Guess what? An analogous zugzwang occurs in this variation too...

4	...	♚xe6
5	♚a2!!	

Readers can work out why Black is now, as some players put it, 'in Volkswagen'. Two crucial variations: 5...♚d6 6 ♘e7! ♘h6 7 ♘f5+! and 5...♚e5 6 ♘f6! ♘h6 7 ♘g4+. In these lines the white knight also manages to prevent the black king getting at the pawn. There is a rare and beautiful unity between the two lines of this study. Such unity is more often encountered in problems, as you will discover later.

Some readers might find the geometry of the above study has greater impact than the paradox. In that case, the valuation would be GPD – who are we to disagree?

And now for something completely different! Just to confuse you, it is Black to play and you must find how White wins:

White is a lot of material up but the question is: can he avoid perpetual check? Black must choose the first move carefully since 1...♛b3+? 2 ♜c4 ♛d3+ 3 ♗d4 and all is over.

1	...	♛a2+!
2	♜c4	♛d2+
3	♗d4	

7.18   GF(P)

Black to move; White wins
R. Kassai, 1959
1st HM, Wiener Schachzeitung

The only way to make progress. There follows a weird, circular unwinding manoeuvre:

3	...	♛g5+
4	♛e5	

Not 4 e5?? ♛g2#.

4	...	♛d8+
5	♜d6	♛a8+
6	c6	♛a5+
7	♗c5	

If 7 ♜c5 ♛a2+ Black will repeat the pattern.

7	...	♛d2+
8	♛d4	♛g5+
9	e5	♛g2+
10	♛e4	♛d2+
11	♛d3+!!	

Giving away the queen with check – some paradox added to the circular flow and geometry. After 11...♛xd3+ 12 ♗d4 ♛f3+ 13 ♚c5 White has a winning position (on material). An entertaining solution, certainly, and also somewhat humorous.

The systematic manoeuvre in the following study by Gorgiev is repeated half a dozen times before a subtle difference ensures White's victory:

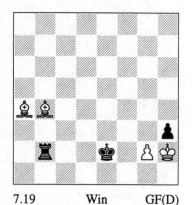

7.19   Win   GF(D)

T. Gorgiev, 1968
First prize, Tidskrift för Schack

As in the Halberstadt, the material balance of two bishops and a pawn versus rook is winning for White. The tactical sequence you are about to see is based on White needing to gain the time to capture the h3-pawn without losing a bishop:

1 ♗c3!

Attacks the rook, thus preventing Black from having the time to play 1...hxg2. 1 ♗a3? ♖a2 2 ♗b5+ ♔d1 would only draw.

    1 ...   **♖a2**
    2 ♗b3!

Not 2 ♗b5+ ♔d1 drawing.

    2 ...   **♖a3**
    3 ♗c4+   **♔e3!**

The best choice. If 3...♔d1, then 4 ♗b4 ♖a4 5 ♗b3+ wins for White, while 3...♔f2 4 ♗d4+ ♔e1 5 gxh3 ♖a4 6 ♗c3+ leads to the same result.

    4 ♗b4

The two bishops, the rook and the king have all moved a square up the board. This geometrical 'translation' is now repeated again.

    4 ...   **♖a4**
    5 ♗c5+!   **♔e4!**

Again the best. If 5...♔f4 6 ♗b3 ♖a5 7 ♗d6+ followed by 8 gxh3 wins. 5...♔d2? 6 ♗b3 ♖a5 7 ♗b4+ fails too.

    6 ♗b5   **♖a5**
    7 ♗c6+!   **♔e5!**
    8 ♗b6   **♖a6**
    9 ♗c7+   **♔e6**
   10 ♗b7   **♖a7**
   11 ♗c8+   **♔e7**
   12 ♗b6!

Breaking the pattern. 12 ♗b8 ♖a8! draws – the edge of the board ending the sequence (13 ♗c9+??). However, just in time, a new possibility has emerged.

   12 ...   **♖a8**
   13 ♗xh3!

winning. No paradoxical moves, but breathtaking flow and geometry make this a natural first prize winner. Only seven pieces, too! The same composer adapted a study by Mattison to produce our next offering.

Note the natural game-like position. Consider yourself a chess genius if you can already see the (forced) stalemate in seven moves. Incredible but true – not that you are or are not a chess genius, but that a position like this can produce such a bolt from the blue.

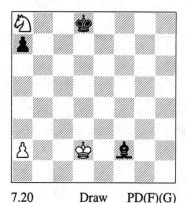

7.20   Draw   PD(F)(G)

T. Gorgiev (after H. Mattison)
Shakhmaty v SSSR 1963

Despite the simplicity of the position, White is in serious trouble because of the trapped knight.

1   a4!

With the idea 1...♔c8 2 a5 ♔b7 3 ♘b6! ♗xb6 4 axb6 axb6 5 ♔c3 drawing. 1 ♔e2? ♗c5 2 a4 ♔c8 3 a5 ♔b7 4 ♘b6 ♗xb6 5 axb6 axb6 6 ♔d3 ♔a6 7 ♔c4 ♔a5 wins for Black. Because of the subtle difference between these two lines, the order of White's first two moves is forced.

1   ...   a5!

Avoiding the above line and threatening to round up the knight. The next move has a deep point (apart from threatening the bishop!) – revealed only five moves later.

2   ♔e2!   ♗g1

2...♗a7 leads to similar play. 2...♗d4 or 2...♗c5? lose time as the white king advances, e.g. 2...♗c5? 3 ♔d3 ♔d7 (3...♔c8 4 ♔c4!) 4 ♔c4 ♔c6 5 ♘c7!. But what has White gained by attacking the bishop, given his next move is just to advance the king anyway?

3   ♔d3   ♔d7!

If 3...♔c8?, then 4 ♔c4 ♔b7 5 ♔b5 draws easily.

4   ♔c4   ♔c6

Now White appears lost. If 5 ♔b3? ♗e3 6 ♔c4 ♗f2 7 ♔b3 ♔b7 8 ♔c4 ♔xa8 9 ♔b5 ♗e1 Black wins. 'Paradox' comes to the rescue:

5   ♘c7!!   ♔xc7
6   ♔b5   ♗b6

The real point of 2 ♔e2! was to prevent the move 6...♗e1! in this position.

7   ♔a6!   ♔c6

Stalemate! A splendid study with a surprise finish, subtle move order and depth, and a flowing white king march up the f1-a6 diagonal to achieve self-immobilization.

Notice, too, the way that all the pieces have either moved into position or been captured during the play. Critics and composers often seek this feature in studies. It is considered a big plus when none of the pieces finish on the same squares that they started. Why should this be so? Our elements give a clear rationale for this criterion. The point of the final position comes as more of a surprise, since none of the preconditions were present at the start – an increase in paradox. Also, the movement of all the pieces tends to improve the flow.

The next study has the honour of being placed 2545th in Kasparian's book *Domination in 2545 Endgame Studies*. At the end of the book Kasparian extends the meaning of 'domination' to include a mauling of the opponent's forces. The sequence of knight checks (designed to destroy the powerful black army) exhibits sensational smooth flow:

7.21   Win   FG(P)

I. Chuiko
Shakhmaty v SSSR 1963

1 ♘d4+   ♚e5

This is about the only choice Black gets in this study, but it is not much of a choice since 1...♚c5 2 ♘d3 is mate!

2 ♘g4+ ♚f4 3 ♘e6+ ♚f5 4 ♘g7+ ♚f4 5 ♘h5+ ♚f5 6 ♘h6+ ♚e5 7 ♘f7+ ♚f5 8 ♘d6+ ♚e5 9 ♘xc4+

One down, several to go! With the rook gone, White goes into reverse gear:

9...♚f5 10 ♘d6+ ♚e5 11 ♘f7+ ♚f5 12 ♘h6+ ♚e5 13 ♘g4+ ♚f5 14 ♘g7+ ♚f4 15 ♘e6+ ♚f5 16 ♘d4+ ♚f4 17 ♘xe2+ ♚f5 18 ♘d4+ ♚f4 19 ♘e6+ ♚f5 20 ♘g7+ ♚f4 21 ♘h5+ ♚f5 22 ♘h6+ ♚e5 23 ♘f7+ ♚f5 24 ♘d6+ ♚e5 25 ♘c4+ ♚f5 26 ♘xb2

White has reached a materially winning position! It is easy to lose one's sense of direction in the midst of all these knight switchbacks. Looking at the way the black king has simply obeyed the cavalry's every whim, it is more a case of 'humiliation' than domination. A new book will probably be needed to establish this new term – *Humiliation in 3669 Endgame Studies* might make a good title!

Tightness and Overall Effect

Generally our elements apply to single moves or to a limited number of moves, but sometimes it is necessary to consider the entire study as a single move set. This is when there is some special 'overall effect' which may well prove to be the 'point' of the work.

The next example will help to demonstrate exactly what we mean by this. It also serves to illustrate the notion of 'tightness' (or 'crispness') which relates to the impact of flow. Unfortunately the notion of tightness is difficult to define and we will only be able to provide you with a not-at-all tight grasp of it...

7.22   Draw   FG(P)

T. Gorgiev
1st HM, Shakhmaty v SSSR 1939

1 ♖a3+

One can deduce this is forced by a process of elimination. No other move deals with the deadly threat of 1...♖f1#.

1 ...   ♔xa3
2 ♔b1

Forced, by the same logic.

2 ...   ♖b2+
3 ♔c1   ♖xb8

4 g5

If 4 f7, then 4...♖f8! or 4 ♔d2 ♖g8! 5 f7 ♖f8!.

4 ...   ♖f8!

To stop 5 f7. Now the white king must march towards the pawns, but precision is needed: 5 ♔c2? ♔b4 6 ♔d3 ♔c5 7 ♔e4 ♔d6 8 ♔f5 ♖a8 is winning for Black, as can be seen in the note to White's eighth move.

5 ♔d2   ♔b4
6 ♔e3   ♔c5
7 ♔f4   ♔d6
8 g6!

If 8 ♔f5, then 8...♖a8 9 ♔g6 (alternatively, 9 g6 ♖a5+ 10 ♔g4 ♔e6 11 f7 ♔e7) 9...♔e6 10 ♔g7 (10 f7 ♖f8) 10...♖a7+ 11 ♔g8 ♖b7! wins.

8 ...   ♔e6

8...♖xf6+ 9 ♔g5 ♔e7 10 g7 ♖f1 11 g8♘+ draws.

9 ♔g5   ♖a8

After 9...♖xf6 10 g7 White has no problems: 10...♖f1? 11 g8♕+ wins while 10...♔f7 11 g8♕+ is a draw.

10 f7   ♔e7
11 ♔h6   ♔f6

The hardest test for White.

12 ♔h7   ♖b8
13 f8♕+   ♖xf8
14 g7   ♖f7
15 ♔h8   ♖xg7

stalemate

So what is so special about that? No big surprises, no paradoxical moves, no particularly difficult or deep moves. The introduction seems a bit violent. What is the point of it all? One has to consider the study as a whole. It is a miniature in which White sacrifices a rook, bishop and two pawns and starts in one corner, yet stalemates his king in the opposite corner! This is a great achievement, with only the black rook controlling the play. Note the precise route of the white king: ♔a1-b1-c1-d2-e3-f4-g5-h6-h7-h8. The way these moves are compelled creates an impressive flow across the board. The corner-to-corner effect is graphically geometrical, but it is the flow and overall effect that make this study stand out. While no single move is unusual, surprising or paradoxical, the overall achievement of the study could be considered any of those three.

It should be admitted, though, that the corner-to-corner effect does depend on a certain arbitrariness in what is considered to be the main line of play. There is not much scope for disagreement over the first few moves, but towards the end of the study a lot depends on the choice of the composer as to what is the main line. There are no cast-iron rules to determine which line should be given priority. We cannot prevent you from considering any sideline you like as the main line, if you really want to. However, sometimes the analysis is 'tighter' than at other times, and the final few moves in the above study are definitely a little bit

'loose', which is a weakness. The tighter the better!

Real 'crispness' depends upon the absence of lengthy supporting analysis, which tends to undermine the flow. Given the constraints of composing an artistic study, this quality is fairly rare ('Crispness comes but once a year').

Complete Studies

By 'complete' we mean simply that a study shows all the four of our elements: paradox, depth, geometry and flow. As pointed out earlier, this in no way implies that the work is 'better' than another which, say, shows only two of them. However, there is a certain all-round strength and balance to studies with a 'bit of everything' that makes them well worth a look. You have already seen a few examples, for instance the Korolkov at the start of this chapter and the Korolkov/Mitrofanov from the geometry section. This section will round off the show, and should leave you raring to have a go at the exercises!

Our first example is by Dutchman W. Korteling:

(see diagram on following page)

With his king far away from the action, White has real problems to solve here. He starts with a surprising check – surprising since it is not usually a good idea to drive your

7.23   Draw   FPDG
W. Korteling
Tidskrift KNSB 1942

opponent's king to a more active position in the endgame.

1 ᾃd8+!

A deep move, the purpose of which is to place the black king on the g-file. Not good enough is the immediate 1 ᾃg4 ♝c6+! 2 ♔b4 g2 when Black is winning.

1	...	♔g7
2	ᾃd3	♝c6+
3	♔b4	g2
4	ᾃg3+	

This is why White first played 1 ᾃd8+. He has wasted one move with the rook but Black has had to make two moves with the king. These two king moves seem to help Black become more active, but in fact they prove irrelevant.

4	...	♔f6
5	♔c5	

This move gains what turns out to be a crucial tempo. The play flows inevitably towards its paradoxical finish...

5	...	♝b7
6	♔d4	h5
7	♔e3	h4
8	♔f2!!	hxg3+
9	♔g1!	

Either achieving a stalemate or the win of both black pawns should the bishop 'undefend' g2. The black king is a tempo too slow defending the g3-pawn. Everything hangs together very neatly in this study, especially the white king's unique route from one side of the board to the other.

In *Tactical Chess Endings* John Nunn describes the next work as one of his personal favourites. We will also give the position, since it displays all our elements with great power...

7.24   Win   GPDF
R. Missiaen, 1974
Second prize, Schakend Nederland

The 'strategy' is clear enough. The material balance is drawn in general, so White must exploit the dynamics of the position to win a bishop.

1 &f3+

After 1 &c8+? &b7 2 &xf8 &xd1 Black draws.

1 ...   &a7

After 1...&b8, the reply 2 &b2 nets a bishop immediately. Now White must choose which bishop to attack.

2 &c3!

After 2 &c8? &d6! Black starts to co-ordinate his pieces. The bishop on b3 has an apparently wide choice of squares, but...

2 ...   &e6!

Domination at work. The alternatives 2...&a2 and 2...&a4 lose to 3 &c8 and 4 &a8+. 2...&f7 3 &c7+ and 2...&g8 3 &c8 are the other possibilities.

3 &c6   &b3!

Not 3...&f5? 4 &f6. Now comes a move of exceptional depth and paradox.

4 &h1!!

Incredibly this moves creates a position of reciprocal zugzwang! The main line will show why White's king is better on h1 than g2.

4 ...   &b4

It is easy to see why the black king cannot move. The light-squared bishop is dominated (see the note to Black's second move) and the dark-

squared bishop has nowhere better than b4, for example 4...&a3 5 &c3 or 4...&g7 5 &c7+.

5 &c1!

Not good enough is 5 &c7+ &a6 6 &b7 &a5!, holding on. Now the threat is 6 &b1.

5 ...   &g8

If the dark-squared bishop moves, then White picks off the other bishop, e.g. 5...&d6 6 &a1+ &b6 7 &b1. After 5...&e6, 6 &c7+ does the job. Now the 'point' of 4 &h1!! is revealed – it opens the g-file.

6 &g1!   &e6

6...&c4 7 &g4 'kebabs' the bishops along the fourth rank.

7 &g7+   &b6

8 &g6

The 'double domination' of the bishops involves very rich geometry with the rook working along almost every rank and file. The reciprocal zugzwang is a real shocker (depth and paradox) – the sort of move that would probably never be found over the board with the clock ticking. There is some smooth flow but, unlike the other elements, nothing exceptional. A sequence of rare beauty!

Although a large number of ideas have been 'used up' by earlier composers, there is still great scope for creativity in study composition. A number of modern studies involve enormously complex ideas, where a high level of analytical skill is necessary to understand the play. Many of the selections for this book conform to our general policy of not obscuring aesthetic elements with difficult play. In other words we have tried to give relatively clear, 'user-friendly' studies. For these reasons we have resorted to a number of older classics. One of the best of the 'new generation' of chess artists is the very talented David Gurgenidze, and we finish off this section with one of his joint compositions:

7.25   Win   DPGF

D. Gurgenidze and L. Mitrofanov
First prize,
Molodoi Leninets 1982

White is material down but Black is tied up defending his king. After any move of the *en prise* rook along the first rank Black will only have pawn moves available. However, you have to see Black's defence to have any hope of finding White's deep and precise first move.

1   ♖b1!!

Even Nimzowitsch never played as mysterious a rook move as this. The point is revealed only on move six.

1   ...   c4

Black's plan is to run himself out of pawn moves and then set up a stalemate defence.

2   ♔c6!

The start of an even more mysterious king march. His majesty needs to get to a8. Well, obviously!

2   ...   h4
3   ♔b7!   h3
4   ♔a8!

4 ♔c6? would only draw after 4...c3 5 bxc3 ♕c7+ 6 ♔xc7 h2!.

4   ...   c3

The immediate 4...♕b8+ 5 ♔xb8 h2 leads to mate: 6 ♘g5 c3 7 ♘e4 c2 8 ♘g3#.

5   bxc3   ♕b8+

It is clear that the white king needed to avoid giving the black queen a safe check. But now the point of the mysterious rook move and king march is revealed: the white rook can swing across with tempo.

6   ♖xb8!   h2

If 6...♗f2, 7 ♖h8 wins or 6...♗d4 7 cxd4 h2 8 ♖b1+ and the d-pawn will be decisive.

7   ♖h8!   ♗f2
8   ♖xh2#

Deep stuff involving some beautiful 'hiding' moves. Notice the interesting path of the white rook

f1-b1-b8-h8-h2, the good use made
of the corners and the mysterious
flowing king march up the long diagonal. The white moves were most
unexpected, yet involved no sacrifice – a more sophisticated form of
paradox in many ways.

Exercises

Although it is useful simply to play
over the solutions to studies (it will
stimulate imagination and help you
pick up patterns), actually solving
them is an even better form of training. Sometimes players are put off
by the difficulty. To misquote G. K.
Chesterton, it is not that studies have
been tried and found wanting, they
have been found difficult and left un-
tried! We hope readers will have a go
at the following exercises, since they
will greatly enjoy finding the solutions for themselves. You can check
you got them right at the back of the
book. White is to play in all positions.

7.26   Win   PDG

T. Gorgiev, 1938
1st HM, VCSPS Chess Club Ty

7.27   Draw   FPG

Finish of study by
J. de Villeneuve-Esclapon
First Prize, Schweizerische
Schachzeitung 1923

7.28   Win   GP(F)
L. Kubbel, 1938
2nd Prize, Chigorin Memorial Ty

7.30   Draw   PFG
L. Mitrofanov
1st Prize, 5-man Tourney 1976

7.29   Win   PG
L. Prokes
First prize, I. Louma Ty 1941

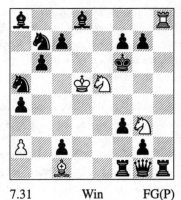

7.31   Win   FG(P)
H. Meyer
A Complete Guide
to the Game of Chess, 1882

8 Art for Art's Sake: the Delights of Chess Problems

'It is easy to be heavy, hard to be light.'
G. K. Chesterton

'Problems worthy of attack prove their worth by hitting back.'
Piet Hein

'What is man before beauty cajoles from him a delight in things for their own sake, or the serenity of form tempers the savagery of life?'
Friedrich von Schiller

The only difference between an orthodox chess problem and a chess position is that the problem always contains a stipulation that White must force mate in a fixed number of moves. This innocent little feature gives composers the chance to thrill their solvers with an enormous range of ideas and effects.

Take Mate in Two, for example. A naïve player might expect that the stipulation is just too limiting. White plays a move, and, however Black replies, it is mate next move. Sounds pretty straightforward? Read on and you will discover just how wrong such an expectation would be. Mate in Two and the game of chess are two very different domains.

Unlike the other chapters in this book, this one is written as much for the problemist as for the player. People with no experience of problems should still be able to follow it, but the going will not be light! We will be looking at the three main schools of problem composition (Bohemian, Logical and Strategic), relating their aspirations to our elements, and exploring some of their aesthetic possibilities. Later, we will also take a brief look at conventions and construction. We hope and fully expect you to find some of the final examples well worth waiting for.

Composing Directions

Historically speaking, there are three major directions, or schools, of composition which are clearly discernible: the Bohemians, the Logical (or New German) School, and the Strategic School. Numerically, this sequence also represents an ascending order in terms of output.

Before we look at some examples of these three major traditions, it is necessary to explain the problemist's special use of the word 'strategy'. This usage is a little odd, because its meaning is actually quite close to 'tactics'! To a problemist, 'strategy' has to do with a device or mechanism, usually geometric in nature, by which a move-set may be categorized or explained. Any of the problems included in Chapter 4 would be examples of good strategic content. A problem which contained very few such devices, or in which they did not form a coherent idea, would be regarded as relatively lacking in strategy.

Bohemian Problems

The Bohemian school of composition is centred round a very restricted interest: **model mates**. A model mate is a mating position with the following characteristics:

1) No square in the mated king's field is guarded more than once, or is blocked as well as guarded;

2) All of the mating side's pieces, with the permissible exception of the king and pawns, participate in the mate;

3) If a piece belonging to the mated side is pinned, it does not matter if it stands on a square in the mated king's field – an exception to rule '1'.

Such checkmates – mates with, as it were, 'nothing to spare' – can be most unexpected. As well as this paradoxical element there is also 'optical logic' geometry in the control of the black king's field.

So much for the letter, let us have a look at the spirit via No. 8.1, by the acknowledged Bohemian leader.

8.1   #3   G(P)(D)

M. Havel
Zlata Praha 1904

The key is **1 ♘e4!** which gives a flight on d7 and threatens **2 ♕e8+ ♔b6 3 ♘c4#**. This is a mate to savour: all White's resources, including the king, are just sufficient to effect the mate. Now look at the variation after **1...a5**, which defends against the threat by vacating a6, but turns out to be a prospective self-block: **2 ♕d6+ ♔b5 3 ♘c3#**. This model is sufficiently similar to the mate in the threat to count as an echo, and because it is on squares of the opposite colour, it is a chameleon echo. The third variation is **1...♔d7**

2 ♔b7! (threatening **3 ♘c5#** which is not a model because c8 is guarded twice and the ♘e3 is a non-participant) **2...♔e6 3 ♕e8#**. One of the best-known models showing a pleasing symmetry.

This work is the very epitome of the Bohemian school. It shows a variety of mates as well as an echo. Although the prospective self-block is a very good variation strategically, the other two mates have no strategic content. One is produced by the threat in a completely straightforward manner and the other comes about by the black king simply walking into a different mating net. A big plus in this particular instance is the outstanding economy – it is a miniature without any white pawns. Also, the key is technically good, although the tiny size of the black force reduces the paradoxical impact.

Bohemian problems can quite often prove difficult to solve, precisely because of this lack of strategy. The positions are designed to show the black king being mated on different squares, and this, together with the comparative lack of black force, often results in a shortage of positional signposts.

No. 8.2 shows a very attractive, but constructionally demanding way of adding interest to model mates through the use of **pin-models**.

The surprising **1 ♖b5!**, giving up a promising-looking ♖+♗ battery,

8.2   #3   G(P)

G. Koziuri, 1st-2nd Prize
Lobusov Jubilee 1990

threatens **2 ♕f6+ ♔xh5** (**2...♘g6** leads to an unimportant dual after **3 ♕g7/♕g5#**) **3 g4#**. Note that the ♘e5 is pinned, making **3...♘xg4** impossible. An obvious defence to this threat is **1...♘xg3**, which makes f4 available to White's queen: **2 ♕f4+ ♔xh5 3 ♗xf7#** – again the ♘e5 is necessarily pinned. Lastly, **1...fxe6** unguards g6, leading to **2 ♕xh7+ ♔g5 3 ♕g6#**, a third pin-model depending upon the pin of the ♘e5, and a clever second use of the ♗g3. The fact that the knight is pinned in all three variations provides this elegant work with exceptional unity. The only slight criticism is that two of the mates are **side-board** models, which are of lesser value than midboard models (reduction of paradox).

Model mates are widely regarded as a special form of economy: with the possible exception of the king and pawns, the mate will necessitate the participation of all available white men, and each white man performs a vital task – no superfluous force is involved in the mate. We can also take the view that models are geometrically interesting: we can take pleasure in the precise way in which the white pieces guard the squares in the black king's field without overlapping in their protection of a single square.

While problems such as 8.2 demonstrate that the Bohemian tradition is far from dead, they are few and far between nowadays. Original ideas are hard to come by, and the relative lack of strategy limits the appeal of problems whose only purpose is to show models. On the other hand, a model mate or two in a work with a completely non-Bohemian point is universally regarded as a most desirable enhancement. An example is No. 4.9.

The Logical School

The Logical or New German school has been going strongly since the early years of the twentieth century. The term 'logical' refers to the way in which the solution is structured. This structure is called a **logical combination** and boils down to the following: in the initial position, White has a potential means of

forcing mate, which is referred to as the main plan; if he tries to execute this plan immediately, Black will be found to possess a refutation. Accordingly, White must first execute a **foreplan**, whereby Black's defence to the main plan is negated in some way.

No. 8.3 is a very clear example.

8.3   #3   D(G)

J. Møller
Skakbladet 1920

White's main plan is highlighted by the try **1 ♕b1?** threatening **2 ♕b8#**, which is refuted by **1...♗g3!**. The key is **1 ♕g7!**, which threatens **2 ♕xd7** followed by unavoidable mate. Black can defend against this by interposing his bishop with **1...♗e7**. This move signifies the success of White's foreplan, which was to **decoy** the bishop. Thus he can now revert to the main plan with **2 ♕b2**, again threatening **3 ♕b8#**. Black no longer has the defence

2...♗g3 at his disposal, but can instead play the analogous **2...♗d6**. Whereas playing ...♗g3 did not harm Black's position, this move interferes with the ♘d7, allowing **3 ♕g2#** since 3...d5 is no longer possible. White's foreplan has forced Black to substitute a bad defence for a good one – a very popular logical idea. Notice the three 'long' queen moves in this solution, which carve a large triangle out of the board. The non-thematic **1...♔b7** does not really defeat the threat: **2 ♕xd7+ ♔a6 3 a8♕#**.

This problem illustrates the most important feature of the Logical School: there is only a single thematic line of play. Within this single line – there are seldom even two thematic variations – the composer expresses his entire conception. Most logical problems are more-movers, enabling both foreplan and main plan to be longer; indeed, some have multiple foreplans, each one negating a counter to a later one or to the main plan. Strategy is not lacking – the interference in 8.3 is very pretty – and the mate is, technically, a model, albeit a rather unimpressive one. But the Logical School utilizes an important reasoning structure of the game as played: you want to execute your plan, your opponent has a counter, so you manoeuvre to remove or undermine that counter before returning to the central idea.

Logical composers are above all else concerned to show this structure in a pristine form, and to this end they apply a very important standard, called **purity of aim**. By this is meant, to express it at its simplest, that the foreplan must *only* have a single purpose in dealing with Black's defeat of the white try or tries. In 8.3, the only purpose of **1 ♕g7** is to decoy the black bishop; the move does not confer on White any other advantage which he did not have before.

The main appeal of logical problems is Depth; their very structure guarantees this. More than in any other kind of problem, it is necessary to solve them to appreciate their impact fully. Look at No. 8.4.

8.4   #5   DP(G)

Stefan Schneider, 1st Place
Austria-Switzerland Match 1977

White achieves nothing with 1 ♖e7 as 2 ♕xe2+ ♗xe2 3 ♖xe2+ is not mate – a well-known situation in which queen and rook are the wrong way around. Thus White's main plan is ♕e8, followed by ♖e7 and ♖xe2+, a geometrical motif often seen in logical problems, and referred to as **doubling**. But 1 ♕e8? is much too long-winded, and frees the black queen to run rampant by giving up the possibility of ♕xd2#. The secret to achieving the doubling is to be able to play ♕e8 with gain of time – a very hard thing to imagine, especially as the move is in the opposite direction to Black's king. This is how it is done:

1 ♔a8!!

A move which is not only deep for the reasons outlined, but also allows a check, which creates a strong flavour of paradox as well. The threat is simply **2 ♖h7!** followed by removing the ♖h2 and ♘g2#; the point of going to a8 is to avoid 2...♖xh7 being check, but in doing so also to avoid b8 because of the potential pin by the black bishop coming to h2 (the reason for avoiding 1 ♔c8? will soon become clear). Black is so tied down that his only possibility is to put White's idea to the test.

1 ...   ♖h8+

White now continues in madcap style:

2 ♕e8!!

Now, if 2...♖xe8+, 3 ♔a7! (not 3 ♔b7? ♖b8+ 4 ♔xb8 ♗h2! – this also explains why 1 ♔c8? would have

been a mistake, because the white king would not have been able to escape the h2-b8 diagonal within the 5-move limit of the problem). Black can now no longer guard g2, and after 3...♖a8+ 4 ♔xa8, 5 ♘g2# is threatened. This can only be prevented by freeing f2, but moving the knight on f2 allows 5 ♘d3#. Therefore, Black must play

2 ...   ♖h2

and now the main plan is executed with **3 ♖e7**, leaving the black army looking on while White goes **4 ♖xe2+ ♗xe2 5 ♕xe2#**.

Diagram 8.5 shows the exact opposite of the doubling we have just seen.

8.5   #7   DGP

H. Grasemann & A. Kraemer,
1st HM, Deutsche
Schachzeitung 1957

The main plan of 1 ♖b8+ ♖xb8 2 axb8♕+ ♕xb8 3 ♕a6+ fails here because, from White's point of view, the ♛g8 and the ♜c8 are the wrong way around; if the rook arrived on b8 instead of the queen then 3 ♛a6 would be mate. White has a foreplan which brings about the reversal of queen and rook:

1   ♘e8!

First the queen is dragged over the critical square f8.

1   ...   ♛xe8

After 1...♜cxe8 2 ♛c7 or 1...♜exe8 2 ♜b8+ the mating is easy.

2   ♗d4!

Guards a7 in order to threaten 3 ♜b8+ ♜xb8 4 axb8♛+ ♛xb8 5 ♛a6+ ♛a7 6 ♛xa7#. Black has no adequate direct defence to this threat and must avail himself of the opportunity given him by White to lash back with a check:

2   ...   ♜c2+
3   ♗f2!!

A lovely rejoinder, whether or not you have seen its point.

3   ...   ♜xf2+
4   ♔h3   ♜f8

Black must restore the protection of his back rank.

5   ♜b8+   ♛xb8
6   axb8♛+   ♜xb8
7   ♛a6#

Although logical problems are, if anything, easier than the average more-mover to solve, an obscure main plan can lead occasionally to ferocious difficulty. Diagram 8.6 looks so innocent, yet hides a remarkably deep idea:

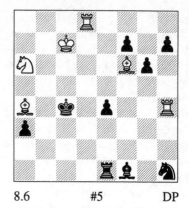

8.6   #5   DP

H. Grasemann
Berliner Morgenpost 1956

1   ♜h3!!   ♗xh3

White was threatening 2 ♜c3# and 2 ♜d4#. If 1...♘g3, then 2 ♜xg3 ♗e3 3 ♜g5 and 4 ♜c5#. After 1...♗d3, 2 ♜d4+ ♔c3 3 ♜dxd3++ ♔c4 4 ♜d4#.

2   ♜d4+   ♔c3
3   ♜d5+   ♔c4
4   ♗c2!!

Threatening 5 ♜c5#.

4   ...   ♔xd5
5   ♗b3#

Only now do we see the purpose of White's superb first move: the ♗f1 had to be decoyed so as not to be available to interpose on c4 and upset this lovely model mate! Of course, the double rook sacrifice is not so easy to spot either.

Somewhat easier to solve, yet of challenging length, is the sort of problem beautifully represented by No. 8.7.

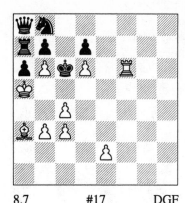

8.7   #17   DGF

Y. Vladimirov, 1st Prize
Macleod Memorial Tourney 1994

White's main plan is ♖f8 followed by ♖c8#, but Black's stalemate must first be relieved. The foreplan is like walking a tightrope, allowing ...♔c5, then checking the king back to c6, all the while re-grouping the forces to make the main plan possible without giving Black the opportunity to unravel.

1	♗c1	♔c5
2	♗e3+	♔c6
3	♗f4	♔c5
4	♖f5+	♔c6
5	♗e5	♔c5
6	♗h2+	♔c6
7	♖f6	♔c5
8	♗g1+	♔c6
9	e3	♔c5
10	e4+	♔c6
11	♗h2	♔c5
12	♖f5+	♔c6
13	e5	♔c5
14	♗g1+	♔c6

15	♖f2!	♔c5
16	♖f8+	

Finally, the move White has been building up to all along. The foreplan has made it possible to play this move with check.

16	...	♔c6
17	♖c8#	

Among the fascinating geometrical effects in this problem is the variety of self-interferences employed by White to relieve the stalemate: the bishop interferes with the rook, and the rook with the bishop; the pawn interferes with both rook and bishop. Because of its length, the problem exhibits a pleasing flow as well. Although Black merely marks time with the king, the three dancing white men perform an intricate counterpoint.

By way of recompense to the king, our next example shows the white king doing all the work. No. 8.8 is also the problem which inspired the tourney won by No. 8.7.

The main plan here is 1 ♔d5 (2 ♔xc4#) 2...♛b4 2 ♔c6 (3 ♔c7#) and Black is unable to hold all the discovered checking squares, e.g. 3...♛e7 4 ♔b5+ and mate next move. However, after 1 ♔d5, there is the simple and effective 1...c1♛! scotching White's plans, for if now 2 ♔c6, the e1-bishop moves away and the ♗h1 comes under fire. What is the foreplan, and how does it put paid to the ...c1♛ defence?

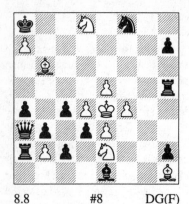

8.8　　　　#8　　　　DG(F)

N. A. Macleod, 1st Prize
Mat 1983

1 ♔f3　　　　♖h4

The best way to defend against the threat of 2 ♔g4#. If 1...♖g5, then 2 fxg5.

2 ♔g2　　　　dxe2

Black had to stop 3 ♔f1#.

3 ♔f3!

White can return to great effect, whereas Black's second move is irrevocable.

3 ...　　　　c1♘

And there you have it. This is a particularly amusing form of *obstruction*: now the pawn can no longer become a queen because it has become a knight!

4 ♔e4　　　　♖h5
5 ♔d5　　　　♕b4
6 ♔c6　　　　♕e7
7 ♔b5+

and mate next move.

This problem is a demonstration of the fact that logical problems are excellent vehicles for geometric ideas which require a number of moves to effect. Our last example of this school is an awe-inspiring strategic-logical achievement.

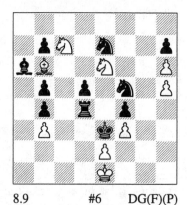

8.9　　　　#6　　　　DG(F)(P)

A. Lobusov & A. Spirin, 1st Prize
E. Zepler Memorial Tourney 1985

The position shows a situation often referred to by problemists as 'White to play', emphasizing the point that, if it were not White to play, Black would be in zugzwang. This is a favourite theme amongst composers of logical problems: in the foreplan, Black is inveigled somehow into allowing White to lose a move. In the present situation, if it were Black to move, a knight would have to give up the protection of d5 or d4, resulting in instant mate. Note that attempting a waiting move with the ♗b6 frees the ♙b7 and subsequently the ♗a6 to make all the waiting moves Black needs.

1 ♘e8! **♞g8**

This is the only move to stop 2 ♘f6 followed by mate on g4.

2 ♘6c7! **♞fe7**

The black knights are hard-pressed to contain the threats of their opposite numbers. If 2...♞ge7, 3 ♘f6.

3 ♘g7!

Threatening 4 ♘xd5+ and 5 ♘f5# or vice versa. If now 3...♞f6, then 4 ♘ce6! and Black cannot prevent 5 ♗xd4# without allowing 5 ♘(x)f5#.

3 ... **♞xh6**

4 ♘ge6 **♞hf5**

5 h6!

Lo and behold, out of nowhere White has acquired a waiting move! The diagram position has been repeated, only there is a pawn missing from h5 and it is not 'White to play'. Mate follows on the next move. Even more remarkable is that, during the solution, the two white knights have swapped places, a graphic motif popularly known by the German word *Platzwechsel*. And, as though this were not enough, the same manoeuvre has been performed by the black knights! A wonderful creation, particularly as the play is so clear in a neat, if slightly heavy position. The prancing of the knights also provides a pleasing impression of flow. Perhaps there is some humour here too, since laughter is quite a common reaction to seeing the solution!

The Strategic School

The Strategic School is easily recognized by the fact that their problems generally have a number of variations. Their interest lies almost entirely in the exploration of a vast treasure trove of geometric or 'strategic' ideas. An idea is displayed a number of times in a problem, creating an artistic effect strongly resembling the 'variations on a theme' of classical music. Strategic problems are mostly short – between two and four moves – because the majority of the themes only require a few moves for their expression, and anyway the longer the problem, the more difficult it is for the composer to control more than a single line of play.

An important feature for which the strategic composer strives is *unity*. In broad terms, this means that he tries to maximize the number of elements shared among the variations. Unity is the rough equivalent for the strategic composer to purity of aim for the logical composer; however, as we shall see, it is frequently impossible to avoid *by-play*, which is essential to the soundness of the problem.

Diagram 8.10 is as good an example of Strategic School ideals as any.

Its fundamental theme is the *half-pin*, which has proved to be one of the most fertile geometric devices in problemdom: the line between the

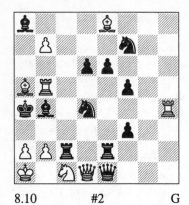

8.10   #2   G

C. Mansfield, 1st Prize
Hampshire Telegraph & Post 1915

♖h4 and the ♔a4 is occupied by two black pieces – when one moves off the line, the other becomes pinned. The key is **1 ♗c7!** threatening **2 ♖a5#**. Any move of the ♗b4 defeats the threat by creating a potential flight square; it also leaves the ♘d4 pinned, thus: **1...♗a5 2 ♖b6#**. This mate not only capitalizes on the fact that the ♘e5 cannot interpose, but also on the blocking of a5 by the bishop, allowing the rook to interfere with the ♗c7 (this is in direct contrast to the logical composer's ideal of purity of aim, which would require the mate to be allowed only by the pin on the ♘d4). Note the enthralling complexity of what is happening in this variation: the ♖b5, in discovering check from the ♗e8, must move in such a way as to maintain control of b4, the square just vacated by the ♗a5, but b7 and b2 are occupied by white pawns, leaving a choice between b3 and b6. But **2 ♖b3+?** unpins the ♖c2, allowing it to interpose on c6, so the only mate is **2 ♖b6** – another case of dual avoidance.

Let us look at the remaining variations. If **1...♗a3**, we have another self-block: **2 b3#**, again depending on the pinning of the ♘d4. In fact, all the moves of the ♗b4 result in mates which depend on this feature: **1...♗d2** allows **2 ♕xc2#** because the ♖e2 is interfered with, while **1...♗c5/♗c3** interfere with the ♖c2, allowing **2 ♖b3#** unpinning the rook, which is unable to interpose – a glorious collection of geometric effects in a single variation!

We now turn to the moves of the ♘d4. By opening the line from the ♖h4, they cause the ♗b4 to be pinned: **1...♘c6** does not defeat the threat: **2 ♖a5#** is still mate, because, although the ♗e8 has been shut off, both protectors of a5 are pinned. **1...♘xb5** is another strategy-intensive variation: by capturing the rook, the knight as well as the bishop is pinned again, this time permitting a new actor to enter the stage: **2 bxa8♕(♖)#** (problem conventions do not count this choice of promotion as a dual). Finally, the knight can divert White's attention by a check: **1...♘b3+** which is met by the strategy-less **2 axb3#** – an example of the by-play we referred to earlier.

The Construction of a Chess Problem

The appreciation of chess compositions can be greatly enhanced by an understanding of the composing process, just as our appreciation of a master game is increased by understanding the reasoning behind their moves.

Let us examine the constructional features of Mansfield's problem. If we consider first the very mild flaw of the unthematic **1...♘b3+** variation, we soon see that the composer was unable to eliminate it because the b3 square could not be blocked owing to the need for **2 ♕xc2#**. In fact, it dawns upon us how clever the composer has been in making use of the white king to ensure that 1...♘b3 is check, thus forcing 2 axb3#, otherwise the threat would not have been prevented and a nasty dual would have resulted.

It is customary among composers to talk about the *matrix* of a problem. This refers to the pieces which are essential to the expression of the idea, and their locations. In Mansfield's problem, the matrix comprises all the white men except the king, the knight and the pawn on a2; the black men include the king, the rooks, the bishops and the ♘d4. We can now examine the justification for the men which are not part of the matrix, for all must have a reason, as demanded by the tenets of artistic economy.

The justification for the white 'extras' is easy: the ♘c1 protects b3 as well as preventing the catastrophic 1...♕xd1+; the ♙a2, together with the king being located on a1 rather than anywhere else, are required for the by-play variation we have already examined.

The ♘f7 is a typical necessity: without it 1 ♗d8 would be a cook. The ♙d6 prevents the ♗b4 moving to that square or beyond, which would result in a 'no solution'. The ♙e6 shields the ♗e8 from the ♖e2. The ♕e1 protects the ♗b4, so that **1...♘c6** does not allow the horrible 2 ♖bxb4#. More controversial are the pawns on f5 and f3. These have the purpose of preventing the ♘d4 from moving to these squares, which would allow not only the threat, but also the rather smart 2 ♖c5#, which does not appear in the thematic variations. Nowadays, composers are generally far more relaxed about duals following moves which do not defeat the threat. However, even by today's standards, we feel Mansfield was correct to add the pawns, because they ensure that the problem is one hundred percent accurate. This is an aesthetic plus worth having, and is an example of the sort of refined judgement sometimes demanded of a chess problem composer.

Conventions

An important concept in the appreciation of problems, as in other art forms, is the distinction between form and content, or, as a problemist would express it, between construction and idea. It is not enough for the composer to present a beautiful idea; he must also endeavour to present it beautifully. The problem genre abounds with rules and conventions, most of which are guides to the ideals of construction. Probably the strictest of these is the rule that an orthodox problem must have an unique solution. If a second solution exists, this is termed a 'cook' (after an eminent American composer of the 19th century, Eugene B. Cook) and renders the problem effectively non-existent. This is surely natural enough: additional solutions cheapen the intended one, however pretty it might be in itself, and we would feel similar disappointment at a brilliancy which represented but one of a choice of wins.

Another natural convention, particularly in shorter problems, is that the key move should not be a check or capture of a piece. Such crudity militates against our desire for depth and paradox; it also usually undermines the difficulty of the problem (if a problem is too easy it ceases to be a problem!). Yet such rules can be bent, provided there is a justification; if a beautiful idea cannot be better constructed, then it is better that it should not blush unseen.

Players may find the following problem rather pointless at first, as well as being too easy to solve! But it was an understanding of constructional difficulty that enabled a tough tourney judge to set aside all the crudities of No. 8.11 (by John Rice) to give it First Prize, because he was aware of the great achievement of constructing a cyclic change two-mover. We must always balance the defects we see in a work by asking ourselves whether its aesthetic achievement can carry them.

8.11 is an example of a well-justified constructional defect.

8.11   #2

J. M. Rice, 1st Prize
Problem Theme Tourney 1961

There are three phases to this problem, and in each we must concentrate on the way in which White deals with the king moves **1...♚c6** (x) and **1...♚e6** (y). In the set play, these are answered by **2 ♕e8#** (**A**) and **2 ♕c8#** (**B**) respectively. But White must get a move on, because Black possesses two much stronger moves, 1...♛xd4+ and 1...b5+. So we try **1 ♘b6++?** (The question mark denotes the fact that this move is a 'try'): now, after **1...♚c6** we get **2 ♕c8#** and after **1...♚e6** comes **2 ♕d6#** (**C**), but after **1...♚e7!** there is no mate. Thus we arrive at the key: **1 ♘f6++!** and now **1...♚c6** (x) gives **2 ♕d6#** (**C**) while **1...♚e6** (y) is met by **2 ♕e8#** (**A**).

This work shows the extremely difficult theme of **Cyclic Change**; the replies to the two black defences **x** and **y** are **A-B** in the set play, **B-C** in the play after the try, and **C-A** in the actual play. At the time, the theme had not been achieved at all; even today it is regarded as something of a task. The use of double-checking try and key moves would probably be justified by this consideration alone, but there is an additional factor. The fact that there are two likely-looking checks goes some way to counteracting the lack of difficulty inherent in checking moves; the solver still has a slightly tricky choice to make. Note also that the *unprovided checks* – black checks in the diagram position against which there is no mating reply – are also a technical flaw, because they

point to the solution. Given the checking try and key, there is little point in doing anything about this, and the composer has quite rightly preferred to maximize the economy of force used, rather than add material to avoid the flaw.

Such works are often dismissed by some problemists – not to mention players – as arid and excessively formal. In our view, this is a mistake; it misses an opportunity for the enjoyment of human ingenuity which is of a very similar order to that displayed in a brilliant combination. Always study the mechanism whereby the composer rings the changes. Consider, for example, the reasoning behind the change of just one of the mates between the set play and the play after **1 ♘b6++?**: in the set play, after **1...♚c6**, **2 ♕c8+** is not mate because the ♝a5 can interpose, but **2 ♕e8#** succeeds because the ♘d5 guards c7. After **1 ♘b6++? ♚c6**, **2 ♕e8+** is not mate because c7 has been unguarded; on the other hand, **2 ♕c8#** is mate because the ♘b6 now shuts off the bishop from c7.

Returning to the consideration of problem conventions, it is frequently unsatisfactory when a black defence leads to more than one mating continuation, called a *dual*. Many compositions of all types contain clever devices whereby the author has eliminated duals whose presence would otherwise have severely reduced the value of the work. In fact, *dual avoidance* has proved to be a rich theme in itself. Consider No. 8.12:

8.12   #2

V. Lider, Second Prize
Tribune de Genève 1983

The key is the nice corner-to-corner move **1 ♕a1!**, which puts Black in zugzwang. If the ♘b2 were removed from the board, White would have the dual mates **2 ♕xe5#** and **2 ♘c5#** because of the opening of the a1-e5 diagonal, but after **1...♘a4** only **2 ♕xe5#** is possible, while after **1...♘c4** only **2 ♘c5#** is possible; in both instances, the defence protects one of the two potential mating squares. **1...♘d3** has a similar effect to a correction, preventing both the previous mates but allowing the new **2 cxd3#**. The same idea is echoed by the ♘d1: its random move opens a line for the queen allowing **2 ♕e1#** and **2 ♕h1#**. **1...♘c3** and **1...♘f2**

separate these mates, while **1...♘e3** prevents both, but self-blocks instead, allowing the **self-interference** mate **2 ♗f3#**. We must also account for **1...d4** producing the switchback **2 ♕a8#** and **1...f4** allowing **2 ♗g6#**.

Traditional and Modern

One of the most interesting developments in the Strategic School has been the evolution of ideas in the two-mover. This was alluded to in the Geometry chapter, where it was characterized as a progression towards abstraction and the relationships between moves. This shift is referred to amongst problemists as a change from the Traditional to the Modern two-mover. As a somewhat crude rule of thumb, traditional two-movers focus on the play after the key, whereas modern ones are concerned with more than one phase, comprising try-play and/or set play, as well as actual play.

Diagram 8.13 shows a half-pin, but in this case it does not form the central idea of the problem.

Any move of the ♗e5, retaining control of f4, will threaten mate by **2 ♘d2#**. Let us try **1 ♗g3?**. If Black pins the knight with **1...♖c6**, the ♖f5 becomes pinned and **2 f3#** results. If **1...♖xf2** the ♖g6 is pinned and this allows White to mate with **2 ♖e8#**. However, **1...f4!** cleverly defeats the threat (by shutting off the ♗g3)

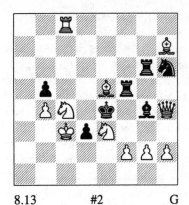

8.13   #2   G

U. Heinonen, First Prize
"Mat" Theme Tourney 1984

without allowing mate, because, although the ♖g6 is pinned, 2 ♖e8+ is not mate because the ♗g4 can now interpose.

Our next attempt to mate by 2 ♘d2# is to protect the ♗e5 with the queen by 1 ♕e7?. Now if Black answers as before with 1...♖c6, 2 f3 is no good because the ♗g4 is no longer pinned, but 2 ♗d6#, neatly shutting off the ♖c6, is possible because of the new battery. If 1...♖xf2, White now has 2 ♕b7#, taking advantage of the inability of the ♖g6 to interpose. This time, Black deals with the try by 1...♖e6! to which White has no answer.

Finally, we come to the key itself, 1 ♕g3!. Against 1...♖c6, White has this time 2 ♕f4#, whilst 1...♖xf2 is now met by 2 ♘d6#.

What does this work present? It consists of three phases, two of which occur as a result of tries, and one is, as always, the actual play. In each phase, Black has two thematic defences, 1...♖c6 and 1...♖xf2, and each time the mates permitted by these moves is different. The half-pin, which underlies all six mates, is a means of drawing them all together into a particularly tight and satisfactory unity.

This scheme, in which the same two (or sometimes more) defences are answered by different mates in at least three phases of the solution, is called the *Zagoruiko Theme* after one of its Russian pioneers. In our view, it is the bedrock of the modern strategic two-mover. It has been developed in many different directions, including reducing the number of mates even to the minimum possible, of which No. 8.11 was the first example.

Problemists often refer generically to the device which allows the mate to occur after a defence as a 'mistake'. (In the Heinonen problem we have just examined, for example, the mistake made by the thematic black defence 1...♖c6 is to leave the other rook pinned.) Because the focus of the Strategic School centres round these devices, its members could be characterized as collectors of mistakes! Amusing as this may sound, such an accumulation is also of considerable interest to the general chess enthusiast, and perhaps it accounts to some extent for the enduring vitality of the Strategic School.

Our last example of the modern two-mover demonstrates that White can also make mistakes.

8.14   #2   GP

J.-P. Boyer, 1st Prize
Thèmes 64 1985

In this diagram White can threaten 2 ♘f4# by playing something to e3, thereby shutting off the ♗c1. If **1 e3?** Black has **1...♘d3!** because 2 ♖xd3+ is no longer mate as the △e3 has interfered with the ♗g1, and control of c5 has been lost. If White tries **1 ♗e3?**, **1...♘d3** now allows **2 ♖xd3#**, but this time the refutation is **1...♘h5!**, because the bishop has interfered with the △e2 and prevented it from mating on the unprotected e4 square. The key is amusingly radical: **1 ♖8e3!**, which surprisingly renders the mates prepared for both defences inoperable by interfering

with both g1-bishop and e2-pawn. Of course, that this move has compensating features that make new mates possible against the original defences: **1...♘d3 2 ♖exd3#** and **1...♘h5 2 ♕g8#**, the latter having been made possible by the departure of the key rook from the a8-g8 line.

There are two serious drawbacks from the aesthetic point of view in this problem. Firstly, there are just two thematic defences, and each is seriously lacking in strategy, the 'mistake' made in each case being a simple unguard. Secondly – and this would be unacceptable to many a traditionalist – the ♗g1 plays no role at all after the key. Can the original and well-unified tries, which represent a white ♗/△ Grimshaw, justify these flaws? You pays your money and you takes your choice.

Longer Strategic Problems

There are a number of strategic themes which require more than two moves to execute. For example, the logical extension of the half-pin is the *third pin*, of which No. 8.15 is a beautifully constructed example.

The key is **1 ♔b1!** which threatens **2 ♖b4+ ♔c5 3 ♖b5+ ♔c4 4 ♖c5#** by avoiding a discovered check from the ♕g8. Black can only defend by protecting c5: **1...♘d7**. This is an example of negative depth, because it turns out that the knight

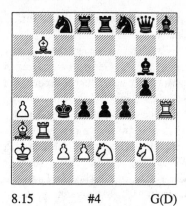

8.15   #4   G(D)

Y. Vladimirov, 1st Prize
Probleemblad 1966

interferes with the ♖d8. White has only to play the next three moves in the correct sequence: **2 ♖c3+! dxc3 3 ♘e3+! fxe3 4 d3#**, the other two pawns having been dragged off the h4-c4 line, the ♙e4 now finds itself pinned.

If Black instead tries **1...♖e5**, the rook will be found to have interfered with the ♗h8. White plays the same moves as before, this time in a different order, so as to avoid the attentions of the pieces whose lines are opened by the pawn captures: **2 ♘e3+! fxe3 3 d3+! exd3 4 ♖c3#**. Finally, **1...♘e6** interferes with the ♖e8, and the final sequence is **2 d3+! exd3 3 ♖c3+! dxc3 4 ♘e3#**. We should, for the sake of completeness, mention the sideline **1...♕(♖)d5** which operates as a self-block: **2 ♗a6+ ♕(♖)b5 3 ♖xb5** followed by **4 ♖c5#**.

A great problem by a leading composer! Note the graphic start position with a neat line of black pieces along the back rank. This work illustrates, not only the third pin, but also a highly fashionable cyclic theme. The second, third and fourth white moves in the thematic variations form the pattern ABC, BCA, CAB. As we have seen, this cyclic arrangement is very highly-prized among two-mover composers. The extra length has enabled it to be achieved without resort to the multiple phases necessitated by the two-mover's brevity.

One of the most basic square effects in three- and more-movers is *obstruction*. This is simply the occupation by a piece of a square to which a piece of the same colour wishes to go. Self-block, which can be considered a special case, is the only type of obstruction possible in two-movers. No. 8.16 shows this with some ingenuity.

The key is **1 ♔d7!** threatening **2 ♕g6+ ♔e5 3 ♘xd3#**. Black defends by protecting d3: **1...♕b1 2 ♘fxd5!** and mate follows by **3 ♘c3#** or **3 ♕f4#**. Piquantly, the queen obstructs the knight on b1; if **2...♘b1** were possible, Black would be able to refute the double threat. Similarly, if **1...♕b3, 2 ♘fxe6!** threatens **3 ♘c5#** and **3 ♕f4#**, and now **2...♘b3** is impossible (**2...♘xe6 3 ♕xe6#**), or **1...♕c4 2 ♘g6!** followed by **3 ♕e5#**

8.16   #3   G

M. Keller, 1st Prize
Schweizerische Arbeiter
Schachzeitung 1968

or 3 ♕f4#, because this time 2...♘c4 cannot rescue Black.

An important feature of problems like Keller's is that they can equally well be claimed as belonging to the logical as well as the strategic tradition. The reason for this is that they have *thematic tries* which emphasize the strategy and enable the content to be construed as a logical combination. In Keller's problem, White can try 1 ♘fxd5?, 1 ♘fxe6? and 1 ♘g6? and these are uniquely defeated by 1...♘b1!, 1...♘b3! and 1...♘c4! respectively. The key represents a foreplan which forces Black to negate one of these defences; White can then execute the appropriate main plan. This illustrates the fact that there is little ideological difference between the two schools, and that, to the onlooker at least, it is more a

question of emphasis than a difference of content.

We have discussed the *Novotny* theme in the Geometry chapter: a white piece plays to the intersection square of two *unlike* line-moving black pieces, such as a rook and a bishop. In three or more moves it is possible to show the same idea with *like-moving* black pieces, such as two rooks, or a bishop and a queen operating diagonally on the same colour. This inherently paradoxical theme is called a *Plachutta*, and is particularly clearly shown, with an extra strategic element, by No. 8.17.

8.17   #6   G(D)(P)(F)

H-P. Rehm, Second Prize
Probleemblad 1962

The black rooks prevent the one-two knockouts by 1 ♘e3+ ♚e5 2 ♘c4# and 1 ♘h6+ ♚e5 2 ♘xf7#. Black also threatens to zap the white battery with 1...g5, so White must act fast with 1 ♗c7!! which threatens

2 ♗xd6+ as well as the advertised
mates, so 1...g5 will not do. **1...♖cxc7
2 ♘h6+! ♚e5 3 ♗d7!**. The point of
the Plachutta: now the ♖b7 cannot
deal with this second nobly self-sac-
rificial cleric, so his brother has to do
the dirty deed instead; this in turn
means that the ♖c7 is decoyed from
guarding c4. **3...♖xd7 4 ♘g4+ ♚f4 5
♘e3+ ♚e5 6 ♘c4#**. After **1...♖bxc7**,
things are just the other way round: **2
♘e3+! ♚e5 3 ♗c6! ♖xc6 4 ♘g4+
♚f4 5 ♘h6+ ♚e5 6 ♘xf7#**.

The parallelism of the two variations is heightened by the way in
which the ♘g4 first travels west to
effect the decoy for the mate in the
north, and then travels north to effect
the decoy for the mate in the west.
These travels by the knight, powered
by a discovered check, to deliver a
distant mate, are examples of a favourite device called the *Siers battery*, which gives such problems a
light but pleasant flow.

Lest you think that things like this
never happen in real chess, perhaps
you have not seen the beautiful No.
8.18?

| **1 ♗c7!!** | **♕xc7** |

The other 'horn' of the Plachutta
in this case is 1...♖xc7 2 ♕b7+!
♖xb7 3 ♖xc5#.

2 ♖xc5+	**♕xc5**
3 ♕b7+	**♚xa5**
4 ♖a1#	

The relationship between Novotny and Plachutta is echoed by that

8.18   W
*S. Tarrasch – Allies
Naples 1914*

between interference (see p.90) and
Holzhausen. Ordinary interference
is between line pieces of unlike motion whereas Holzhausen is between
line pieces of like motion. Again,
this cannot be shown in just two
moves since the interfering piece as-
sumes guard over the mating square.
A double-Holzhausen is shown in
No. 8.19, which is particularly in-
structive for its game-like material
balance and disposition of forces.

White concludes the king-hunt
which has evidently been in progress with **1 ♗c6**, with the threat of **2
♕xa6+ ♚c5(b4) 3 ♕b5#**. Black can
defend against this by vacating d6,
but the black queen must keep control of e5. If Black tries **1...♕c7**, the
loss of the guard on a3 allows the
Novotny **2 ♘e3+!** followed by knight
mates on a3 or d2, or, if **2...dxe3, 3
♕c3#**. The only way the queen can

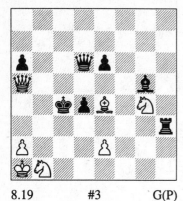

8.19   #3   G(P)

G. Bouma, First Prize
Schakend Nederland 1984

prevent the Novotny is to prepare to capture the knight on e3: **1...♕f4** achieves this but interferes with the ♗g5, allowing the queen to be dragged away from e5 by **2 ♘d2+! ♕xd2 3 ♘e5#**. The parallel variation sees the queen interfering with the rook: **1...♕g3 2 ♘a3+! ♕xa3 3 ♘e5#**. Once again, we should account for all defences: **1...♖b3 2 axb3+ ♔xb3 3 ♕a4#**.

There is a viewpoint which holds that the three-mover is the ideal length for strategic problems. The reasoning behind this is that three moves are few enough to enable the composer to incorporate a good number of variations on a theme, while they are sufficient to carry most of the effects which we have been looking at, and more. Also, as we have seen, the three-mover is a suitable vehicle for patterns, which,

in the two-mover, often depend on set and try play which strike the solver as unconvincing. Those who advance this view could do a good deal worse than quote No. 8.20 in evidence.

8.20   #3   GP(D)

W. Jørgensen, First Prize
Arbejder Skak 1950/1

The key is the stunning **1 ♗e6!!** which increases the black king's flights to three and the possibilities of the ♙f7 to four.

Now, a regular solver would instantly recognize that the main content of the problem comprises the *Pickaninny* theme, the name given, during a less politically-correct age, to the maximum four variations possible by a black pawn. So let us first get the non-thematic possibilities out of the way: **1...♔c5** and **1...♔xc7** are met by the short mates **2 ♕xc7#** and **2 ♗xe5#** respectively, and **1...♔xe6** is met by **2 c8♕+** and if **2...♔d6**,

then **3 ♛c6#**, or if **2...♜/♞d7**, then **3
♞d4#**. The first thematic variation to
consider is **1...f6**. It is clear that this
does nothing against **2 c8♛** followed
by **3 ♛c6#**, which, as you would
guess, is the threat. Much more
promising is **1...fxe6**, which, although it admittedly blocks e6, has
the great merit that 2 c8♛? is stalemate! Two can play at that game,
however, and the under-promotion **2
c8♜!** forces mate after the obligatory
2...♚d7 by **3 ♛d8#**. Another self-
stalemating attempt is **1...fxg6**, which
has the merit, from Black's point of
view, of not blocking e6. Unfortunately, leaving the ♝e6 on the board
has its drawbacks, and White has **2
c8♝!** ♚c7 **3 ♝xe5#**. Finally, **1...f5**
very cleverly defeats the threat, because after 2 c8♛? f4! a mate in one
is nowhere to be seen. As always,
there is a down-side to the black defence; on this occasion it is the prospective self-block on f5, allowing **2
c8♞+!** ♚xe6 **3 ♛xe7#**, or here
2...♚c7 3 ♝xe5#.

This problem not only shows
one of the best-loved graphic
themes, the Pickaninny, but it also
shows all four possible promotions
of a single pawn. This theme is universally known by the German word
Allumwandlung (literally, 'all con-
versions'). The extended geometry
involved here is clear: the four
moves of the black f-pawn are
matched up with the four possible

promotions, creating a beautiful conceptual pattern. No true problem
lover could remain unmoved.

Exercises

See how well you do on the following three problems. They are not
easy, but they are well worth the effort. Solutions are at the end of the
book.

8.21   #2   PG
*B. P. Barnes, 2nd Prize
Ring Tourney, Evening News,
Brian Harley Award 1959*

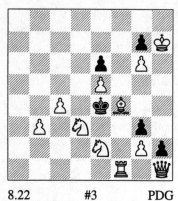

8.22   #3   PDG
C. A. L. Bull (after Sam Loyd)
Natal Mercury 1915

8.23   #12   DFG
H-P. Rehm, 3rd Prize
3rd FIDE Tourney 1966

9 The Weird and the Wonderful – Unorthodox Problems

'There is but one step from the sublime to the ridiculous.'
Napoleon (attributed)

For our final chapter, we take a look at just a few of the composing genres developed in the unceasing quest for spectacular chess. The ones we shall sample are Helpmates, Selfmates, Series-movers and lastly Retrograde Analysis. Each represents a variant of the game and of 'orthodox' compositions, yet each in its own way enhances our enjoyment of the elements and offers different fields for exploitation by the composer.

Helpmates

In the helpmate, White and Black cooperate to mate Black in a fixed number of moves. Unless otherwise stated, Black moves first and, unlike any other genre, it is the black move which is given first in each move-pair. One implication of the helpmate form is that a line of play contains a half-move more than orthodox problems; for example, in a Helpmate in two, Black moves, then White moves, then Black moves, then White mates. A second implication is that helpmates do not have variations in the normal sense. Thus, in order to obtain the effect of 'variations on a theme' which is so desirable to the strategic composer, various devices are resorted to, including permitting more than one solution, or using some method of **twinning**.

No. 9.1 is a splendid example of excellent thematic content allied to impeccable economy of material.

9.1   H#2   PG
Two solutions
*F. Abdurahmanović &
M. Mladenović, 2nd Prize
Arnhem TT 1981*

The solutions are as follows:

1 ♕d6+ ♘e6+ 2 ♔d5+ ♘e5# and 1 ♕f3+ ♘f5+ 2 ♔e4+ ♘b2#.

In both solutions, all the moves are checks. This is paradoxical, because one would expect checks to both White and Black to be disruptive to the co-operation between the two sides. Excellent unity is provided by the two prospective self-blocks with the queen, and by the mates involving the two batteries which share the ♘c4 as the front piece. Such geometric correspondence between the lines of play is typical of many good helpmates.

The paradox of material also has a special flavour in the helpmate form. The surprising No. 9.2 might well prove quite hard to solve if you were not aware of this.

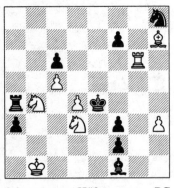

9.2   H#2   PG
Two solutions
G. Bakcsi
1st Prize, Feenschach 1966

The solutions are:

1 ♗xd3+! ♘c2 2 ♔f4 ♖g4# and 1 ♖xb4+! ♘b2 2 ♔d5 ♖d6#.

In both cases, a white knight is captured – with check, moreover – for the sole reason that it prevents the black king from entering the mating net. The question we are by now accustomed to ask about the paradox of material arises again: why is it that only these solutions work? In the helpmate, the question has an intriguing angle, because we would expect the material that is removed to be easy to use for mating purposes when both sides are co-operating.

Again, the play in the two lines is closely related: Black captures a knight with check, the other knight interposes, the black king moves into position and White delivers mate, the remaining knight guarding a flight square.

The two-move helpmate is capable of a huge range of geometric expression. No. 9.3 is a charming interpretation of the organ pipes:

a) 1 ♗g7 (interfering with the ♖h7) 1...♗xe5 2 ♖g6 (interfering with the ♗h5) 2...♗f6# (shutting off both bishop and rook).

The second solution is based on a twin in which the white king is placed on g5 and a new Helpmate in two exists. The solution is easily seen because it is the exact parallel of 'a':

9.3   H#2   G

(a) Diagram (b) w♔g8→g5
M. Myllyniemi, 1st Place
Nordic Championship 1967

9.4   H#4   GF

(b) ♗d7→d4 (c) ♗d7→d3
M. Vukčević, Special Prize
Magyar Sakkszovetzeg 1979

b) **1 ♗g6 ♘xe5 2 ♖g7 ♘f7#**. The geometrical content speaks for itself here, but note how the position of the white king determines the order of the black moves, and incidentally protects f4 in 'b'.

Now take a look at the splendid sub-miniature triplet No. 9.4.

The solutions run:

a) **1 ♔a5 ♔e7 2 ♗a4+ ♔d6 3 ♖a6+ ♔c5 4 ♕b4+ axb4#**.

b) **1 ♗e5 a4 2 ♗c7+ ♔d7 3 ♗a5+ ♔c6 4 ♕b5+ axb5#**.

c) **1 ♖a8+ ♔c7 2 ♔a7 a4 3 ♗a6 a5 4 ♕b6+ axb6#**.

This little sparkler has a great deal to recommend it: three echo-mates, each of which is an *ideal mate* – a model mate in which every piece on the board, black and white, is used – as well as play which manages to retain interest in spite of the solver's

foreknowledge. Yet we feel that it has something extra which is, perhaps, a special attraction of such works: flow. Even though it is a mere four moves long, there is a strong feeling that one can lay the three solutions end-to-end in the sequence 'a' to 'c' and produce a twelve-mover in which the pieces swirl up the board in a flowing movement. This end-to-end effect seems applicable only when there is great unity between the different solutions.

The next example is a move shorter and has corresponding play as well as echo-mates.

(see diagram on following page)

Yet we believe that it, too, has the same quality of flow, because the unified solutions again progress, rank by rank, up the board:

9.5 H#3 GF(D)
Three solutions
F. Abdurahmanović & O. Catić,
2nd Prize, Mat 1981

9.6 H#4 GP(D)
(b) a1=h8
J. Kricheli, 1st Prize
Ideal Mate Review 1983

1 ♔b6 e5 2 ♔c7 e6+ 3 ♔c8 e7#
1 ♗d8 f4 2 ♔d6 f5+ 3 ♔d7 f6#
1 ♗e7 g3 2 ♔d6 g4+ 3 ♔e6 g5#.
The (D) symbol here relates to the two prospective self-blocks by the black bishop on d8 and e7.

The helpmate can also be a very successful vehicle for Bohemian dreams. No. 9.6 achieves a symmetry between the orthogonal and diagonal both in terms of play and mates, which is sheer perfection.

The position solves as follows:

a) 1 ♖d6 ♔f4 2 ♖a6! ♔f5 3 ♔c6 ♔e6 4 ♖b6 ♖c8#. Note the cute waiting move by the black rook.

Now, the legend 'a1=h8' means that these two squares trade places, that is, the board is turned upside down! As a consequence, the pawn now guards the square on which the mate occurred in the first solution,

but it no longer guards the mating square of the second:

b) 1 ♖f2 ♖h1 2 ♗d1! ♔e6 3 ♔f3 ♔f5 4 ♗e2 ♖h3#. This time it is the bishop which makes the waiting move, producing a perfect echo mate at right angles to the first. Again, the special value of these mates is that they are *ideal mates*. A breathtakingly beautiful work.

The helpmate can well be used to produce a range of graphic effects. Look at the solutions to No. 9.7, which manages to dispense with the services of all but one white pawn:

1 ♔f6 ♔g2 (amazingly, this is a waiting move) 2 ♔g7 f6+ 3 ♔h8 f7 4 ♖h7 f8♕#

1 ♔d5 fxe6 2 ♔c6 e7 3 ♔b7 exd8♕ 4 ♔a8 ♕xc8#

1 ♔d4 fxe6 2 ♔c3 exd7 3 ♔b2 dxc8♕ 4 ♔a1 ♕c1#

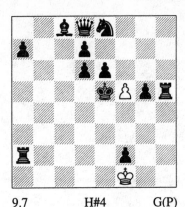

9.7   H#4   G(P)
Four solutions
F. Abdurahmanović
1st/2nd Prize, Mat 1978

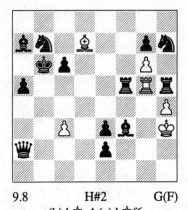

9.8   H#2   G(F)
(b) b♔e4 (c) b♔f6
V. Rudenko & V. Chepizhny,
2nd Prize, Olympic Tourney 1984

1 ♔f4 f6 2 ♔g3 f7 3 ♔h2 fxe8♕ 4 ♔h1 ♕xh5#

The king is mated in all four corners – a formidable feat in itself, given the ultimate in white economy, and here achieved with satisfactory variety in the play.

Diagram 9.8 takes the Loshinsky Magnet to even greater heights:

The solutions are:

(a) **1 ♖b5 ♖c5 2 ♖d5 ♖xc6#**
(b) **1 ♖c5 ♖d5 2 ♖e5 ♖d4#**
(c) **1 ♖d5 ♖e5 2 ♖f5 ♖e6#**

A magnificent conception! Have you ever seen three rooks behave in such a manner? A black rook is followed three times by the white rook, which is followed by the other black rook! In addition, not content with this grandiose effect, the composers have provided three pretty, unified and exact echoes, in which one rook

performs an interference and the other a self-block.

No. 9.9 is an example of the way in which a longer helpmate can deliver a powerful flow impact.

9.9   H#10   FD(P)(G)
L. Zoltan, 2nd Prize
Miniature Tourney
Tipographia TE 1969

The sparse force emphasizes the delicious accuracy of each one of the twenty half-moves:

1 &f2 &c7!

The bishop has to give the king access to e3, but its choice of destination foresees events eight moves ahead.

2 &e3 &g5
3 &d4 &f4
4 &d5 &e3

The route which the white king is constrained to take is a subtle demonstration of chessboard geometry.

5 &c6 &d4
6 &b7 &c5
7 &a7!

Beginning a cute triangulation. What makes it surprising is the elaborateness of the manoeuvre and the fact that there is no alternative sequence whereby the king can arrive at his destination in time, whilst also allowing White to get his moves in.

7 ... &xb5
8 &a8 &c6
9 &a7 &b6+
10 &a6 b5#

A very light work, but possessed of all four elements in some measure and a welcome break from the intricacies of strategy.

Our final helpmate shows something a little different:

(a) 1 &f7! &b2 2 c3+ dxc3 3 &b3+ cxb3#

(b) 1 cxb3 e.p.!. There is a convention of problem chess stating that

9.10   H#3   GP(D)
(b) ♙b5→a3
H. Aloni, 1st Prize
Israel Ring Tourney 1962

if one can prove that White's last move must have been an initial double move of a pawn (here b2-b4), then the *en passant* capture is allowed. In this case the b-pawn could not have come from b3, where it would have been giving check. The white king could not have moved either because b2, b3, and d4 are the only vacant squares it could have moved from, and, in each case, the king would have been in an impossible check. Note especially the case of b2: we have to ask ourselves what was Black's last move, to discover that the ♙a3 could not have played to its square on the previous move. This process of proving something about the legality of a position is called *retrograde analysis* (or *retro-analysis*).

1...&xd3! 2 &xd2+ &c4 3 &a5 cxb3#.

Usually, the 'special move' (castling, en passant, promotion) is the centre-piece of the problem and constitutes the major – if not the sole – aesthetic attraction. In en passant problems particularly, we would also expect the construction to show at least a little strain because of the retro-analytical requirement. In Aloni's work, the special move is unusually well integrated and the problem has plenty of artistic content. Even the ♗e5 is required for reasons other than making the retro-analysis work (it ensures that the white king could not have come from d4 in (b)): It prevents a nasty cook in (b) by 1 ♕e1/f1 ♔d4 2 ♕b1 ♔xc4 3 ♕b3+ cxb3#. In the actual solution, the hesitation by the king, making a waiting move in a direction away from the action, is not much less of a surprise than the en passant. In (a), Black's first move has a hint of depth – about as much as you can expect in a three-move helpmate with such light material. Above all, the problem possesses a satisfying unity by virtue of the mates being delivered by the same pawn on the same square, but capturing a different piece.

Selfmates

In a selfmate, White plays first and forces Black to mate White in a fixed number of moves. No. 9.11 will give some of the flavour of the intriguing kind of strategy involved.

9.11   S#2   G(P)
W. Weber, 1st Prize
Ring Tourney, Deutsche
Schachblätter 1949

If it were Black to move, 1...♔b6 would be mate, but he would strenuously avoid making this move if given the choice!

The key is **1 ♘a4** which is a pure waiting move. Black's only legal moves are with the pinned queen, and each one makes a different error:

1...♕xb2 allows the queen to be recaptured whilst simultaneously releasing the b6 square with **2 ♘xb2**, leaving Black a single legal move, **2...♔b6#**.

Running Black out of alternatives except for a mate is one of the two ways selfmates operate. The other technique is to check the black king in such a way that the reply has to be a mate of White. The remaining variations of the problem use this method.

1...♛b4 unpins the white queen but maintains a guard on c4, allowing **2 ♕a6+!** which forces **2...♚xa6#**.

1...♛b5 is the 'star' variation. It prevents 2 ♕a6+, but this time White has the clever **2 ♘xc5+! ♚b6#**, because from b5 the queen pins the ♘c5, preventing it from interposing on b7.

Finally, we have **1...♛b6**, guarding e6 and allowing **2 ♗c8+! ♚xc8#**. This 'un-block' is, in fact, the opposite of the self-block in orthodox problems.

This distinctive slant on geometric devices is one of the main attractions of the selfmate. No. 9.12 shows this with great sophistication.

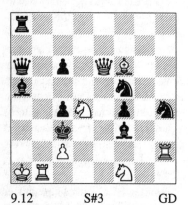

9.12   S#3   GD

V. F. Rudenko, 1st Prize
Gazeta Czestochowa 1977

The key is **1 ♖h3!**, which, by unguarding the ♙c2, threatens **2 ♘b5++!**

♚xc2 3 ♕xc4+ ♗c3#. The rook has to pin the ♗f3, else there is the refutation 1...♗e2!. Now, because Black has a double-barrelled battery on the a-file, the threat cannot be ducked by moving the queen or the rook off the file. Capturing the ♘d4 with 1...♘xd4 is a side variation; the c2 square is now unprotected, allowing the neat **2 ♕e1+ ♚xc2 3 ♕d2+ ♗xd2#**.

The remaining two defences protect the ♙c4: **1...♘d6 2 ♘xc6+! ♚xc2 3 ♘b4+ ♗xb4#**. The reason why this works is that the ♘d6 interferes with the ♕e6 – if it were not for this, 3...♗xb4 would not be mate because of 4 ♕xa6. Similarly, **1...♘e3 2 ♘xf3+! ♚xc2 3 ♘e1+ ♗xe1#**. This time, the ♘e3 interferes with the ♖h3, preventing it from interposing on a3. These interferences of Black on White cannot, of course, be used positively to force a mate in an orthodox problem. The two variations are rounded off by the device contained in the threat, which has a normal shut-off of Black by White.

This problem, even though only a three-mover, is an excellent illustration of negative depth. The moves 1...♘d6 and 1...♘e3 turn out to be damaging to Black only on the third move. The fact that the white knight is obliged to remove a black piece (♙c6, ♗f3) from the line on which the black knight interferes increases the obscurity of Black's error.

On top of all this complexity, you might still have the energy to spot the neat effect of having the a5-bishop deliver mate on all the squares between e1 and b4.

No. 9.13 is a typical modern blockbuster which shows a particularly powerful combination of geometry and depth.

9.13   S#5   GD(P)(F)
V. Alaikov, 1st Prize
Tungsram Tourney 1980

The key 1 ♕c7! sets up a second battery and so threatens 2 ♘xg5+ (opening the line of the ♗h6 to d2!) 2...♔f4 3 ♘e6+ ♔e5 4 ♘xc4++ (the second battery fires, sending the next knight on his way) 4...♔e4 5 ♘d2+ exd2#, at last exploiting the opening of the line of the ♗h6 to d2.

The obvious way to meet this threat is by playing 1...♗xg7, removing the bishop from the fatal diagonal. But, as you no doubt guessed, this puts the bishop in a position to

be dragged (kicking and screaming, no doubt) to a mating square: 2 ♘xd4+ ♔f4 3 ♘e6+ (again this knight returns to the stables, having cleared the line, and the second knight takes over to deliver the finish) 3...♔e5 4 ♘b5+ ♔e4 5 ♘c3+ ♗xc3#.

The last variation begins 1...♖a2, which prepares to meet the 5 ♘d2+ of the threat with 5...♖xd2!. This makes the mistake of guarding the ♙e2, allowing the prancing knights to reverse their roles: 2 ♘xc4++ ♔e4 3 ♘d6+ (the knight returns to d6, having removed the protection of d3) 3...♔e5 4 ♘c5+ ♔f4 5 ♘xd3+ ♘xd3#.

A memorable work, featuring positive depth in the threat, set off by the negative depth in the two variations, scintillating battery-play, reversal of the knights' roles in parallel variations, all topped off by multiple switchbacks of the knights.

In common with all genres, the selfmate has often been used to display entertaining graphic effects. No. 9.14 is an impressive example.

Players will readily recognize the stand-off situation of the pawn configuration in the lower right quadrant of the board. It prevents White from losing a move, which would oblige Black to mate by ...axb3#. The solution is as follows:

1 g3!
White frees e3 for later use.

9.14   S#10   GDF(P)
J. Balazs
Blathy Memorial 1941

1   ...   f3

Not 1...fxg3? 2 fxg3 and Black's only legal move is mate.

2   ♖e3+

The rook occupies the freed square, but what is the purpose?

2   ...   ♚f7

3   ♖b4!

Black's last move has unpinned the rook, which repays the favour by interfering with the ♗a3, allowing the king to shuttle back. As yet, the point of this elaborate little square-dance is lost in the mists of the future.

3   ...   ♚f8+
4   ♖c4+   ♚f7
5   ♖c5   ♚f8+
6   ♖d5+   ♚f7
7   ♖d6   ♚f8+
8   ♖de6+   ♚f7
9   ♖e7+   ♚f8+

The rook has arrived at the top of the staircase, which means that the black king is now, at last, starved of a move.

10   ♖b3!

The rooks have traded places and somehow White has lost a move! The law says Black must now play:

10   ...   axb3#

The staircase and Platzwechsel fit in beautifully here with White's deep method of losing a move. The relative length of the solution provides a flow effect which is considerably enhanced by the careful single-stepping of the two protagonists.

Series-movers

In series-mover problems, one side plays an uninterrupted series of a fixed number of moves, after which the other side makes a single move to fulfil the stipulation; during the course of the series, checks are illegal, except on the final move.

In spite of their artificiality, series-movers are great fun and fully capable of embodying the four elements. Moreover, they represent a kind of thinking very familiar to players, who are accustomed to developing a plan, particularly in the early middle-game, comprising a sequence of moves for their side. Series-movers put you in control of the position; all you have to do is construct the plan!

No. 9.15 is a series helpstalemate,

of the same type as the amazing composition 5.8.

9.15   SH=19   PGFD
P. Kahl
Die Schwalbe 1955

To recap, what is required here is for Black to play a sequence of nineteen moves, after which White plays a single move stalemating Black. Given that Black is in possession of his full birthright of pieces, this looks like a very tall order: **1 ♘cb4 2 c2 3 c3 4 c4 5 ♘c5 6 ♖d3 7 ♖1d2 8 ♗d1 9 e2 10 e3 11 e4 12 e5 13 ♘e6 14 ♗c5 15 ♕d4 16 ♔d5 17 ♗d6 18 c5 19 ♘c6 ♖d7** Stalemate.

This extraordinary problem possesses the four elements in good measure. It is founded on a paradox: how can it be possible to parcel up the entire black army in a mere nineteen moves? It is deep, because all but the last few moves have a point which is hard to visualize in advance. It achieves a highly ambitious geometric theme, an elaboration of the Platzwechsel in which there is a *cyclic shuffle* of the black pieces; that is, piece A makes room for piece B, which makes room for piece C ... until piece P makes room for piece A. In spite of the extreme intricacy of the geometric idea, the flow of the problem is also good. In particular, the order of moves is cleverly constrained. For example, the ♘d3 must traverse c5 on its way to e6, because f4 is taboo owing to the illegal check. The knock-on effect of this circumstance on the rest of the solution is fascinating to unravel. A truly awesome work!

Has it crossed your mind to try your own hand at composition? For encouragement, we offer an account from one of your authors (J.L.), of the making of a serieshelpmate.

9.16   SH#33   FGP(D)
J. Levitt
The Problemist 1994

In this problem, your task is to find a series of thirty-three black moves in a row (neither giving nor walking into check), so as to reach a position where White can mate in one. (If you find a solution in less than thirty-three moves, you have 'cooked' the problem.)

It is not easy to solve; if you can manage it in less than an hour, you will be doing better than several masters and grandmasters who have tried it! The difficulty is due to depth, the final mating position being quite hard to spot.

Since there is no immediate mate possible (the king cannot get to a8 for the purpose of setting up d5-d6# without capturing the ♖a1, thus defeating the purpose!), it is necessary to promote the black d-pawn. To do this Black must remove the ♙d5 and all its defenders. The solution runs as follows (the moves given are all by Black):

1 ♔b2 2 ♔xa1! 3 ♔b2 4 ♔xc3! 5 ♔xc4 6 ♔b5 7 ♔a6 8 ♔b7 9 ♔xa8! (Black must take either the ♗a7 or the ♘a8 to obtain a path to the ♗h1) **10 ♔b7 11 ♔c7 12 ♔d6 13 ♔e5 14 ♔f4 15 ♔g3 16 ♔h2 17 ♔xh1! 18 ♔g2 19 ♔f3 20 ♔e4 21 ♔xd5!**

So where is the mate? The astute reader might have noticed that the black king has visited three corners already...

22 ♔e6 23 d5 24 d4 25 d3 26 d2 27 d1♗! 28 ♗c2 29 ♗xh7! 30 ♔f7

31 ♔g8 32 ♔h8 33 ♗g8 and White mates with **♗d4#**.

As I remember it, the genesis of this problem went something like this: I woke up one morning with an idea in my head. Two minutes later, the final twelve moves of the problem were ready! It would have been possible to present this final stage as a miniature, but I decided to try to extend it. The ♗h1 came next and then the idea to have the king visit all four corners. The hard work was just beginning! Technically, the difficulty in composing such problems is keeping the solution unique – this also applies to move order. There must never be two ways to reach the goal. For example, if a king on a1 must go to b3 during the course of the solution, the problem would be ruined if there were a choice of getting there via b2 as well as a2. The reader might find it interesting to play through the solution again, seeing why each move is precise.

Several hours and a couple of phone calls to John Nunn later, the problem was cast in its final form. Aesthetically, the solution contains all of our four elements. There is always paradox in capturing white pieces when it is White who is supposed to be delivering mate, but the main one is undoubtedly that of the ♖h7. This rather surprising destruction of white force has been too big a hurdle for many would-be solvers.

The solution flows for thirty-three moves and the hidden final mate has already been mentioned (depth). The most striking geometrical effect is the black king's visiting of the four corners of the board. There is also an *excelsior* – the black pawn making its full-length journey to promotion – as well as an under-promotion to a bishop, for those who like that sort of thing. In addition, the final mate is economical, leaving no 'extras' on the board.

Perhaps the composer is over-partial to his own work, but this position has given me more pleasure and sense of achievement than any single game I have yet played. Unfortunately, it is rather better technically than most of my games too!

A Step Backwards: Retrograde Analysis

For our final offering we take a backward look – but of a very creative kind. For the field of retrograde analysis is all about the presentation of positions whose history has to be unravelled, sometimes as far back as the initial position of the game. We have already had a foretaste with No. 9.13. In that case, it was possible to prove that Black could capture en passant because White's only legal last move had to be the double jump of a pawn from its initial square. Many retrograde analysis problems

are concerned with *proof games*, in which the solver must discover the unique 'game score' leading to the diagram position.

A pretty case in point is No. 9.17.

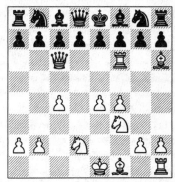

9.17   W   GP(D)(F)
Position after Black's 12th move.
How did the game go?
U. Heinonen
The Problemist 1991

We have here the position after twelve moves of a legal game of chess, and we must discover how the game went. How does one tackle such a problem? With careful, painstaking logic. The first stage should be to count the minimum number of white moves involved in reaching the diagram position:

♙s on c4, e4, f4	1 move each	3
♘s on d2, f3	1 move each	2
♗ on h6	1 move	1
♕ on c6	2 moves	2
♖ on f6	4 moves	4
Total		12

Why four moves for the rook to get to f6? Since the rook can only get out after the queen's bishop and knight are developed, the route has to be a1-c1-c3-f3-f6 (four moves). So there is no time to waste. Black, meanwhile, can have moved only his knights and rooks. Move-order logic now predominates and, as you will see, miraculously restricts Black to just one surprising possibility.

There is no white d-pawn in the final position. It had no time to move, so it must have been captured on its original square. This capture must have been performed by a black knight. After the knight moves away, White plays the sequence of moves:

A) ♗h6, ♘d2, ♖c1, ♖c3, ♖f3, ♖f6, f4, ♘(g)f3.

This sequence comprises eight moves. It follows that the black knight must have captured the d-pawn and moved away all in the first four moves. The first three black moves are 1...♘f6, 2...♘e4, 3...♘xd2. Meanwhile, White cannot waste his first four moves. He must play c4, e4, and queen to c6 in some order. The e-pawn is still on the board, so it cannot have been captured by the black knight *en route* to d2. It is now possible to deduce the first four moves by each side:

1 c4 ♘f6 2 ♕a4 ♘e4 3 ♕c6 ♘xd2 4 e4 ♘b3.

The queen must go via a4 to get to c6 in two moves. The move 4...♘b3

is necessary since the knight must get out of the way of the ♗c1 immediately, it cannot capture any white piece, and cannot go to f3 as this would be check, preventing 5 ♗h6.

We are close to the answer now. In the final position, there are white pieces on h6 and f6 and a black knight on g8. In the sequence of moves above, A), White plays ♖f6 in six moves' time, so Black has only five moves to get a knight to g8. The knight currently on b3 simply cannot get back in time. What about the other knight? The squares c6 and e4 are unavailable owing to enemy occupation, which leaves a unique route:

5 ♗h6 ♘a6! 6 ♘d2 ♘b4 7 ♖c1 ♘d5 8 ♖c3 ♘f6 9 ♖f3 ♘g8 (just in time) 10 ♖f6.

Finally, the other knight must get back to b8. Again, there is only one way. Meanwhile, White completes his deployment:

10...♘c5 11 f4 ♘a6 12 ♘gf3 ♘b8.

So there we have it! We have proved that the black knights have swapped positions! There is a geometrical symmetry about this interchange (Platzwechsel) and it is surprising, that is, paradoxical, too. However, the main interest lies in the 'flow' of logic involved in the solution. The tension is maintained right until the end. One can also talk of the depth of the whole manoeuvre, even if no single move is especially deep (5...♘a6! is probably the deepest). Real foresight is needed to determine the right move order for White.

It is difficult to apply our elements precisely here because we are dealing with an unusual type of problem, a retrograde analysis problem. In particular, the notion of depth is turned on its head. As in a detective story, the evidence (the position of the pieces) is there for everyone to see, but it takes skilful deduction to uncover what the black knights have been up to. The problem has the attraction of a complex puzzle.

Those who doubt the artistic value of such a problem will not find it hard to attack. Is it not just a trick, a gimmicky ploy? It is possible to attack any work of art, and you will have to judge for yourself. Even if it is just a 'glorified card trick', it is an extremely clever one!

The Cambridge mathematician G. H. Hardy viewed chess from a very mathematical perspective. In his autobiographical book *A Mathematician's Apology* (1940), he tried to justify the value of a life spent studying mathematics. In it he had a go at chess problems:

'A chess problem is simply an exercise in pure mathematics (a game not entirely, since psychology also plays a part) and everyone who calls a problem "beautiful" is applauding mathematical beauty.'

And later:

'A chess problem is genuine mathematics but it is in some way trivial mathematics. However ingenious and intricate, however original and surprising the moves, there is something essentially lacking. Chess problems are unimportant.'

It is fruitless to argue with somebody taking such a narrow perspective. Perhaps Shakespeare would not be valued highly either, since his work would not even qualify as genuine mathematics? We hope the examples in this book have given the reader every reason to disagree with Hardy, but maybe he is best answered by another mathematician, Augustus De Morgan:

'It is easier to square the circle than to get round a mathematician!'

Exercises

Three unorthodox problems for you to solve. In No. 9.18, there is an unusual twinning mechanism. First solve the diagram as a normal helpmate in two. Then remove the white knight on e6 and solve the new helpmate that results. Then remove the rook on d7 without replacing the knight for another helpmate. Finally remove all the white pieces for the last instalment!

No. 9.19 is a series helpmate in which there are two solutions, one of which is especially tricky.

No. 9.20 is a hard selfmate; most practical players will probably find this a real challenge!

9.19   SH#8   GF(P)
2 Solutions
B. Lindgren
Mat 1984

9.18   H#2   GP(F)
(a) Diagram (b) Remove ♘e6
(c) Further remove ♖d7
(d) Further remove ♗c8
G. Bakcsi, First Prize
Magyar Sakkszov. 1985

9.20   S#3   PGDF
D. G. McIntyre
Alain White Album 1920

Solutions to Exercises

Game

Ex. 6.7:

After **30 ♘e4!!** Black resigned. (30...♖xc1 31 ♘g5 mate). Had there been a black pawn on e4, I suspect my opponent would not have missed it. As in the Kasparov-Short example, a 'sacrifice' on an empty square!

Ex. 6.8:

White forces mate by **1 ♕h6+!!** **♔xh6** (1...♔h8 2 ♕xh7+! ♔xh7 3 hxg6+ ♔g7 4 ♖h7 mate) **2 hxg6+** **♔g5** (or 2...♔g7 3 ♖xh7 mate) **3 ♖h5+!!**.

Sacrifices on empty squares which give check to the opposing king are not quite so paradoxical, but giving away as much material as in this example is pretty unusual.

3...♔xh5 4 f4+ ♘xe2 (others are no better) **5 ♘f6+! ♔h6 6 ♖h1+ ♔g7 7 ♘e8+ ♖xe8 8 ♖xh7+ ♔f6 9 ♖xf7 mate**.

A twentieth century answer to the Evergreen game, involving extreme paradox of material, with three sacrifices on empty squares.

Ex. 6.9:

1 f6!! ♖xe2 (if 1...gxf6, 2 g7 ♖g2 3 ♗g5!! ♖xg5 4 ♕xg5 ♕xe2 5 ♕g1

wins) **2 fxg7 ♖xd2 3 ♗xd2 ♕e2 4 ♔c1 1-0**.

Tal supported his eye for brilliancy with deadly accurate analysis. It is not enough just to see the idea; you must also see precisely why it works.

Studies

Ex. 7.26:

This position is from a study by Gorgiev (1938). We have, as in the next example, removed the introductory play since it was, in fact, unsound. What is left is the climax of the study only, which should make it a bit easier for solvers.

1 ♔d7!!

But not too easy. To find this deep move, and to avoid the more obvious 1 ♔e7? one has to appreciate that after 1 ♔e7 ♔g8 the position is a mutual zugzwang.

1 ... ♘f6+!

Black tries a stalemate defence. After 1...♔g8 2 ♔e7 ♘c5 3 ♘f6+ ♔h8 4 ♔f7 ♘e6 5 ♘g4 ♘d8+ 6 ♔e7 ♘c6+ 7 ♔f8 Black will be mated.

2 ♔e7!

Not 2 ♘xf6? stalemate. Now play divides into two unified variations. Firstly 2...♘g8+ 3 ♔f8! ♘xh6 4

♘d6 with another mutual zugzwang. Secondly, our main line.

2 ...   ♘xe8
3 ♔f8!

With yet another mutual zugzwang. Subtle play with optical logic and paradoxical twists thrown in.

Ex. 7.27:

From a study by J. de Villeneuve Esclapon. White, a rook down, must attack the black pieces:

1 ♔g5   ♖h2!

If 1...♖b6 then 2 ♗e5 with 3 ♗d4 to follow a black knight move.

2 ♗e5

Attacking rook and knight.

2 ...   ♖f2

Defending rook and knight!

3 ♗f4

Attacking the knight and preparing 4 ♗e3+ should the knight go anywhere other than d4.

3 ...   ♘d4
4 ♗e3

Black now defends his two pieces in the only way possible:

4 ...   ♖f5+
5 ♔g4   ♖d5
6 ♔f4

Threatening 7 ♔e4. Black rushes his king to the defence.

6 ...   ♔b6
7 ♔e4   ♔c5

It seems Black has secured his winning material advantage. However, the turbulent flow comes to an abrupt paradoxical finish:

8 ♔d3!

With a positional draw – we have reached diagram 7.8.

Ex. 7.28:

A study by L. Kubbel. Accurate play is needed to force a win, but the real point is the geometric effect of having the black king mated on both sides of the board!

1 ♘f8+   ♔e8

If 1...♔c8 then 2 ♖c1+ ♔b8 (alternatively, if 2...♔d8 then 3 ♘e6+) 3 ♘d7+ and White delivers mate on the a-file.

2 ♘e6!   ♖g8

If 2...♖h7, 3 ♖d8+ ♔f7 4 ♘g5+ wins.

3 ♘c7+   ♔f7
4 ♖f1+   ♔g7
5 ♘e6+   ♔h6
6 ♖h1#

This time White mates on the h-file. This study makes a good talent test for your ability to analyse at chess.

Ex. 7.29:

In some ways the easiest to solve, but did you see all three thematically linked variations?:

1 d7 ♖h8 2 ♗g8!.
1 d7 ♖d1 2 ♗d5!.
1 d7 ♖a1+ 2 ♗a2!.

All avenues of approach for the rook are negated by a time-gaining bishop sacrifice. A neat study by Prokes.

Ex. 7.30:

A study by Mitrofanov. Paradoxically White must block his own pawn:

1 ♔e6!

Threatening 2 ♔d5. The alternative 1 ♔e4? would not save the game after 1...c6!.

1 ...   c5

After 1...♗d2 2 ♔d5 ♔d3 3 ♔c6 ♗d8 4 e6 draws.

2 ♔d5   ♗e7

It looks hopeless for White, but now there is a surprising circular chase:

3 ♔e6   ♗f8
4 ♔f7   ♗h6
5 ♔g6   ♗f4

5...♗f8 6 ♔f7 just repeats.

6 ♔f5   ♗g3

So as to meet 7 e6? with 7...♗h4. If 6...♗xe5, 7 ♔xe5 picks off the last pawn.

7 ♔e4!   ♗h4
8 ♔d5   ♗e7
9 ♔e6

'Perpetual motion'! Consider yourself a top-class solver if you managed this one.

Ex. 7.31:

1 ♘g4+ ♔e7 (1...♔g6 2 ♘e5+ ♔f6 3 ♘g4+) **2 ♘f5+ ♔d7 3 ♘e5+ ♔c8 4 ♘e7+ ♔b8 5 ♘d7+ ♔a7 6 ♘c8+ ♔a6 7 ♘b8+ ♔b5 8 ♘a7+ ♔b4 9 ♘a6+ ♔c3 10 ♘b5+ ♔d3 11 ♘b4+ ♔e2 12 ♘c3+ ♔f2** (12...♔e1? 13 ♘d3#) **13 ♘d3+ ♔g3 14 ♘e4+**

♔g4 15 ♘e5+ ♔f5 16 ♘g3+ ♔f6 17 ♘g4+.

Superb smooth flow. The small white army holds the draw with a repetition on the grand scale. This position is also given in Lasker's *Manual*, where Lasker describes it as 'highly humorous'. If you trace out the path of the black king, you will find it forms a chessboard approximation to an ellipse. The theme of this study was first achieved over seven hundred years ago – an Arabic position, with a similarly grand perpetual, appears in the 'Alfonso' manuscript of 1283.

Orthodox Problems

Ex. 8.21:

With **1 ♔b3!!**, White walks into a veritable battery of checks. The threat is **2 ♕b4#**. If the bishop discovers check randomly, for example **1...♗xg5+**, the 'crosscheck' by **2 ♘fd3#** is possible. Black's bishop can put paid to this possibility with **1...♗xf2+**, but this loses control of the white rook, allowing the charming **2 ♘f3#**, guarding d4. Black can correct this error with **1...♗d4+**, but this is a self-block, allowing the double-check **2 ♘ed3#**. A simple capture crosscheck occurs after **1...♖b6+ 2 ♕xb6#**. Finally, **1...♔d4** is met elegantly by **2 ♘xc6#**. A traditional crosschecker from Barry Barnes, one of Britain's leading modernists. The interplay of the three batteries provides excellent geometric entertainment. One of the reasons for this problem's renown is its impeccable economy. Such problems with between eight and twelve men are known as 'Merediths'.

Ex. 8.22:

1 ♖g1!! (waiting). A stunning key putting the rook *en prise* and doing the very opposite of giving the queen more air by smothering her completely. The sole purpose of the move is to be able, after **1...♔f5**, to continue with the equally extraordinary **2 ♘f2!!** leaving Black with two possibilities: **2...gxf2 3 g4#,** finally demonstrating the key's deep point – the rook protects the pawn! The alternative **2...hxg1♕ 3 ♕h5#** is more humdrum. Now look at the alternative move **1...hxg1♕**; obviously, this opens a line for the white queen, but even then the continuation **2 ♘c5+!** scarcely leaps to the eye. If **2...♕xc5** we discover that the black queen has compensated for the capture of the knight by the clearance of White's back rank, making **3 ♕b1#** possible. If instead **2...♔f5**, we have a small flaw in the dual mate by **3 ♕h3#** or **3 ♕h5#**. The final variation occurs after **1...♔xd3**; the white rook now throws itself into reverse gear and streaks across the board to make room for the queen with a sublime Bristol manoeuvre: **2 ♖a1!!**. Now

2...♔xe2 is answered by **3 ♕f1#**, while the alternatives see the queen marching down the red carpet rolled out before her by the rook to deliver **3 ♕b1#**.

Ex. 8.23:

An amusing diagram in which Black stands stalemated.

1	♗f5!	♔f3
2	♗g4+	♔f2
3	♗c8!	♔f3
4	♗b7+	♔f2
5	c6	

This is the point of White's bishop manoeuvre, but what is the point of the point?

5	...	♔f3
6	c7+	♔f2
7	♗c8!	♔f3
8	♗g4+	♔f2
9	♗f5	♔f3
10	♗e4+	♔f2
11	♗d6!	♔e3
12	♗c5#	

Thus the purpose of advancing the c-pawn was not to promote it, but simply to clear the c5 square (depth). Note the extended switchback of the e4 bishop (geometry and smooth flow). A curious feature of this problem is that not a squeak is heard from the black organ-pipes!

Unorthodox Problems

Ex. 9.18:

a) **1 ♔g4 ♖g7+ 2 ♔h3 ♘f4#.**

b) **1 ♔g6 ♖d8 2 ♔h7 ♗f5#**.

c) **1 ♔e4 c3 2 ♔d3 ♗f5#**.

d) **1 ♔e6 c7 2 ♔d7 c8♕#**.

The disappearing white pieces are very entertaining – try to figure out why the solutions to (b), (c) and (d) do not work in their predecessors! However, the real attraction of this work is the 'double starflight' created by the moves of the black king.

Ex. 9.19:

a) **1 g1♘ 2 ♘e2 3 ♔g2 4 ♔g1 5 ♘c1 6 a1♕ 7 ♕a8 8 ♕h1, ♗d4#**.

b) **1 g1♗ 2 ♗e3 3 ♗c1 4 a1♖ 5 ♖a4 6 ♗f4 7 ♔e3 8 ♖e4, ♖b3#**.

The mid-board mate in (b) is particularly difficult to find. The Allumwandlung is achieved with superb economy and precision.

Ex. 9.20:

1 ♖e7!

This obscure move threatens the startling king march **2 ♔d5+ ♔xb5 3 ♔e6+ ♘c5#**. Black can deal with this threat in several ways:

1) **1...♗b1** destroys the ♗+♘ battery, so that 3...♘c5+ is no longer mate. **2 ♔c3+!** yet again uses one battery to set up another. **2...♔a5 3 ♔xd3+ ♘d2#**. Now we see that 1...♗b1 was a case of negative depth, in that the bishop on c2 is pinned and unable to interpose on b3. Note the fiendish ingenuity with which the mating net has been cast, particularly the way the black knight achieves so much with one move.

2) **1...d2**, so that 2 ♔d5+? can be met by 2...♔a5!. **2 ♔d3+! ♔a5 3 b6+! ♘c5#**. Another double check, this time with the rook and knight.

3) **1...dxc2** prepares to meet 2 ♔d5+? with 2...♘xd4!. **2 ♘b6+! axb6 3 ♖a7+! ♘a5#**. More negative depth, since 1...dxc2 unpinned the black knight enabling the final mating move.

Beautifully constructed, with a deep opener, turbulent flow and intricate geometry. The white king proves – paradoxically for a selfmate – to be a moving target. A problem in the grand manner with which to bid the reader farewell.

The composer, Donald McIntyre, was co-author David Friedgood's original chess problem mentor in Cape Town during the early sixties.

Bibliography

Periodicals:

British Chess Magazine
New in Chess
Informator
American Chess Journal
Inside Chess

EG
The Problemist
Diagrammes
Shakhmatnaya Kompositsiya
ChessBase Magazine

Books:

General works on chess:

Em. Lasker, *Lasker's Manual of Chess,* Dover 1960
A. Avni, *Creative Chess*, Pergamon 1991
D. Bronstein, *The Chess Struggle in Practice*, David Mackay and Co., 1978
G. Kasparov, *Learn Chess with Garry Kasparov*, B. T. Batsford 1993
G. Kasparov, *New World Chess Champion*, Pergamon 1986
D. Hooper & K. Whyld, *The Oxford Companion to Chess*, O.U.P. 1987
V. Vuković, *The Chess Sacrifice*, G. Bell and Sons, 1968
J. Nunn, *Solving in Style*, George Allen & Unwin 1985
J. Nunn, *Secrets of Rook Endings*, B. T. Batsford 1992
J. Nunn, *Tactical Chess Endings*, George Allen & Unwin 1981

Books on the Endgame Study:

G. Kasparian, *Domination in 2545 Endgame Studies*, Raduga 1987
G. Kasparian, *Zamechatelnye Etiudy*, Izdatelstvo 'Ayastan' 1982
A. Roycroft, *Test Tube Chess*, Faber 1972
H. Lommer & M. Sutherland, *1234 Modern End-game Studies,* Dover 1967
H. Lommer, *1357 End-game Studies*, Pitman 1975
I. Chernev, *Practical Chess Endings*, Faber 1962
G. Nadareishvili, *V Poiskakh Krasoty*, Izdatelstvo 'Sabchota Sakartvelo' 1986
J. van Reek, *Chessmen in the Endgame Study*, Alexander Reub Vereniging voor Schaakeindspelstudie 1992

Books on Chess Compositions in general:
N. Petrović (ed.), *FIDE Album*, 1977-1979, 1980-1982, 1983-1985, Sportska tribina
R. Kofman (Ed.), *Shakhmatnaya Kompositsiya 1974-76*, Fizkultura i Sport 1978
V. Chepizhny (Ed.), *Shakhmatnaya Kompositsiya 1977-82*, Fizkultura i Sport 1983
Y. Aloni, U. Avner (Eds.), *The Art of Israeli Chess Composition*, Israel Chess Problem Circle 1983
B. Barnes, *Comins Mansfield MBE: Chess Problems of a Grandmaster*, British Chess Problem Society 1976
B. Barnes, *Pick of the Best Chess Problems*, Eliot Right Way Books 1976
B. Barnes, *White to Play and Mate in Two*, Eliot Right Way Books 1991
G. Bakcsi (Ed.), *Ungarische Schachproblemanthologie*, Corvina Kiado 1983
J. Breuer, *Beispiele zur Ideengeschichte des Schachproblems*, Die Schwalbe 1982
A. Chéron, *Le Joueur d'Echecs au Pays des Merveilles*, Diffusion Payot 1982
F. Chlubna and K. Wenda, *Problempalette II*, Dr. K.Wenda Eigenverlag 1991
W. Dittman, A. Geister, D. Kutzborski, *Logische Phantasien*, de Gruyter 1986
Engel, Schulz, Kniest, F. Giegold, *200 Problematische Einfälle und Ideen*, Feenschach 1982
M. Lipton, R. Matthews, J. Rice, *Chess Problems: Introduction to an Art*, Faber and Faber 1963
D. McIntyre, *Some Problems for my Friends*, South African Chessplayer 1957
G. Murkisch, *Rätselvolle Schachaufgaben*, Wilhelm Heyne Verlag 1980
J. Rice, *An ABC of Chess Problems*, Faber and Faber 1970
J. Rice & A. Dickins, *The Serieshelpmate*, 1978
J. Rusinek, *Sto Kompozycji Szachowych*, Aula Medycyna 1991
W. Sidler, *Problemschach*, W. Sidler Eigenverlag 1968
K.-H. Siehndel (Ed.), *Problemschach*, Sportverlag Berlin 1985
W. Speckmann, *Perlen der Schachkomposition, Walter de Gruyter 1985*

Index of Players and Composers

References are to page numbers.
Suffixes have the following meanings: c – composer; w – player of white pieces; b – player of black pieces.

Index of Openings, Themes, and Definitions

References are to page numbers.
Bold type signifies a leading entry
or definition.